CONIECTANEA BIBLICA (CUND)

Present editors
Samuel Byrskog (Lund), Göran Eidevall (Uppsala), Ola Wikander (Lund)

The ConB Series has published cutting-edge scholarship in English, French, and German since 1966. The following list represents a selection of monographs in English that have appeared since its inception.

Lars Hartman: *Prophecy Interpreted.* 1966.
Birger Gerhardsson: *The Testing of God's Son (Matt 4: 1-11 & Par).* 1966.
Bertil Albrektson: *History and the Gods.* 1967.
Tryggve Mettinger: *Solomonic State Officials.* 1971.
Birger Olsson: *Structure and Meaning in the Fourth Gospel.* 1974.
Tryggve Mettinger: *King and Messiah.* 1976.
Stephen Westerholm: *Jesus and Scribal Authority.* 1978.
Bengt Holmberg: *Paul and Power.* 1978.
Lars Hartman: *Asking for a Meaning.* 1979.
Tryggve Mettinger: *The Dethronement of Sabaoth.* 1982.
Fredrik Lindström: *God and the Origin of Evil.* 1983.
Birger Gerhardsson: *The Gospel Tradition.* 1986.
Lilian Portefaix: *Sisters Rejoice.* 1988.
Håkan Ulfgard: *Feast and Future.* 1989.
Staffan Olofsson: *God is my Rock.* 1990.
LarsOlov Eriksson: *"Come, children, listen to me!"* 1991.
Åke Viberg: *Symbols of Law.* 1992.
Samuel Byrskog: *Jesus the Only Teacher.* 1994.
Fredrik Lindström: *Suffering and Sin.* 1994.
Tryggve Mettinger: *No Graven Image?* 1995.
Mikael Winninge: *Sinners and the Righteous.* 1995.
Göran Eidevall: *Grapes in the Desert.* 1996.
Jonas Holmstrand: *Markers and Meanings in Paul.* 1997.
Anders Eriksson: *Traditions as Rhetorical Proof.* 1998.
Antti Laato: *"About Zion I will not be silent."* 1998.
Tina Haettner Blomquist: *Gates and Gods.* 1999.
Rebecca Idestrom: *From Biblical Theology to Biblical Criticism.* 2000.
Dag Oredsson: *Moats in Ancient Palestine.* 2000.
James M. Starr: *Sharers in Divine Nature.* 2000.

Jesper Svartvik: *Mark and Mission.* 2000.

Anders Gerdmar: *Rethinking the Judaism-Hellenism Dichotomy.* 2001.

Tryggve Mettinger: *The Riddle of Resurrection.* 2001.

Anders Runesson: *The Origins of the Synagogue.* 2001.

Mikael Tellbe: *Paul between Synagogue and State.* 2001.

Thomas Kazen: *Jesus and Purity Halakhah.* 2002 (2010).

Runar M. Thorsteinsson: *Paul's Interlocutor in Romans 2.* 2003.

J. Peter Södergård: *The Hermetic Piety of the Mind.* 2003.

Martin Modéus: *Sacrifice and Symbol.* 2005.

Tommy Wasserman: *The Epistle of Jude.* 2006.

Åke Viberg: *Prophets in Action.* 2007.

Göran Eidevall: *Prophecy and Propaganda.* 2009.

Per Rönnegård: *Threads and Images.* 2010.

Thomas Kazen: *Issues of Impurity in Early Judaism.* 2010.

Rikard Roitto: *Behaving as a Christ-Believer.* 2011.

Tal Davidovich: *Esther, Queen of the Jews.* 2013.

Ola Wikander: *Drought, Death, and the Sun in Ugarit and Ancient Israel.* 2014.

Ola Wikander: *Unburning Fame.* 2017.

Oral Law of Ancient Israel

Robert D. Miller II, OFS

LEXINGTON BOOKS/FORTRESS ACADEMIC
Lanham • Boulder • New York • London

Published by Lexington Books/Fortress Academic

Lexington Books is an imprint of The Rowman & Littlefield Publishing Group, Inc.
4501 Forbes Boulevard, Suite 200, Lanham, Maryland 20706
www.rowman.com

86-90 Paul Street, London EC2A 4NE, United Kingdom

British Library Cataloguing in Publication Information Available

Library of Congress Cataloging-in-Publication Data

Names: Miller, Robert D., II, author.
Title: Oral law of Ancient Israel / Robert D. Miller II.
Description: Lanham : Lexington Books/Fortress Academic, [2021] | Series:
  Coniectanea Biblica | Includes bibliographical references and index. |
  Summary: "Ancient Israel's legal system was both oral and written, its
  law both preserved in written forms and performed orally. By unpacking
  this system, Robert D. Miller II, OFS, sheds light on its practitioners,
  venues, verbal forms, and connections to neighboring peoples"—Provided
  by publisher.
Identifiers: LCCN 2022027697 (print) | LCCN 2022027698 (ebook) | ISBN
  9781978715219 (cloth) | ISBN 9781978715233 (paperback) | ISBN
  9781978715226 (epub)
Subjects: LCSH: Tradition (Judaism) | Customary law—Iceland. | Oral
  tradition—Iceland.
Classification: LCC KB211 .M55 2021 (print) | LCC KB211 (ebook) | DDC
  340.0933/4—dc23/eng/20220801
LC record available at https://lccn.loc.gov/2022027697
LC ebook record available at https://lccn.loc.gov/2022027698

Contents

Preface

Ancient Israel was neither an illiterate nor a writing society. It was a society where writing was the medium for some discourse and not others, where written texts were performed orally and rewritten from oral performances. This study looks at law and jurisprudence in this oral-and-literate ancient Israel. Using Iceland as an ethnographic analogy, it looks at how law was practiced, performed, and transmitted; at the way written artifacts of the law fit into oral performance and transmission; and at the relationship of the detritus of law that survives in the Hebrew Bible, both Torah and Proverbs, to that earlier social world.

Chapter 1 states the target of the study: the legal system of ancient Israel, the kingdoms of Judah and Israel prior to the Babylonian Exile in the 6th century. In addition to understanding orality in ancient Israel in general, scholars now know much about how narrative and mythic-poetic oral "literature" in Israel was performed, textualized, performed from text, re-oralized, and re-textualized. Much of this understanding has come from ethnographic analogies to ancient Israel from early Iceland. The world of the Eddic and Skaldic poets, of *Nornagests þáttr*, is the oral-and-written hybrid society of "Pre-exilic" Israel and Judah, as this chapter thoroughly explains. How do laws work in an oral-and-written society like ancient Israel? How is law "performed," preserved, modified? The first chapter sets out these questions to be addressed.

Chapter 2 presents to non-specialists the current understanding of law in early Iceland. Specific attention is given to how scholars gain access to this legal world, through what sources; to the relationship of the extant written "laws" to legal practice of the pre-literate period; and to how the law was "performed." The relationship of orality to writing as well as the ways in which foreign written and oral law were incorporated in Icelandic practice are also presented, relying on the latest scholarship.

A short "Interlude" acknowledges some possible shortcomings in using Iceland as an ethnographic analogy. By brief excursus into law in the migration-period Germanic Gothic kingdoms, the elements elucidated in chapter 2 are secured. A brief "Résumé" then summarizes the insights from the ethnographic analogy and brings them under the rubric of customary law as understood by the "legal realism" school of thought.

Chapter 3 is the heart of the study—indeed, it might be viewed as its conclusion: a full presentation of the legal system of ancient Israel. It begins by describing how law and jurisprudence would have operated in Iron Age Israel, involving both oral performance and written artifacts, and identifying the tradents and "performers" of that law. Performative schemas are presented drawing on both archaeological evidence and the Hebrew Bible. The nature of the laws found in the Hebrew Bible merits special attention and is explained through the ethnographic analogies. It has been long known that the legal material in the Hebrew Bible, and presumably ancient Israelite law, borrowed from Ancient Near Eastern law. This chapter explains how this happened and how this borrowing relates to the nature of Israel's customary law.

Chapter 4 is an addendum of sorts, which moves the discussion of the ancient Israelite legal world from laws to proverbs. The place of proverbs in customary law is explained, drawing on the ethnographic analogs of the early chapters, with some additional comparative material from Africa. This leads to discussion of the book of Proverbs in the Hebrew Bible, its relationship to ancient Israelite law and the legal sections of the Hebrew Bible.

As chapter 3 contains the proper conclusions or results of this exploration of oral law in ancient Israel, the book ends with a short recapitulation—a snapshot of a performative schema of oral jurisprudence in Pre-Exilic Israel.

There are numerous individuals and organizations that I owe many thanks to for their help in this enterprise. Support for the research of this book came in part from a Confraternity of Christian Doctrine/Catholic Biblical Association "Biblical Scholarship and Biblical Literacy Promotion Grant" that enabled me to undertake a scholar-in-residence at the Snorrastofa Cultural and Medieval Study Centre in Reykholt, Iceland. During that time, I was granted privileges at the University of Iceland, thanks to my longtime collaborator, Professor Terry Gunnell. My work was aided and refined by the questions, discussion, and suggestions of Frog, Sandra Jacobs, Paul Joyce, David Shepherd, Sarah Ferrario, Craig Smith, Bob Mullins—the excavator of Abel Beth-Maacah, William Ian Miller—a veteran authority on Icelandic law, and the newer generation of Norse world scholars Simon Nygaard and Yelena Sesselja Helgadóttir. A Spring 2020 PhD seminar on Law and

Proverbs allowed the invaluable insights of Howard Jung, World Kim, Brian Meldrum, José Nieto, Dimas Pele Alu, and Jonathon Riley, to contribute to this work, even when COVID-19 moved the seminar to an online platform I had no experience with! Another doctoral student, Joshua Roye, provided extensive, thorough editing, for which I am most grateful.

Chapter One

Approaches to Ancient Israel's Legal World

Despite centuries of serious scholarship investigating the laws of the Hebrew Bible and the social history of ancient Israel, we have no clear picture of the reality of legal practice and jurisprudence in the Iron Age kingdoms of Judah and Israel. The Hebrew Bible is full of what seem to be laws, arranged in what might be codes, and references to judges and trials appear in the books of the prophets and Psalms, but scholars have given only passing attention to what a trial might have been, to who judges were and how someone became one, to how the laws were enacted, promulgated, and enforced. Little has been determined, and few have taken seriously the interplay between orality and writing in ancient Israel.

As I have shown elsewhere, Israel and Judah in both the Pre- and Post-Exilic periods were oral-and-literate hybrid societies.[1] On the one hand, considerable evidence suggests literacy beginning in the late Pre-Exilic period, including numerous administrative seals, vulgar script, and writing by common soldiers and landlords.[2] Indeed, the number of inscriptions increased dramatically beginning in the mid-8th century. On the other hand, epigraphic remains from Palestine are primarily ostraca, broken pieces of pottery. Most ostracon texts are ephemeral letters or economic documents kept for a short time before being transcribed, if at all, onto something archival. Literature—or a code of law—could not be accommodated by ostraca, and we have only two examples of ink-written West Semitic literary texts—the 5th-century "Story of Ahiqar" on papyrus and the texts related to the prophet Balaam on a wall plaster at Deir Allah in the Jordan Valley.

1

ORAL-WRITTEN ANCIENT ISRAEL

We know that even in Egypt, after centuries of literacy, texts describe fictional audiences *listening* to oral performance, suggesting that the poems were intended for audiences rather than single readers. So, too, in long-literate Mesopotamia, as late as the 8th century, texts like the *Song of Erra* refer to vocal performance by singers (5.49.53–54).[3] This means that in the Ancient Near East, "Writing was thus designed as a complement to oral communication."[4] Israelite literate audiences, too, preferred and even expected to experience their literature orally.[5] It is a situation found all over the world: writing and oral performance are not mutually exclusive.[6] Thus, David Carr accurately describes Israel as an "oral-written" society.[7]

Oral literature was performed literature. A mode of thought distinct from the literary is operative in performing oral literature, demanding recourse to a performance criticism that furnishes the distinct set of tools needed to investigate this material. Paul Zumthor writes, "Insofar as it engages a body thru the voice that carries it, rejects any analysis that would dissociate it from within its social function and from its socially accorded place—more than a written text would."[8] Most biblical scholarship of the past century, however, has focused on literary genres and the *Sitze im Leben* in which they were used, while more recent scholars have focused on literary, textual stylistic features. As I have argued elsewhere, we cannot understand oral literature without performance criticism that focuses on the dynamic complex of actions in performance.[9]

Since we have no access to the complete performance schemas of ancient Israel, we must reconstruct them on the basis of Ancient Near Eastern comparative material and, even more so, ethnographic analogy. The folklorist Lauri Honko writes, "The only way out of this dilemma seems to be more and better empirical studies on living oral epic traditions, a careful comparison of the results and their cautious application to other epics whose performance contexts will always remain poorly known but may be elucidated with the help of comparisons."[10]

Ethnographic analogy has been the mainstay of folkloric research for a century. Ethnographic analogy has been the mainstay of anthropological archaeology, too, and its detractors have been vocal for as long.[11] Franz Boas warned us against nomothetic laws based on ethnographic analogy as early as 1896.[12] *If* analogies are broadly based, clusters of correspondence rather than isolated parallels; *if* we use primary sources for ethnographic analogies rather than secondary treatments; and *if* we map the entire source culture onto the subject culture and admit where there are non-correspondences, then ethnographic analogy is an incomparable heuristic tool.[13] This means that an extensive treatment of oral law in some ethnographic analog is required.[14]

FROM ISRAEL TO ICELAND

We will need to be specific with ethnographic analogy. In *Oral Tradition*, I found it most useful to bring in analogies from Iceland. Biblical scholars have a long history of interest in the Icelandic literature, and with good reason.[15] As with Israel, the original context of Icelandic literature's composition and recitation are lost to us, reconstructible only through scenes created in a text itself much later than the material's origin.[16] As with the Hebrew Bible, some scholars argue for primarily written origins and others maintain the texts are written versions of oral tradition.

Having previously explored the operation of narrative and poetry in ancient Israel's oral-and-written culture, law's idiosyncrasies remain to be seen. Legal material found in the Hebrew Bible, and the laws of ancient Israel, however much or little those two correspond to each other,[17] cannot—I judge—be explained *other* than as artifacts of an oral-and-written society. One cannot, for example, begin with exposition of the social complexity in ancient Israel and then work on the basis of analogies (or mere "reasoning") about how "ancient village laws" in general work.[18] This old, evolutionary model of law gave way some time ago in the face of the legal pluralism ethnographic exploration revealed.[19] Rather, the medium of communication is of paramount importance, as Marshall McLuhan famously recognized.[20] Ethnographic analogy provides the best elucidation of how law works in oral-literate societies; one cannot simply opine obiter dicta about oral law.[21] Since we want analogies that are broadly based clusters of correspondence rather than isolated parallels, mapping the entire source culture onto the subject culture, this means that an *extensive* treatment—nearly a third of the present volume—of oral law in Iceland is required.

NOTES

1. Robert D. Miller II, *Oral Tradition in Ancient Israel*, Biblical Performance Criticism 4 (Eugene, OR: Cascade, 2011).

2. Miller II, 46.

3. Karel Van der Toorn, *Scribal Culture and the Making of the Hebrew Bible* (Cambridge, MA: Harvard University Press, 2009), 13.

4. Sara J. Milstein, *Tracking the Master Scribe: Revision through Introduction in Biblical and Mesopotamian Literature* (New York: Oxford University Press, 2016),

7; Jacqueline Vayntrub, *Beyond Orality: Biblical Poetry on Its Own Terms*, The Ancient Word 2 (London: Routledge, 2019), 79, 85.

5. Contra Vayntrub, *Beyond Orality*, 79.

6. Van der Toorn, *Scribal Culture*, 14.

7. David M. Carr, 'Torah on the Heart', *Oral Tradition* 25 (2010): 19.

8. Paul Zumthor, *Oral Poetry*, Theory and History of Literature 70 (Minneapolis: University of Minnesota Press, 1990), 28.

9. Robert D. Miller II, 'Performance of Oral Tradition in Ancient Israel', in *Contextualizing Israel's Sacred Writing: Ancient Literacy, Orality, and Literary Production*, ed. Brian B. Schmidt (Atlanta: Society of Biblical Literature, 2015), 175–96.

10. Lauri Honko, 'Comparing the Textualization of Oral Epics', *Folklore Fellows Newsletter* 13 (1996): 2; Rosalind Thomas, 'Performance Literature and the Written Word', *Oral Tradition* 20 (2005): 5.

11. Alison Wylie, *Thinking from Things* (Berkeley: University of California Press, 2002), 136.

12. Franz Boas, 'The Limits of the Comparative Method of Anthropology (1896)', in *Race, Language, and Culture* (New York: Macmillan, 1949), 275–77.

13. Wylie, *Thinking from Things*, 150; Timothy Insoll, *Archaeology, Ritual, Religion* (New York: Routledge, 2004), 84, 89; Mark Aldenderfer, 'Envisioning a Pragmatic Approach to the Archaeology of Religion', in *Beyond Belief: The Archaeology of Religion and Ritual*, ed. Yorke M. Rowan, Archaeological Papers of the American Anthropological Association 21 (Hoboken: American Anthropological Association, 2012), 27; David S. Whitley, 'Rock Art, Religion, and Ritual', in *The Oxford Handbook of the Archaeology of Ritual and Religion*, ed. Timothy Insoll, Oxford Handbooks (Oxford: Oxford University Press, 2011), 318–19; Marc Verhoeven, 'The Many Dimensions of Ritual', in *The Oxford Handbook of the Archaeology of Ritual and Religion*, ed. Timothy Insoll, Oxford Handbooks (Oxford: Oxford University Press, 2011), 127.

14. Already explored by Albrecht Alt, *Essays on Old Testament History and Religion*, Anchor Books (Garden City: Doubleday, 1968), 131.

15. In addition to the parallels in terms of the uses of writing and forms of literature, Iceland was not a natural growth of a single folk community but a society that emerged from disperate clans whose link was at first only local proximity and perhaps common worship, in many ways similar to most models of Israel's ethnogenesis; James Bryce, *Studies in History and Jurisprudence*, vol. 1.1 (New York: Oxford University Press, 1901), 296–97.

16. Robert D. Miller II, *Oral Tradition in Ancient Israel*, Biblical Performance Criticism 4 (Eugene, OR: Cascade, 2011), 31–35.

17. Douglas A. Knight, *Law, Power, and Justice in Ancient Israel*, Library of Ancient Israel 9 (Louisville: Westminster John Knox, 2011), 52.

18. Berend Meyer, *Das Apodiktische Recht*, Beiträge zur Wissenschaft vom Alten und Neuen Testament 213 (Stuttgart: Kohlhammer, 2017), 120–21; and Elizabeth Bellefontaine, 'Customary Law and Chieftainship: Judicial Aspects of 2 Samuel 14.4–21', *Journal for the Study of the Old Testament* 38 (1987): 47–72 from outdated anthropological theory; Niels Peter Lemche, 'Justice in Western Asia in Antiquity, or

Why No Laws Were Needed', *Chicago-Kent Law Review* 70 (1995): 1705–10, from ethnographic analogy; Bernard S. Jackson, 'Law in the Ninth Century: Jehoshaphat's "Judicial Reform"', in *Understanding the History of Ancient Israel*, ed. H. G. M. Williamson, Proceedings of the British Academy 143 (Oxford: Oxford University Press, 2007), 374–75; and Knight, *Law, Power, and Justice in Ancient Israel*, 96, 98–99, 101, 128–29, from "reasoning"; also Rami Arav, 'Do Biblical Laws Reflect a Tribal Society?', *The Torah.Com* (blog), 13 September 2019, https://www.thetorah.com/article/do-biblical-laws-reflect-a-tribal-society. Knight also misunderstands how orality works, espousing a "Great Divide" between oral and writing societies; Knight, *Law, Power, and Justice in Ancient Israel*, 102, 110.

19. G. C. J. J. van den Bergh, 'The Concept of Folk Law in Historical Context', in *Folk Law*, ed. Alison D. Renteln and Alan Dundes, vol. 1, Garland Folklore Casebooks 3 (New York: Garland, 1994), 18–19; Raymond Westbrook, 'The Laws of Biblical Israel', in *The Hebrew Bible: New Insights and Scholarship*, ed. Frederick E. Greenspahn, Jewish Studies in the 21st Century (New York: New York University Press, 2008), 106; and Bernard S. Jackson, 'Evolution and Foreign Influence in Ancient Law', *American Journal of Comparative Law* 16 (1968): 373.

20. Robert K Logan, *McLuhan Misunderstood: Setting the Record Straight* (Toronto: Key, 2013), 63. I am not, however, suggesting we schematize cultures according to "sensory ratios"; for which, see Marshall McLuhan, 'Alphabet, Mother of Invention', *Etc., A Review of General Semantics*, January 1977.

21. As does Douglas A. Knight, 'Tradition-History-Criticism: The Development of the Covenant Code', in *Method Matters: Essays on the Interpretation of the Hebrew Bible in Honor of David L. Petersen*, ed. David L. Petersen, Joel M. LeMon, and Kent Harold Richards, Society of Biblical Literature Resources for Biblical Study 56 (Atlanta: Society of Biblical Literature, 2009), 112–15.

Chapter Two

Icelandic Oral-Written Law

According to the majority of early sources, the earliest phases of Icelandic legal history are somewhat turbid. A "Thing" or legal assembly was first held in 901 at Thigness, which archaeological research may have uncovered at Kjalarnes.[1] Various other regional Things followed.[2] In 927, Úlfljótr, who would become the first Lawspeaker (*Lögsögumaður*), travelled to Norway to learn law.[3] He returned to Iceland in 930 with a form of the Norwegian Gulathing law, known as *Úlfljótslög*,[4] although no texts suggest this was written.[5] In the meantime, his foster-brother selected the site of Thingvellir for the first Althing, or all-Iceland Thing.[6] Úlfljótr was made Lawspeaker and Thorsteinn Ingólfsson made Allsherjargoði, ostensibly over-chief of the island but with very little real executive power.[7]

Annual midsummer (i.e., white-night) Althings attracted artisans, arabbers, and merchants, juggling troupes and drinking booths,[8] but the Althing was primarily a legislative assembly, deciding legal points and granting exemptions. It also elected the Lawspeaker, selected from accomplished poets and lawyers, whose duty it was to recite the law in its entirety over the course of three years.[9]

For legislative purposes, the Althing acted through a committee of 144, only one-third of whom had the right to vote, called the Lögrétta.[10] The Lögrétta was presided over by the Lawspeaker, who was also expected to answer anyone who asked him what the law was at any time, and his substantive canon interpretation was final.[11] If the Lawspeaker left out something in his recitation of the law and no one objected, it was no longer part of the law.[12] Nevertheless, he delivered no judgments and had no power of enforcing a decision.[13] And the Althing was neither a general assembly of all citizens nor a congress of delegated representatives.[14] New laws were passed not by majority vote, "but as a covenant between free individuals . . . nobody was considered bound by anything he himself had not agreed to."[15]

Throughout the island, serving the chiefs, were lawmen or legists (cf. *Njáls Saga,* 142).[16] In fact, knowledge of the law was essential for every chief, as chiefs were perpetually *pendent lite,* engaged in litigation.[17] This was of necessity since, in a sense, all law was civil and depended on private enforcement.[18]

In 965, the country was divided into Quarters, each of which had its own Thing (*Grágás* 1.38, 241). A fifth "Quarter" was added in 1005. There were thirteen district Things (Kjalarnessthing, Thverarthing, etc.), and thirty-nine local Things, each presided over by a chieftain-priest known as a Goði.[19] Yet Iceland really had no government, as well as no police or even means of raising an army.[20] As a scholion to Adam of Bremen's *History of the Archbishops of Hamburg* put it, "Among them there is no king, but only law."[21]

Úlfljótrslög was unwritten, remaining the oral law of the island—with minor emendations in 994 and 1006 and the addition of an ecclesiastical "Tithe Law" in 1096—until 1117.[22] At that time, the same period when records of laws were made in parts of Scandinavia, the Lawspeaker Bergthor Hrafnsson and "other wise men" dictated the laws to Hafliði Masson, one of the *spakir men* with legal expertise, who wrote out the resultant *Hafliðaskrá,* ratified by the Althing (*Book of Icelanders* chap. 10; *Story of the Conversion* [*Kristni Saga*], chap. 16).[23]

Although written, this law was not really "codified," and law as practiced remained quite divergent and independent.[24] Nor do any written versions of *Hafliðaskrá* exist today. What are extant are 13th-century copies of the *Grágás* or "Grey Goose" Laws (the name dating to the 16th century when they were mistakenly re-applied from a Norwegian collection).[25] Presumably, these codify the earlier laws of Iceland. The *Grágás* itself—and at least one vellum fragment—goes back to about 1150.[26] The oldest (and most complete) written copy of the full text is the *Codex Regius* manuscript from 1250.[27] There are about 130 other copies, the most important being Staðarhólsbók, from 1265, which contains two other texts,[28] and the less complete Skalhóltsbók.[29] Neither *Codex Regius* nor Staðarhólsbók is an official law code; both are private lawbooks.[30] Moreover, the *Grágás* claims there were many manuscripts containing recorded laws in Iceland.[31]

Grágás was the law of the island until the Norwegian throne began to assert control. In 1271, King Magnus Hakonarson sent a lawbook called Járnsíða to replace Icelandic law.[32]

This is the traditional account, and it has many problems, especially with regard to Úlfljótr. That story derives primarily from Ari Thorgilsson's 1130 *Book of Icelanders,* and as we shall see, this document cannot be taken as historically accurate.[33] This is especially true with regard to Úlfljótr's supposed dependence on Norway and Gulathing Law—which bears little resemblance to the *Grágás* (e.g., the *Grágás* replace capital punishment with outlawry; *Grágás* 1.86 vs. *Gulathingslög* 152).[34] *Grágás* are in many ways quite "literary," with evidence of Roman legal influence.[35] We will return to both Ari's slanted account and to Roman and other foreign influence below.

In spite of its indebtedness to literary documents, *Grágás* contains much customary law.[36] The *Grágás* is massive in comparison to other Germanic lawbooks.[37] As a constitution, it is too simplistic and omits too much; on the other hand, its turgid structure and puzzling arrangement make it unwieldy.[38] This characteristic results from a "proliferation of enactments on matters of minor significance."[39] This proliferation comes from it not being merely the Lögrétta who amended old laws and, although the *Grágás* does not say how, enacted new laws, but also private individuals introduced new laws at the Law Rock at the Althing.[40] "Scribes acting on their own initiative may have added many clauses, fleshing out entries in order to satisfy their own personal, and probably clerically oriented views."[41] No one had a monopoly on lawmaking; written texts that contradicted or expanded *Hafliðaskrá* joined survivals of pre-1117 law and written alternative opinions from after 1117.[42] Since no distinction was made between these multiple origins of law,[43] the resultant text is a mixture of entries from different periods, some of them contradicting each other.[44]

Moreover, *Codex Regius* and *Staðarhólsbók* (and textual fragments) differ in order, word choice, and somewhat in content.[45] This is probably the result of there being no "official" version of *Grágás*: copies were all privately owned, and lawmen felt comfortable inserting new material at will.[46] And, as William Miller writes, "Others besides scribes wrote law in Iceland. Icelanders loved law. It was both serious business and great sport. . . . Some people kept their own manuscripts of laws, which may have been faithfully remembered, but then again may have been exercises in writing or proposing legislation."[47] On the other hand, some manuscripts duplicate even scribal errors, indicating direct copying.[48]

Grágás differs from Gulathing Law and every other Scandinavian law collection "in almost all respects,"[49] "in every field."[50] *Grágás* gives no provision for national defense, rules of evidence and court procedure are dissimilar, and there is neither capital nor corporal punishment.[51] The syntax and literary style is not that of Norwegian law (or Nordic law in general).[52] *Grágás,* unlike Norwegian laws, treats all free men and free women on the same level, regardless of social or economic status.[53] Gulathing Law does not mention lawmen.[54] Gulathing Law's Thing was composed of delegates nominated from each district, while the Althing was purely aristocratic: *goðar* and those nominated by their liege-lords to provide convincing arguments as needed.[55]

On the other hand, some of the laws themselves seem to presuppose a setting in Norway, not in Iceland.[56] The Icelandic Lögrétta is directly taken from Gulathing Law.[57] The requirement that manslaughter done in anger can possibly avoid a penalty if the perpetrator summons witnesses to the scene of the crime immediately is in both *Gulathingslög* 151, 156, and *Grágás* 1.86–89. Both *Gulathingslög* 61–62 and *Grágás* K112 allow for semi-emancipated slaves. In *Gulathingslög,* the slave is ritually set on his owner's coffer, and he then remains a dependent freeman; *Grágás* calls these "spade freedmen."

Ari Thorgilsson's scenario is that Úlfljótr travelled three years in Norway and returned with a law based on the Gulathing Law. The *Tale of Thorstein Bull's Leg,* par. 1, from *Flateyarbók*, as well as other texts, omits the reference to the Gulathing.[58] *Landnámabók* claims that Thorleifr the Wise was Úlfljótr's uncle, and *The Book of Icelanders* says Thorleifr was one of the originators of Gulathing Law.[59]

Gulathing was one of three legal districts into which Norway was divided, each of which had its own separate law. The oldest manuscript of *Gulathingslög* is *Codex Rantzovianus*, dated to 1250–1300,[60] centuries after Úlfljótr. On the other hand, some of the laws in Gulathing Law claim to be creations of Olaf II Haraldsson, who reigned 1016–1030.[61] So, is it possible that the lack of correspondence between the two is owing to the lack of a 10th-century form of the law of Gulathing.[62]

On the other hand, scholars now doubt much in Ari's story, including the figure of Thorleif.[63] Ari came from a Norwegian family, and throughout his work takes pains to insist on Iceland's direct link to Norway.[64] On this, we know Ari was wrong; Denmark, for example, played a huge role in Iceland's settlement, and Iceland's land-tenure system is the Danish "gode," not the Norwegian "odel."[65] For Ari, almost everyone who came to Iceland was Norwegian; this is ideologically motivated and cannot be accepted.[66] Iceland's "Norwegian-based" law is likewise a part of Ari's fabrication.[67] It is even possible that Úlfljótr himself is a constructed Moses figure.[68]

Nevertheless, we should not entirely discount the story of Úlfljótr. *Gulathingslög* and *Grágás* do have similarities, and much connects Iceland to Norway: even the spatial terminology of Iceland (*inn, ut, upp, ofan*) is Norwegian.[69] Moreover, Ari uses named sources, the families of whom would have been his living peers; his text shows signs of oral transmission, with many digressions hardly befitting fiction.[70]

As we shall see is true of Old Testament law and Ancient Near Eastern law, *Grágás* is not a treatise on the law and its application. The *Grágás* is, considered on its own, a compendium of minute distinctions on a wide variety of issues in daily life, some of which may "be more the product of the wishes of the law-making elite than the society at large."[71] Many of the provisions were never applied, or only loosely.[72] Instead, its rules served as guidelines for future judgements of the parameters of permitted action.[73]

LAW FROM THE SAGAS

Another potential source for understanding the Icelandic legal system is the corpus of Icelandic sagas, as well as other narratives like *Landnámabók*, the *Book of Settlements*. Reliance on the sagas for information on law declined steadily from the 19th century to the end of the 20th, only to see an uptick in recent decades.[74]

William Miller tends to take the sagas as a reliable source,[75] which suggests (from *Njáll's Saga and Ljósvetninga Saga*), "Law loomed large in imagination and life for more than just the chieftain class. Even pauper children found in lawsuits the subject matter for plays ... and servants from neighboring farms would get together to hold mock courts."[76] In fact, Miller considers "the sagas, in most instances, are to be preferred to *Grágás*" when they disagree, because of their accord "with what we know about dispute processing in other preindustrial societies."[77]

Robert Avis, likewise, relies on *Njáll's Saga* in particular to understand Icelandic law.[78] Njáll is a great lawman because he can match the institutional manifestation of the law with his own idea of what the law ought to do.[79] On the basis of the sagas, Avis understands Icelandic law not "as a social superstructure, a concept that sits above and regulates characters and texts, and instead emphasizes its corporate consensual nature ... a mediating space, rather than a structure."[80]

Hannah Burrows, however, notes that veracity of detail is not a prime concern of the saga writers.[81] Legal disputes form the grist for sagas like *Njáll's* for literary effect, which might even be to comment satirically on the state of the law.[82] In *The Saga of the People of Eyri*, for example, legal technicalities seem to be invented by the saga author because certain laws with certain punishments are needed for the plot.[83] Evidence that sagas depict law only as fits their narrative needs we see also in *Laxdæla Saga,* which has eight scenes set at the Althing or local Things, and only one even refers to court cases; their function as legal meetings is irrelevant for the plot.[84] The exact same thing happens in *Sturlunga Saga.*[85] Burrows concludes that while the sagas can and should be studied for legal information, this must take full notice of the techniques and purposes to which that legal matter is put.[86]

We shall return to how law and the legal profession are described in the sagas, but some of it is curious. Thus, in the *Saga of Havard of Isafjord*, when a whale washes up on the Icelandic shore, the people "accept the Lawspeaker's verdict" without any Thing, suggesting a far more expansive executive role.[87] *Njálls Saga*, 142, suggests there were laws known only to one or two learned legists at a time in Iceland, that nevertheless were considered binding if they were dusted off and brought out in a case:

> "There are more great lawyers alive today than I thought," replied Skapti. "I can tell you that this is so precisely correct that not a single objection can be raised against it. But I had thought that I was the only person who knew this specialty of the law now that Njáll is dead, for to the best of my knowledge he was the only other man who knew it."[88]

On the other hand, legal formulae appear in *Njálls Saga,* 142, identical to *Grágás*: "A man who kills someone or inflicts an internal wound or brain wound or marrow wound" (*Grágás* 1.86).[89] As many writers have noted, the sagas suggest law was the national pastime of Iceland (e.g., *Njálls Saga,* 142).[90] *Ynglinga Saga* (par. 8) even has its Euhemerized King Odin establishing "the same law in his land that had been in force in Asaland" immediately upon his migration to Scandinavia from Troy.[91]

Sagas preserve language clearly borrowed from regular legal discourse. Thus, *Njálls Saga,* 142, has Mördr Valgarðsson name witnesses with this formula: "To testify that I reserve to myself the right to correct any mistakes I may make in my pleading, whether overstatements or errors. I reserve to myself the right to amend any of my pleading until I have given my case its proper legal wording. I name these witnesses on behalf of myself or whomsoever else may require the benefit of this reservation."[92] This hardly reflects a historical speech, but the literary artifact has borrowed from the legal literary (although oral) artifact.

Far less attention has been paid to legal information to be found within Eddic and Skaldic poetry. As I have discussed elsewhere, these are important sources for pre-conversion Icelandic traditions.[93] We should also consider the *þættir* short stories, which form the building blocks of many sagas. Finally, Icelandic ballads, though later than sagas, often derive from oral variants to the written sagas.[94] This is especially clear when the same ballad is known in Iceland, Denmark, and Norway, for instance.[95]

In the Eddic poem "Thrymsqviða," the gods hold a Thing to decide how Thor and Loki can get Thor's famous hammer back from the giant Thrym (par. 15).[96] In "Baldrs Draumar," they hold a Thing to discuss Baldor's nightmares (par. 1). Similarly, the gods hold a Thing for the Last Judgement in the Skaldic poems "Harmsól" 32/1, by Gamli kanóki (Gamlkan), and the anonymous Skaldic poems "Líknarbraut" 27/1, and "Lilja" 72/1.[97]

Hróa þáttr heimska or the *Tale of Roi the Fool* suggests the role of learned lawman was not solely male, as Sigrbjörg, daughter of the famed Swedish Thorgnýr the Lawspeaker, proves to be Hrói's best advisor—and the fact that she is a woman receives no comment.[98] The story also illustrates how even in a setting where a king presides over a Thing, it is the Lawspeaker who has the final decision.[99]

"Þorleifs þáttr járlaskálds" is a short story found in the *Flateyjarbók* manuscript from 1390 and in MS *Izlenzkum fornritum* 9, purporting to deal with events of about 1000.[100] It tells of a man named Thorgarðr coming to Iceland at the Althing, describing "his mound" as being north of the Law Rock in the hollow of Öxará.[101] More importantly, the story provides (par. 8) an etiology (one of several) for the saying, "So a man got a thief in the Thingvellir."[102]

Many such idiomatic phrases include references to Things, especially in Skaldic poetry. "Sneglu-Halla þáttr, relating events of 1050, is preserved in Flateyjarbók manuscript and the 13th-century *Morkinskinna*.[103] It contains (par. 10) a Skaldic poem that was recited at the Gulathing in Norway in the following situation.[104] The skald Sneglu-Halla is asked by King Harold at the Gulathing in Norway how he fares with women; Sneglu-Halla answers, "The Gulathing is good; we both seduce as we please."[105] Sagas, too, reproduce such Thing-related proverbs: "Danger is near where might can sway the Thing" from *Frithiofs Saga* chap. 2.[106] Even modern-era folkloric collections of Icelandic proverbs contain many examples, regularly punning the word "thing": "Often a defect is a good 'Thing'"; "There the youngsters stand up to the Thing, those who speak for their own gain"; "A heel is not an Althing, but it is ridden."[107]

LAW FROM THE PRELITERATE PERIOD

There are several specific issues regarding Icelandic law that merit further exploration. One of these is the relationship of the written laws of Iceland to the law of earlier, preliterate periods. There was, indeed, such a period. As Gisli Sigurðsson points out, there is not "a shred of evidence" that laws were written before 1117.[108] So, this is an important question even if, as I must insist again, the oral and written coexisted until the end of the 13th century.[109]

As Helgi Kjartansson writes, "The law doubtless comprised an important body of oral lore which was shared and developed by acknowledged experts who deliberately passed it on to their successors. . . . The law was—in contrast to modern statute law—based on tradition rather than active legislation."[110] Oral law was not a set of preserved formally adopted rules, however, but manipulated tradition.[111] Nevertheless, similarities in written law suggest an unbroken chain of transmission over many centuries.[112]

What, then, in *Grágás* might date from the earliest times, even from Úlfljótr? Now is not the time to revert to Parry-Lord Oral Formulaicism and look for such "evidence of orality" in *Grágás*.[113] Deixis such as that described above is evidence of oral *performance*, not oral derivation.[114]

As Hannah Burrows writes, "Three-and-a-half centuries of development, adaption, changing and diverging conditions and, for *Grágás* at least, the potential of around 150 years' worth of literary editing, means that there is little on which to base a confident reconstruction of what the laws collected by Úlfljótr in around the year 930 might have been like: length, scope and style are lost to us."[115]

A passage in the early 14th-century *Hauksbók* redaction of *Landnámabók* 1.313–15, also found in *Thorðarbók*, an appendix to *Landnámabók* (chap. H268) preserved in two manuscripts from 1670 (previously, misleadingly, called the *Younger Melabók*), and in "Brot af þorðar sögo hreðu" 14.230–32 from *Landnámabók* chap. S329–30, and in "Thorsteins þáttr uxafóts" from the *Flateyjarbók* MS (1.249), claims to be part of *Ulfjotslög*.[116] Nevertheless, it is thought by many scholars to be a "learned construct of *c.*1200."[117] On the other hand, accounts in the *Íslendingabók* seem to provide some support for its authenticity, or at least its currency before 1200, since it also appeared in the now lost *Styrmisbók*.[118] This passage preserves the account of Úlfljótr travelling to Norway for three years and, without reference to the Gulathing, returning with a law. Here are the three main clauses excerpted:

> Men should not have ships in the sea, but if men had, they would take off their heads before they came into the land, and not sail with a gaping head or a shining head, so that land-guardians would fall. . . .
>
> When a man needed a court to solve a law... he should say, "Help me now, Freyr and Njord and the almighty Áss, whom I will so accuse, or defend, or bear witness, or judgements judge." . . .
>
> The land was divided into quarters . . . there men were diligent to preserve the courts of understanding and righteousness; they were to be jailed, and to guide the trials, for they were called goði, who should also pay a toll to a temple, which is now a church.[119]

This supposed *Ulfjotslög* legislates three things: that ships must remove their mastheads so as to not offend the spirits of the land; an oath formula; and quarters and tolls. The wording sounds Christian, although it need not be—even the word for the toll in the last law.[120] The ship law matches *Egils Saga* and the social conditions of Úlfljótr's time.[121] The wording of the oath, however, sounds "Trinitarian" and the phrase "Almighty Áss" [*ass hin almattki*], which must refer to Thor (see below), sounds Christian.[122] And yet, its wording does not look like typical Icelandic Christian anti-pagan satire, which preferred to remove all references to the "pagan" sacred (e.g., Sturla Thórðarson, Oddr Snorrason OSB, and Gunnlaugr Leifsson OSB).[123] In fact, actual Christian Icelandic creeds such as those of Skapti Thoroddsson, as found in *Njáls Saga*, and as in *Grágás* 1a.3, 22, are decidedly non-Trinitarian, almost Modalist/Sabellianist.[124] Triads of Norse gods appear in *Voluspa* 8, 17–18, 20, and *Skáldskaparmál*, although the triad Thor, Freyr, and Njörðr is not attested elsewhere and Njörðr never otherwise appears in a triad of male gods.[125] "*Hinn almáttki Áss*" resembles Tacitus's use of *Regnator omnia deus* ("god sovereign of all") for a god usually identified with Týr (Germania chap. 39).[126] Jón Aðalsteinsson concludes that all three clauses in "Þorsteins þáttr uxafóts" are pre-1200, and that the first clause is even older.[127]

Another section of the laws, known as Baugatal and dealing with the division of wergild, may also belong to *Ulfjotslög*.[128] That, too, "is very dubious, highly controversial,"[129] and sagas from all periods and regions of Iceland suggest these laws were rarely observed.[130]

On the other hand, Burrows also considers it unlikely that all trace of the pre-written law was erased in 1117 or later editing of *Grágás*.[131] We should not doubt the ability of the law to endure fairly faithfully from the time of pure orality to the *Grágás*. The Lawspeaker had 144 men to act as control on the laws, and as Gunnar Jonsson notes, orally preserved methods of Viking navigation proved remarkably effective without sextant or astral guidance.[132]

PERFORMANCE OF LAW

A second topic for finer-grained study is the relationship after 1117 between written law and the practice of law—in other words, "where legal traditions mix oral tradition and written text."[133]

As I have argued elsewhere, there is no "literacy revolution"[134]; all Jack Goody and Walter Ong suggestions that the "Great Divide" transition from oral culture to literature culture entails radical shifts in power and culture must be abandoned.[135] A version of such a divide undergirds the scholarship of Peter Foote on Icelandic law.[136] Foote argues that by the time of the *Grágás*, "The written word has quite supplanted the memorized word in the realm of legal authority in Iceland."[137] His argument rests on a regulation in *Grágás:*

It is also prescribed that in this country what is found in books is to be law. And if books differ, then what is found in the books which the bishops own is to be accepted. If their books also differ, then that one is to prevail which says it at greater length in words that affect the case at issue. But if they say it at the same length but each in its own version, then the one which is in Skalholt is to prevail. Everything in the book which Haflidi had made is to be accepted unless it has since been modified, but only those things from the sayings of other men learned in law which do not contradict it, although everything in them which restores things left out or makes things clearer is to be accepted. (1.213)[138]

His interpretation of this is that only recorded laws were to be accepted as binding, "even though nobody really knew whether they had ever been adopted in the *Lögrétta*."[139] The Lögrétta, then, "in the early 13th century, probably by the end of the twelfth," no longer had the ability to make laws.[140] Foote admits that *Haflidaskrá* "had nothing like the status of a code"[141] and that it contained prescriptions that were outdated from the start, and that other written sources of law were used, some of them even non-Icelandic, including "collections of *nymæli*; slips and scraps with formulas and special articles."[142] But the "oral age" had given way to a "generation brought up entirely on the study of texts."[143] Much of that study had come through the Church, especially the study of canon law like Pseudo-Isidore and Burchard of Worms's *Decretum*.[144]

William Miller also believes that writing fundamentally changes legal culture,[145] that "oral sensibilities . . . becom[e] literate sensibilities,"[146] and that this section of *Grágás* indicates oral law's authority has given way to written, especially since "variants in oral law would have a way of fading away . . . but the written variant versions did not die."[147]

Miller, however, notes a passage in the 13th-century Norwegian *Speculum Regale*: "We ask all good men who hear this book to give it careful thought and study; and if there should be aught which seems necessary to the work but has not been included . . . let them insert it in proper form and connection. And if they find any matters which seem to impair the work . . . let them discreetly remove all such and thus."[148]

There is, moreover, another interpretation of this clause in *Grágás.* First, this clause assumes other written texts were in circulation alongside *Haflidaskrá* and that they disagreed with it regularly.[149] The clause does not conclude by placing ultimate authority in a text; the considered opinion of lawmen is still conclusive: "If there is argument on an article of law and the books do not decide it, the Law Council must be cleared for a meeting on it. The procedure for that is to ask all the chieftains and the Lawspeaker at Law Rock before witnesses to go to the Law Council" (*Grágás* 1.191).[150] As Sigurður Lindal writes, the abstract law all of these efforts try to fish out is "the good old unwritten law which the chieftains skilled in law retained in their memories. The law referred to must have been unwritten because the chieftains were not summoned to give their ruling *unless the books did not decide.*"[151]

Second, when this clause was drafted, no longer would the Lawspeaker compare his own remembered version of the law with other legal experts: he now had to compare manuscripts. That does not mean, however, that oral performance of the law ceased, or that reiterative recital ended.[152] In fact, Ari's description states that the written law was read in the Lögrétta law council, *not* at the Law Rock, where the Lawspeaker continued to recite the law annually.[153] As Helgi Kjartansson writes, "Pre-recital consultation was adopted . . . and oral recital went on. Meanwhile, the law was being privately codified, using a variety of informants, and collected in ever-larger and ever-more diverse legal manuscripts."[154] In fact, "Whether in its final stage it was still done from memory or from a written text . . . we would not know because their language does not distinguish between recital from memory and recital from a written copy . . . or a bit of both, if the lawspeaker's memory was supported by written notes."[155] Moreover, there is no indication than the Lawspeakers between 1117 and 1139 were even literate, and even as late as 1180 literacy was not a prerequisite for being the Lawspeaker.[156] In any case, the whole of the law was not written down in 1117 and we do not know how much later it actually was.[157]

On the other hand, there may have been written legal memoranda, possibly with runic letters, from a very early period.[158] From Sweden around 900, the Oklunda runic inscription serves to publish legally that a man named Gunnar had followed the refuge law correctly after committing a crime.[159] Even earlier, the Swedish Forsaringen rune ring, now dated to the 800s, actually spells out laws.[160]

How then did the written relate to the oral? How was the law performed? In the *Book of Icelanders,* both the Lawspeaker's recital of the oral law at the Althing and the reading out of written law are described in Icelandic by the same verb, *segja upp* ("pronounce, proclaim").[161] The text of the *Grágás* itself gives indications of performance in such deictic expressions as "here" and "today."[162] Thus, the written law contains remnants of a text that was written to be performed orally or a word-for-word imitation of such performances.[163]

In addition, many sections of *Grágás* contain rhyming, alliteration, and other apparatuses that would on the one hand only be evident in oral performance and on the other hand function in such performance as mnemonic devices for both performers and audience.[164] Thus, Hans Fix catalogues *alþing eða várþing* (1.99.4; 112.16; 136.25; 137.2; 2.179.8), *fé ok fjör* (1.239.19, 21; 2.189.19), *fé eða færi* (1.70.18, 21, 27; 2.8.5; 10.2, 27; 11.1, 18; 18.21; 19.20; 25.4), *fiskja ok fygla* (2.183.13), *geldr eða graðr* (2.193.15), *gera eða mæla* (1.135.12; 136.6), *hann eða hon* (2.32.15; 42.20), *lög eða lof* (1.211.9; 212.8; 213.12); *sækjandi ok seljandi* (1.208.17), and many others.[165]

Alliterative mnemonic words predominate in sections that would be most likely to be performed: nominating judges, for instance.[166]

Grágás also contains Christian legal formulas, Tryggðamál and Griðamál, once in *Codex Regius* at *Grágás* 1a.205–207 and in *Staðarhólsbók* at *Grágás* 2.406–407. They also appear in *Heiðarvíga saga*, chap. 33, and in *Grettis Saga*, chap. 72.[167] There is a closely related though shorter version in *Staðar-hólsbók* at *Grágás* 2.405–406. These are versified legal formulas.[168] They combine metrical poetic mnemonic elements with prose text.[169] Moreover, the eleven-line section in *Codex Regius* that Elizabeth Jackson calls the "Everywhere List," seems to be very old—Migration Age, given parallels in Snorri's *Skáldskaparmál* (chap. 108) and the 8th-century Old English "Maxims I" found in the *Exeter Book*.[170] Even some later pieces in *Tryggðamál*, especially in the *Codex Regius* version, must predate the laws' arrival in Iceland and therefore belong with Úlfljótr's Law, since they require a Norwegian context.[171]

In addition to such poetic devices, orally performed written law in Iceland employed small narratives and proverbs, to which we shall return.[172]

According to the *Book of Icelanders*, training in the law remained entirely oral even after *Hafliðaskrá*.[173] Nor does anything suggest the Lawspeaker possessed a copy of any lawbook after this time.[174] If one looks at a listing of the Lawspeakers, few had any connection to the Church or its associated "book culture," until well into the 13th century.[175]

Several Lawspeakers have extant Skaldic poems attributed to them.[176] The longest-serving Lawspeaker, Skapti Thoroddsson (1004–1030), was poet to Norwegian royalty.[177] The "second-wisest" Lawspeaker after Skapti was Markus Skeggjason (1084–1107), instrumental in the Title Law of 1096, well known as poet to Danish and Swedish kings.[178] The author of the *Third Grammatical Treatise*, an essay on poetics, was the Lawspeaker Óláfr hvítaskáld Thórðarson (1248–1250, 1252), poet to Norwegian, Swedish, and Danish nobility.[179] Lawspeaker Sturla Thorðarson (1251) was the author of *The Saga of Icelanders*, *The Saga of Grettir the Strong*, *The Saga of Haakon Haakonarson*, and the Skaldic poem "Hrafnsmál."[180]

This overlap with poets suggests the oral skills of poet and lawman were similar; mastery of law meant special training in oratory.[181] Once literacy was more widespread, the oral and written supported each other in poetry as well as in law, throughout the wider Scandinavian world.[182] According to sagas, young aspiring legists in the 11th century went to apprentice with experts like Njáll Thorgeirson and Skapti Thóroddsson (e.g., *Njáll's Saga* 27, 142).[183] Nevertheless, the profession was not regulated as it was in Medieval Wales, for instance: there was no colleague control and no specialized literature apart from the laws themselves.[184]

Men said to be good at remembering the oral law (*Book of Icelanders* chaps. 1, 9) often also have religious roles, such as the second Allsherjargoði, Thorkell máni Thorsteinsson (*Landnámabók* chap. 59).[185] Another example is Thorgeir Ljósvetningagoði, the individual ultimately responsible for deciding Iceland would accept Christianity (*Book of Icelanders*, chap. 7).[186] He makes this decision, which has been delegated to him by both the pagan and Christian adherents, after mysteriously retiring "under a cloak" while lying on the ground for some time to deliberate (*Story of the Conversion* [*Kristni Saga*], chap. 12).[187] Much debate surrounds this unusual procedure. All over the North, individuals go "under cloaks" for shamanistic experiences: *Geirmundar þáttr*, *Hálfs Saga*, *Thorsteinn Oxfoot's þattir*, *Egils Saga*, *Vatnsdæla Saga*, *Hávarðar Saga Ísfirðings*, *Finnboga Saga*, and others.[188] Andrea van Arkel cites a procedure outlined in the *Key of Solomon*, a pre-15th-century grimoire, for a magic divinatory carpet, made of new wool under a new moon, beneath which a man goes from midnight to sunrise, lying on the ground while incense burns, emerging at dawn to reveal the answer to all.[189] Thorgeir's behavior thus bridges ritual and legal, illustrating the sacred role of legal agents.[190]

None of this should exclude the importance of laymen with good memories.[191] In the 1270s, a farmer named Loden of Ulvkälla was brought to the Swedish Althing to recite orally forty-one boundary markers he knew.[192] *Hälsinge Law* calls such men "Memory Men" (*Codex Iuris Helsingici* §7; 12; 14.4; 16).[193] The 1413 *Diplomatarium Suecanum* #17767 records lawmen consulting two such Memory Men at a Thing about twelve such stereotyped lists.[194] Several such lists are preserved on Swedish runestones.[195]

Early juridical documents detail oral performances of the law. One example is a 1309 boundary rights transfer described in the *Diplomatarium Islandicum* 3.9, 54–55; 3.10–13.[196] Here, the written word is read aloud, nuncupative.

Grágás is and is not customary law.[197] Nowhere in the *Grágás* is custom invoked.[198] On the other hand, all the evidence from *Grágás* and from written legal fragments of earlier Scandinavia indicate legal custom, not comprehensive laws, were the norm.[199] Yet, as we have seen for early Sweden, oral customary law regularly involved written legal artefacts.[200]

We should also devote some attention to the nature of the Althing itself, as well as other "Things." The Thing is not an institution unique to Iceland; Things were a regular legal venue across the Nordic world, possibly as early as the 6th century.[201] Rune stones from 10th- to 11th-century Sweden mention the creation of Things at several locations, including Gamla Uppsala, Uppland, and Södermanland.[202] Inscriptions indicate other Things at Vallentuna, Bällsta, and Aspås.[203] Danish Things met at Viborg and Øresund.[204] Sheltand had a Lawthing, although the situation on Orkney is less clear.[205] The Faroe Islands had a Thing at Torshavn, Streymoy (Tinganes Peninsula), as well as lesser

Things at í Køltrum in Borðoy and Storagil in Suðuroy.[206] Scotland's Western
Isles had things,[207] and even Greenland had a Thing at Gardar.[208] The version
of the *Saga of the Jómsvíkings* in Flateyjarbók claims that King Sveinn tjú-
guskegg established "Thingamannaleið" at London.[209] Some have argued that
this might only mean a muster of soldiers, but Sven Aggeson argued it was
a proper Thing.[210] Multiple place names contain the element *t[h]ing* across
this region, which may indicate a former Thing: Delting, Nesting, Aithst-
ing, Lunnasting, Sandsting, Thveitathing, and Raudarthing in Shetland, and
Tingwall and Dingieshowe in Orkney.[211] The area of Bury St. Edmunds, the
East Danelaw, which remained Danish until 917, had Thingoe Hundred, and
another Danelaw Thing was probably at Weeting in Norfolk.[212]

Great care went into the selection of a site for a Thing, both in Iceland
(*Book of Icelanders*, chap. 2),[213] and in the Faroe Islands (*Færeyinga Saga,*
chaps. 24–25, 41).[214] Gotland Law (par. 11), Gulathing Law (chap. 91), one
of its Norwegian counterparts, Frostathing Law (1.2), as well as *Egils Saga,*
describe Things as round, enclosed by a perimeter hurdle within which weapons were barred.[215] The 13th-century Norwegian *Hirðskrá* Law, with parallels
to the 11th-century law of the Jomsvikings found in the *Saga of the Jómsvíkings,* 16,[216] prescribes high-seats to be prepared for the attending noblemen.[217]
Heimskringla has King Óláfr Haraldsson assemble nobles on such seats, with
farmers behind them standing and sitting "on hillocks and mounds" in a circle.[218] In *Frithiof's Saga,* the impromptu Thing held at the grave of King Beli
of Sogn is likewise described as rings within rings of men—over a thousand
in total.[219]

Archaeological excavation of Things at Anundshög and Gamla Uppsala
in Sweden, the Frostating at Tinghaugen and the Gulathing site at Florid in
Norway are theatre-like, with wide open areas.[220] These range from 2,475 m^2
at Arkel to 168,750 m^2 at Gamla Uppsala.[221] Thorsteinn Gunsjonsson, following the 19th-century scholar Guðbrandur Vigfússon, considers the Law Rock
to be the oldest element of a Thing, with its role in recitation and sentencing,
the circle (*rétta*) secondary, and the theatrical plain (*völlr*) latest, although
little evidence supports this.[222]

As far as procedure, we have seen that the Icelandic Althing departed
from the representative approach of Gulathing in being an assembly of all
the chieftains. Shetland's Lawthing also followed this all-landowners policy.[223]
There, too, the lawyers (*lögréttu-men*) played a key role.[224] Hirðskrá Law
claims that a horn blast summoned the people to the Thing.[225] *Heimskringla*
has everyone stand when Thorgnyr the Lawspeaker begins speaking.[226]

Although the Lawspeaker office was common to all of Scandinavia, the
Icelandic version has some idiosyncrasies found also in Gotland.[227] Gotland
Law has the advantage over *Grágás* of being more securely dated to an early

period.[228] Given its brevity, recitation of the entirety from memory over three years becomes quite reasonable.[229]

Rituals also appertained to Things. Several Swedish Things were also shrines.[230] As we have seen, within a Thing's boundary, a truce was enforced, as the Swedish Law of Uppland and *Prose Edda* attest.[231] Restricted entry to the Thing enclosure, along with wood and stone monuments that lined the entryway, produced a "monumental choreography," confirmed by written references to ritual processions (Eddic poems "Grímnismál," 30, and "Völuspá"; Skaldic poem "Ynglingatal"; *Ynglinga Saga*).[232] The ritual nature of the Thing site may also have a connection to the location's selection in the first place: the Lawthing site at Torshavn in the Faroes was once the main shrine of Thor.[233] Tynwald Hill on the Isle of Man and Thingvellir in Iceland both show signs of pre-Christian religious activity.[234]

Archaeological remains and descriptions of Thing-goers in *Landnámabók* (chap. 207, 93) suggest those attending wore atypical costuming, perhaps mythological in nature.[235]

THE FUNCTION OF LAWBOOKS

As for the use of the written law, as we have said, *Grágás* is not a treatise on the law and its application. Its provisions never applied or only loosely. This is clear not only from the sagas, but also from extant verdicts: in Iceland and in Norway, even as late as the 13th century, verdicts rarely mention lawbooks or only vaguely.[236] In the 15th century, references do exist, but those are still infrequent: in 1401, 1472, 1480, and 1497.[237]

Like *Grágás*, Gotland Law, too, has no structure. It is not organized into sections. Civil law is interspersed with criminal law, and the same topic (e.g., property law) is treated in multiple sections.[238] Whole sections of the law are ignored or missing.[239] Laws and legal processes attested in *Guta Saga* are absent or contrary in Gotland Law.[240]

How then did the lawbooks function? First, legal codices themselves were tokens of power,[241] present in court as objects for display.[242] Second, some form of the written law served as *aide mémoire* for the Lawspeaker, and the alliteration, rhythm, and so on of *Grágás* and Gotland Law contributed to this employment.[243] Third, the format of *Grágás'* laws—a legal question "spun out in pragmatic fashion, more by accumulation than by systematization. With its series of imagined circumstances [so that] an indefinite extension could be envisaged."[244] Instead of beginning with legal principles, imagined hypothetical scenarios are played out with different parties involved, and that allows for future legal reasoning to extrapolate new cases, the procedures and principles already set by example even if not spelled out explicitly.[245] *Grágás* was, then, not so much a law code as a textbook for legal education, "juristic exercises, some of which may have actually constrained the vagaries of practice . . . some having, as far as we can discern, no effect at all on the practice and the main purpose of which seems to have been nothing more than the satisfaction of a juristic and aesthetic urge."[246]

Finally, it cannot be forgotten that the *Grágás* text and Gotland Law are each a mishmash of layers, from multiple periods of origin.[247]

BORROWINGS FROM FOREIGN LAW

We have seen how Ari exaggerated the Norwegian origins of early Iceland, both legal and demographic. We have also noted some differences between Icelandic law and its supposed ancestor, *Gulathing Law*. Although legal innovation was, as noted supra, a key element of Icelandic legal culture, scholars are also aware that Icelandic law borrows from other legal traditions. This is important for an analogous understanding of Israelite law: such as the ways in which "foreign" law became incorporated into the native legal heritage.[248] In the case of Iceland, two foreign legal traditions figure significantly, one "folk" and one "literate," the former less well documented than the latter.

What I am calling a folk element foreign to Iceland is the possible presence of elements from the Celtic world that may have worked their way into Icelandic law. There are two different ways in which this may have happened.

The first is the pre-Norse occupation on Iceland of Irish (and Scottish) monks, known as Papar. The *Book of Icelanders* records that Irish monks or "Papes" were in Iceland before the Norwegian settlers, fleeing upon their arrival (chap. 1.5).[249] *Landnámabók* mentions Papey and Papyli in Iceland and Kirkiuboer, where Papar had previously dwelled (31–32). Although the evidence of Landnámabók might be disputed as potentially a feature of medieval Icelanders projecting Christianity on the island back into the settlement period, Theodoricus's *Historia de Antiquitate Regum Norwagiensium* claims that a few Irish had lived in Iceland at some point before the settlement, leaving behind books and utensils.[250] The *Historia Norwegiae* says that prior to the Vikings, Orkney was inhabited by Picts and Papae, which it oddly suggests were African Jews.

Prior to these texts, the 9th-century Irish writer Dicuil claims Irish hermits had lived in Thule, probably the Faroe Islands, since the early 700s and observed accurately the length of February versus July days.[251]

Place name evidence has been much debated in connection with the question of early Irish presence in Iceland. Etymologies are debated for Old

Norse "Papar." Earlier scholarship suggested Old Irish, borrowing ultimately from Latin *papa*, in the sense of "cleric."[252] Certainly, in Old Irish, *popa/ pobba* held the meaning of "father" as a respectful secular or clerical form of address.[253] Óengus of Tallaght uses Papa for Irish hermits in his 9th-century *Martyrology*.[254]

Place names formed from the *Papa(r)* are found from the Scottish islands to the Faroes.[255] In Iceland, this includes Papey Island, Papafjord, the Papos confluence, Papyli settlement, Papi pool, Papafell Mountain, Papakross cliff carving, and Papahellir cave.[256]

The archaeological evidence for the Papar is much debated. Small bells and bronze pins found associated with cave habitations of the early 9th century in southwestern Iceland decorated with crosses are markedly similar to sites in western Scotland.[257] The crosses at Heimakletter on Vestmannaeyjar Island, in particular, look like a design taken from St. Columba in Argyll.[258] Archaeological survey at Seljaland and excavation of Kverkathellir Cave showed farming prior to the Settlement tephra layer of 871, and pairing volcanic ash layers of palagonite in 2001 confirmed this dating.[259] Christian gravestones on the Faroe Islands also date to this period.[260] "Symbol stones" have been found at many of the *Papa-* locations: Pabay on the Isle of Skye, Papley on South Ronaldsay in the Orkneys, at Pabbay and Paibles in the Hebrides; somewhat related Cross Slabs appear at Papa Stronsey, Papa Westray, North Ronaldsay, and Papleyhouse (Eday) in the Orkneys and Papil Geo (Noss) in the Shetlands.[261]

On the other hand, some of the *Papar* names are undoubtedly from as late as the 19th century.[262] Many of them show no signs of habitation prior to the Norse.[263]

At the same time, some have argued that the reference in the *Voyage of Saint Brendan* is not to Iceland but to rocky outcrops off the Atlantic coast of Ireland and Scotland.[264] Even the accounts of Thule in Bede's *On the Reckoning of Time* and Dicuil's *De mensura Orbis terrae* to nightless days could be further south than Iceland or the Faroe Islands.[265] Some have argued that the *Papa* names were coined by Vikings *after* the Settlement period in response to the Gaelic interactions of the North Atlantic described below, or in an effort to link Christianity to earliest Iceland, with no connection to the pre-Settlement period.[266]

This would, however, be no justification for *Historia Norwegiae*'s Jewish African Papar. Nor would it account for the location of Papar names only away from the Scottish and Irish mainland, often precisely where Pictish and Gaelic churches have been found,[267] nor the absence of Old Norse terminations like *-garth, -ston, -by,* and *-bister* in the vicinity of Papar place names.[268] Nor would it explain why the Icelandic *Papar* names are only found in the Southwest of the island.[269]

Of course, if the Papar were all driven out by the arrival of the Vikings, what impact could they have made for Icelandic laws?[270] Their departure may be one more of Ari's fictions, however: a land emptied so Norwegians could create *ex nihilo*.[271] Archaeological evidence suggests some of the native Christian lay population survived, as well as a rudimentary organization from the pre-Settlement period.[272] Thus, we need to look at the Viking-period Celtic community.

The second way in which Celtic law could have entered Iceland is after the Viking settlement. It is well known that Irish slaves were brought to Iceland in great numbers.[273] DNA analysis done in 2000 found that 62.5 percent of the original female settlers were of Gaelic origin,[274] and this DNA figure misses altogether the hybrid Hebridean Norse-Gaels to be discussed below.

However, Irish settlers in Iceland were not all slaves. *Hauksbók* devotes much attention to Irish settlers (chap. 307), tracing several back to Cerball mac Dúnlainge, king of Ossory (also the *Sturlubók* version of *Landnámabók* written by Sturla Thórðarson, chaps. 208, 366, and 392).[275] Two percent of the names in *Landnámabók* are Gaelic.[276] A Gaelic-named Hebridean living in Iceland named Gilli appears in *Gold-Thorir's Saga*; another named Anakol is in the *Saga of the Men of Flói*; Rígr from the Eddic poem "Rígsthula" is Gaelic; even the great lawman Njáll has a Gaelic name.[277]

Finally, even Norse settlers of Iceland had already come into contact with various Gaelic legal traditions in parts of the loose "Viking Commonwealth" that stretched from Scandinavia across the Shetland, Orkney, Hebrides, and Faroe Islands to Iceland—a contact unbroken throughout the Middle Ages.[278] This contact included interaction that created a hybrid Celtic-Norse ethnic group known as the Norse-Gaels in the Hebrides.[279] Over the course of the 10th and 11th centuries, Old Norse became increasingly Gallicized in the Hebrides.[280] Many people of the broad commonwealth were bilingual in Norse and Gaelic, a bilingualism on which a joke in the 13th-century *Saga of Bishop Jón of Hólar* depends.[281]

Sigurður Lindal and others have argued that the Icelandic legal system was a mix of the various legal traditions the settlers had known before.[282] This would have included significant Celtic elements from Shetland and Orkney in particular, but also Dublin.[283] *Melabók* indicates the Kjalarnes Thing was established in part by Örlygr Hrappson, foster son of a Hebridean bishop, and Helgi Bjólan, son of Ketill Flatnose—probably the Caittil Find who was leader of the Norse-Gaels and ruler of Dál Riata.[284] Ketill's family provided leadership to an entire migration of Norse-Gaels to Iceland (*Laxdæla Saga*, *Erybyggja Saga*),[285] re-invigorating the Gaelic element when his daughter Auðr the Deep-minded married Óláfr the White, King of Dublin.[286] From this family come Gaelic names (*Bjólan* < *Beolan, Feilan* < *Faelan*), as well as many of the first Icelandic Christians.[287]

There is reason to believe Lindal is correct, since Gaelic influence in Icelandic literature and custom is well established.[288] Indeed, literature was shared across the "Viking Commonwealth": the Norse mythological story of Wayland the Smith occurs in Anglo-Saxon England four hundred years before it appears in a Norse version, in Iceland.[289] For our purposes, Iceland borrowed much folklore from Ireland.[290] *Jarls' Saga* is filled with Celtic elements.[291] The *only* non-Scandinavian element in the speech of the North Atlantic is Gaelic.[292] Pre-Christian water consecration prevalent in Iceland (e.g., *Saga of King Heidrek the Wise*) although unknown in Scandinavia could have derived from Celtic Christians.[293] Even structures of prayers seem to have spread from Ireland via the Hebrides to Iceland and eventually Greenland.[294]

So what aspects and elements of Icelandic law suggest Celtic origins? The Irish legal system, for which we have evidence from the 7th century on, is known as Brehon Law, and no work on it prior to the pioneering scholarship of D. A. Binchy is of any value.[295]

The key transmitters of the law were hereditary poets, *Filid*, who were both professional academics and satirical bards.[296] The *Filid* were also involved in court proceedings and nomography, working alongside clerics on the earliest datable law text, the *Cain Fhuithirbe* or Law of Fuithirbe from the late 7th century.[297] But these *Filid* were the same people who before the coming of Christianity we know as druids, as is made clear in the later introduction to the collection of customary legal texts, the 8th-century *Senchus Mar*.[298]

As would be expected of the work of oral poets, the law texts are frequently alliterative and metrical.[299] They have as their basis archaic snippets of rhythmic poetry called "*Roscad,*" labelled as quotations from the *Fenechas*, designed for oral performance.[300] Some of these legal poems appear in more than one text.[301] In fact, even after literacy spreads in Ireland, legal "schools"—family homes of known legal experts—continued to re-inforce oral performance practices.[302] Other signs of oral performance are deictic phrases and the use of imperative or second-person statements.[303] As Robin Stacey writes, "The lawbooks are literally saturated with references to performances."[304]

Notable in the laws themselves is preference for depriving the guilty of rights rather than execution as punishment for murder or other serious offences.[305]

Thus, potential contributions to Icelandic law from the Celtic world include the pivotal role of priest- and poet-lawmen, the poetic form of the law texts, the strong performative element of legal procedure, perhaps even the emphasis on outlawry as an alternative to capital punishment—although we will see this is a common element of Continental law, too. None of this can be verified, but matters are different when we turn to Icelandic law's borrowing from "learned," literary legal material.

The second external source in Icelandic law is Continental canon law. Canon law was well known in Scandinavia already in the 11th century.[306] According to the 13th-century *Gesta Danorum* of Saxo Grammaticus, both Archbishop Anders Sunesen of Lund and his brother studied abroad around the year 1200. In Iceland, the oldest ecclesiastical statutes were those used around 1100 by Bishop Ketill of Holar and Bishop Thorlakr Runolfsson of Skalholt.[307] Unfortunately, Latin fragments were of so little interest to the 19th-century collectors of early Icelandic manuscripts that we do not know the extent to which canon law was known in Iceland.[308] Nevertheless, the earliest writings in Iceland were ecclesiastical, and we know canon law influenced provincial laws in other Nordic lands.[309] Scholars have recently begun to note several sections of "secular" law in the North demonstrably beholden to canon law.[310]

The extreme is the work of Elsa Sjöholm, who argues that every element of Scandinavian laws is the 14th-century result of the reception of Continental, especially canon law.[311] She does not believe anything in the Norse lawbooks derives from customary law, oral tradition, or indigenous Viking law. Stefan Brink and others have refuted this extreme of the argument, showing as we have seen how Swedish law, for instance, relies on older legal customs attested in runes, in Tacitus's *Germania* (which Sjöholm dismisses entirely), and archaeologically.[312] Moreover, Sjöholm ignores the possibility that any written copies of Scandinavian laws existed prior to the oldest manuscripts that happen to have survived.[313] The laws closely fit the local natural environments they claim to govern, hardly likely for literary borrowings from the Continent.[314]

We know Norse canon law was written in Norway and Iceland in the early 1100s and in Denmark and Sweden around 1200.[315] According to Theodoric the Monk's 1180 *Historia de Antiquitate Regum Norwagiensium,* 16, King Óláfr II Haraldsson and Bishop Grimkell, who was English, promulgated Norwegian canon laws as early as in 1020.[316] This was Western canon law: the three major works of Ivo of Chartres, transmitted via Poland.[317] Yet canon law, too, remained largely oral down to the 13th century.[318]

Nevertheless, we should be thinking of influence not of Roman Canon Law, but of Byzantine. Scandinavian kings always were on better terms with the Byzantine Empire than the Holy Roman Empire, a result of intentional Byzantine foreign policy.[319] In *Morkinskinna* from the early 13th century, King Sigurðr I Magnússon speaks perfect Greek at the court of Alexios I Komnenos, but does not know which Holy Roman Emperor reigns at the time.[320] The Varangian Guard that served the Byzantine Emperors from the 10th to the 14th centuries was composed largely of Northmen, which included alongside those from Rus and even the British Danelaw Icelanders, the one Anna Komnene names "Nabites" at the 1081 Battle of Dyrrhachium in her *Alexiad*.[321] Harald Hardrada served in Constantinople and brought many goods back with him.[322] Runes found in Sweden record returning Varangian Guards, and excavations in Sweden, Gotland, and Denmark give evidence of trade.[323] Russia, too, legally very strongly Byzantine, could have served as a cultural intermediary between Constantinople and the Viking world.[324]

"Armenian hermits" who appear in Ari's *Book of Icelanders* and *Kristni Saga* and in the 12th-century *Veraldar Saga* ("Saga of the World") are not Armenian at all, but betray terminology that comes from the 9th-century Byzantine Emperor Leo V the Armenian.[325]

As far as art, most suggested Byzantine art in Scandinavia and Iceland can be eliminated as Italo-Byzantine art that could have come via Germany or France.[326] One important exception is the 11th-century carved fir panels from Bjarnastaðahlíð in Skagafjörður on Iceland's north coast.[327] Although found in a secular building, this Last Judgement scene is described by the art historian Selma Jónsdóttir as "wholly Byzantine."[328] Apparently, similar panels, even larger, stood in the Hall of Flatatunga until the 19th century.[329] The scene is identical to examples found in Byzantine manuscripts, icons from Mount Sinai St. Catherine's, and Torcello, Venice.[330] Selma Jónsdóttir suggests the carvings could have been copied from illustrations, the result of either Icelandic pilgrims to the East, foreign bishops in 11th-century Iceland, or even the aforementioned "Ermsker" preachers.[331]

Literary influence can also be shown.[332] Ari's treatment of the Last Judgment in the *Book of Icelanders* is Byzantine.[333] The *Langfeðgatal* genealogy, from as early as the 12th or perhaps even 10th century, traces back Scandinavian nobility to Priam of Troy, in contrast to early Anglo-Saxon genealogies.[334] Alexander Bruce considers this might attest to contact with Byzantium as early as in the Migration Period.[335]

Law in the Byzantine Empire—really at this point indistinguishable from "Orthodox" canon law,[336] although the division between "Catholic" West and "Orthodox" East would not have been nearly as clear at the time as it is in hindsight—included the *Ecloga* (726), *Prochiron* (872), *Eisagoge* (880), *Basiliscs* (900), *Epitome* (921), as well as the *113 Novels* Leo VI the Wise added to the *Basiliscs* (ca. 890),[337] and the *Nomokanon in Fourteen Titles* Theodore Bestes added to them in 1090.[338] All of these were set to replace the Justinian Code,[339] whose use was now forbidden.[340] The *Eisagoge* is unique, since unlike the other collections, it introduced new laws.[341] At the same time, customary law played a major role in the Byzantine legal system; as Patriarch

Nikephoros I wrote, "*Quid alium enim est lex nisi scripta consuetudo? Sicuti vicissim consuetudo est lex non scripta,*" "What is law, other than written custom? Contrariwise, custom is unwritten law."[342]

Hans Henning Hoff argues that *Hafliðaskrá* is heavily influenced by Byzantine Law,[343] and that much of that material appears in *Grágás*.[344] The scrivener Hafliði's family had several members who had spent time in Byzantium.[345] Hoff compares both Latin and Greek laws with *Grágás* , finding close parallels to both in terms of content and procedure (e.g., the use of *regulae iuris*),[346] with the strongest parallels being with Byzantine and Byzantine-filtered Roman law.[347] As specific examples, the *Ecloga* 17.49 provides for banishment instead of capital punishment for one who kills in hand-to-hand combat.[348] The legislation in *113 Novels* 70 on homicide reiterates this, matching *Grágás* 88, while *Novels* 25 manumission regulations match those in *Grágás* 112. Imitation of canon law, however, need not be only a matter of contents: the 1180 Danish *Witherlogh* (Lex Castrensis) is "wholly un-Roman" in content but imitates canon law in its phraseology.[349]

Yet one has to ask how much access Scandinavians of any sort would have had to Byzantine law itself. How much contact did average Byzantines have with their own law?[350] Ioannis Konidaris's research indicates that even high-ranking prelates had minimal knowledge of the actual contents of the laws.[351] Only the most powerful elite had such access,[352] and in this sense it is clear the connections are stronger between powerful Icelandic families and the nobility of Dublin and the Hebrides than they are with the Byzantine court.

* * *

INTERLUDE: GOTHIC LAW AS CONTROL

Before the ethnographic analogies of Icelandic law are applied to ancient Israel, an objection should be raised. Iceland corresponds closely to Israel in terms of literacy, in terms of the interplay of literacy and orality, an oral-and-writing culture. However, when it comes to law, the isolation of Iceland could be the spanner in the works. Iceland was never invaded, a self-contained polity that could dispense with "providing for the common defense," and thus, as we have seen, with central administration.[353] Moreover, the population of Iceland was very low: 60–70,000 people over an area of 40,000 square miles.[354] These idiosyncrasies could impel the creation of completely different legal institutions.

Ideally, following my 2012 *Oral Tradition in Ancient Israel*, one could appeal to traditional Arabic law, given the use I made then of Arabic epic oral poetry.[355] No Arabic legal tradition exists apart from Islam, however, rendering it impossible to use as a comparand. I will therefore briefly glance at Gothic law as a check on our comparison with Iceland.

First, it must be made clear that "gone with the wind is the idea of 'Germanic Law.'"[356] Jakob Grimm began his career as a student of legal history and his work on folklore was largely a response to the belief that the *Volkgeist* was preserved in a nation's customary law.[357] Grimm continued to work on Germanic law, arguing it had been transmitted orally.[358] Scholarship in the 19th and much of the 20th century held to the notion that customary law endured unchanging in oral societies, preserved in poetic form.[359] Because all Germanic languages seemed to have the same inventory of legal terms and phrases, Grimm and others believed all speakers of Germanic languages inherited a very old, homogenous *germanisches Urrecht*.[360] At one time, *Grágás* was readily included in this unity.[361] Since 1961, this idea has been increasingly debunked and can no longer be sustained.[362]

I am not, therefore, arguing that we can look at Gothic law because it belongs with Icelandic and other Viking law to a massive entity of Germanic law. I am instead bringing Gothic law in because while the Nordic laws are the youngest of the so-called *Leges Barbarorum,* the Gothic are the earliest: that is, the Visigothic *Codex of Euric* (475–480), *Breviary of Alaric II* (506), and *Lex Visigothorum* (654), Burgundian *Liber Contitutionem* (517), Lombard *Edict of Rothair* (643).[363] No Ostrogothic equivalent has been discovered.[364] The Gothic are thus the oldest legal systems with many of the characteristics of Icelandic law we are interested in[365]—the earliest Things, their Þeihs[366]—but without Iceland's isolation. As Ditlev Tamm writes, "The comparative aspect based on reflections on the institutions and the language of the laws are still valid and should guide us when we try to grasp the essence of Nordic medieval law."[367]

On the other hand, sometimes, precise similarity to Nordic Law is present: Lombard legal traditions are closer to the Nordic than to the German.[368] Whether this is because the Goths were originally *from* Gotland in Sweden, is debatable.[369] The Thing of All Geats did sit in Skara, Västergötland, from pre-Christian times.[370] The 13th-century *Saga of Bósi and Herraud* indicates Odin was worshipped under the name Gautr in Gotland, an area Alfred the Great knows by that name in the 9th century.[371] On the other hand, Arne Christensen argues extensively against any connection, the Goths' supposed northern origins being a mythic invention of Cassiodorus, so Goths and Geats are unrelated.[372] In any case, the ethnic origins of the Goths would have been quite complex in a world of Scythians, Sarmatians, and Alans, without boundaries.[373]

Visigothic laws later than Euric can probably be removed from considerations, although earlier scholarship argued for long-term oral customary continuity with the "Germanic base."[374] Spanish sources from the time of the Muslim invasions of Visigothic Spain show judicial institutions unmentioned in the Visigothic law codes and often directly opposite practices.[375] When the Goths arrived in Hispania, some 300,000 Visigoths met 12–15 million indigenous Iberians; the customary law that resulted was not Germanic but heavily Roman.[376] Pre-Hispanian Visigothic law is Euric's Code, of which only a sixth survives and much of that unintelligible.[377] This is unfortunate, since it exemplifies the durability of law that embraces custom, as its influence shows up in the present laws of the state of Texas.[378] Likewise, the Frankish laws—Salic, Ripuarian, and so on—are not a good source because their contents and dating are suspect.[379]

Although no Germanic ur-law unitary tradition existed, there are multiple commonalities in the legal texts of the early Gothic Germanic peoples.[380] Identical clauses are found in every example.[381] In fact, the various legal systems—Visigothic, Salic, and so on—were mutually accepted.[382] Turning to specific examples, the law of the Langobards or Lombards is "usually regarded as a statement of almost pure Germanic [sic] custom."[383] They emphasize the policy of *wergild,* a tariff charged for various forms of assault between equals dependent on the severity (*Rothair's Edict,* 12–14).[384] This seems to be already present for Tacitus's *Germani* (*Germania* 12, 21).[385] Compurgation is the main method of proof in determining rights of a party in a suit.[386]

Many written artifacts of law were promulgated by kings. In those cases, kings made a *portion* of customary law their own as an aspect of assertion of royal authority.[387] That the law was customary before its textualization is an assumption, admittedly, but one made by most scholars today.[388] The kings did not "draw the attention of the users" to the laws' continuation or emendation of customary law.[389] On the other hand, several legal texts were not ascribed to a king.[390]

In the end, what was produced were no more "codes" than was *Grágás*—certainly not in the sense of Justinian's *Code.*[391] The Gothic codes are disorganized and contradictory.[392] As Patrick Wormald writes, "Some legal manuscripts make arrant nonsense." . . . They "must have had hair-raising results if their work was ever produced in court."[393] Most manuscripts of these texts were done by private individuals, not royal officials.[394] Like *Grágás* and the other Nordic "law codes" we have seen, the written texts had a purpose "more or less regardless of its actual value to judges sitting in court."[395] Actual judicatory cases, as in the Norse world and the Ancient Near East, rarely make reference to written law.[396]

Since we know that functioning law in the Gothic kingdoms was quite efficient, these characteristics of the written laws must indicate that normal judicial procedure and legislation were oral activities.[397] Judges (e.g.,

Ostrogothic) regularly appeal to customary law for their decisions.[398] This is not because these were illiterate societies,[399] and the increase in literacy shows no relationship to increase in citations of written law.[400] Writing law had a distinct, unrelated purpose.

Like the Icelandic counterpart, Gothic law "codes" regularly incorporate material of a literary origin, especially Roman canon law.[401]

* * *

RESUMÉ: ORAL-WRITTEN CUSTOMARY LAW

We can now summarize the comparative evidence. The law comprised a body of oral lore shared and developed by acknowledged experts who deliberately passed it on to their successors. The law was based on tradition rather than active legislation. Oral law was not a set of preserved formally adopted rules, however, but manipulated tradition.

On the other hand, there may have been written legal memoranda, possibly with runic letters, from a very early period.

Nevertheless, similarities in written law suggest an unbroken chain of transmission over many centuries, preserving some authentic elements in writing that derive from oral law, some of it earlier than the written text. Moreover, the written law contains remnants of a text that was written to be performed *ore tenus* or a word-for-word imitation of such performances. Laws contain rhyming, alliteration, and other apparatuses that would on the one hand only be evident in oral performance and on the other hand function in such performance as mnemonic devices for both performers and audience.[402] In addition to such poetic devices, orally performed written law employed small narratives and proverbs. Lawmen overlap with poets, which suggests the oral skills of poet and lawman were similar; mastery of law meant special training in oratory. Men said to be good at remembering the oral law often also have religious roles. None of this should exclude the importance of laymen with good memories.[403]

Great care went into the selection of a site for a Thing: round, 2,475 m^2 to 168,750 m^2, enclosed by a perimeter hurdle within which weapons were barred, high-seats prepared for the attending noblemen, with farmers behind them standing and sitting on hillocks and mounds in a circle. Things were sacred locations, with ritual actions and perhaps even ritual costume. Such legal liturgy serves both to conserve the law and to reinforce its authority.[404]

We are dealing with customary law, at least as viewed according to Legal Realism.[405] That is, it is an assembly of legal usages that acquires obligatory force in a socio-political group by the repetition of public acts and enduring over a relatively long span of time.[406]

Customary law regularly employs "oral skills, memory, and testimony, as well as the various iconographic . . . elements of legal procedure."[407] Customary law need not be unwritten *parol*, but its relationship with written artifacts of law is distinct, as we have seen.[408] Maunier calls it "*droit écrit-oral.*"[409] Lawbooks are by no means rare in customary legal cultures—it is not a matter of illiterate societies[410]; such books are depositories for interwoven mixtures of material and glosses.[411] Even where diachronic development does not go into these lawbooks, because law and customs are not sharply delineated, the "laws" "are porous and malleable. Because they have no clear definition, it is difficult to differentiate one rule from another, and, in consequence, to classify rules according to type. If rules cannot be classified, they cannot be arranged into a system, and, without the discipline of a system, rules may overlap and contradict one another."[412]

In customary law, when a case arises for which no valid law can be adduced, jurists extrapolate from laws that have been put into practice under the assumption that they are putting forward existing law not hitherto explicitly expressed. They are discovering law, not making it.[413] This will be important in the discussion of Israelite law that follows.

We have just considered the presence of kernels of the oral law in the written law. But what is the function or nature of the whole codes, the corpus of written law? How then, did the lawbooks function? First, legal codices themselves were tokens of power, present in court as objects for display. Second, some form of the written law served as *aide mémoire* for the Lawspeaker. Third, the format of these laws—a legal question spun out in pragmatic fashion, more by accumulation than by systematization; "an intricate but pattern-less tracery of variant detail"[414] with its series of imagined circumstances so that an indefinite extension could be envisaged—suggests that hypothetical scenarios are being played out with different parties involved to allow for future *casus incogitatus* legal reasoning to extrapolate new cases, the procedures and principles already set by example even if not spelled out explicitly.[415] Thus, the "codes" were not so much law codes as textbooks for legal education, juristic exercises.[416]

In Owen Barfield's description, those exercises are analogous to metaphor formation: like the movement from literal to simile to metaphor, customary and common law develops by means of fictions, fictions drawn out of a people's social life.[417] From the fiction, principles are drawn that can be applied in new situations.[418] Sometimes those principles are even explicitly added. "Has new law been made?" Barfield asks; "It is much the same as asking whether new language has been made when a metaphor disappears into a 'meaning.' . . . 'Substantive law has at first the look of being gradually secreted in the interstices of procedure.' This is particularly true of an unwritten system."[419]

Of course, the "codes" might be used by officials, as well, but as part of "research into a general body of principles for the correct solution of a specific problem to which they might be applied—and indeed, much new law grew up in this way over time."[420] In this way, the written "law" becomes, as Oliver Wendell Holmes said, "the witness and external deposit of our moral life."[421] Indeed, the Hebrew term *'ēdût,* favored by the so-called Priestly Writer, derives from the root meaning of "witness" (Gen 31:52; Exod 31:18; Deut 31:19; Josh 22:27, 34; 24:27; Ruth 4:9–10; Sir 34:23; 36:20) and signifies law precisely because the written law is (like Joshua's stone in 24:27) a physical, permanent witness to the covenant made with God (Exod 31:18; Deut 31:26).[422]

Customary law does not necessarily need to have been approved by sovereign authority.[423] In that sense, judiciary power precedes legislative power, and real legislation codifies what is already in force.[424] As we have seen, the design of the so-called codes facilitates extending existing law to cover new cases *casus omissus.*[425] Nevertheless, elites are certainly involved in this process: they, not some vague *Volk,* are the ones extending and applying.[426] Customary law may have specific social actors who transmit law from one generation to the next.[427]

Both the actual oral or oral-and-written customary law and the written so-called law codes also incorporate foreign material, borrowed from literature both oral and written of other peoples,[428] especially from more cosmopolitan, heavily literary societies. That this incorporated material is largely written—and may not be customary at all—does not annul the customary nature of the target legal system.[429]

But alongside this kind of borrowing, there is a more fluid lack of boundaries with customary law, as we saw with the Gothic laws.[430] "In the course of contacts—involving conflicts, or co-operation—between people, human groupings, communities of people, and human societies customary laws have been coming into touch more quickly and easily than have written laws, thereby influencing one another, mutually or unilaterally."[431]

Moreover, these so-called codes are each a mishmash of layers, in part because they come from multiple periods of origin.[432] But that is not the only reason. "The particularistic mass of common [i.e., customary] law is notably resistant to large-scale systematization or to clear logical structure within any attempted systematization."[433]

Finally, as in *Úlfljótslög,*[434] it is typical in customary law for matters that we would not consider "law" to be treated of a piece with law: customs and conventions are not seen as distinct from customary laws.[435] "Life is seen as a network of relations dominated by custom, and in this custom one does not distinguish between what relates to the law and what relates merely to convention."[436] Especially the conduct of spiritual life is likely to be treated alongside economics and governance.[437]

Even when societies do adopt codification—and it will be argued that Pre-Exilic Israel and Judah did not—it may be at times that a written statute enables the recognition of a customary law, while at other times a truer codification still does not end the customary law. It merely means that the code and the custom both have the force of law, but one is particular while the other remains amorphous.[438] I would contend that even after Post-Exilic Jews understood that a written text could make law as well as describe it, they formally preserved the theory that written law was merely declaring the law that already existed.[439] Moreover, as we shall see in the Ancient Near East, customary law gives judges the power to compel results quite unlike that which the legal rule strictly applied would require.[440]

NOTES

1. Stefan Brink, 'Law and Legal Customs in Viking Age Scandinavia', in *The Scandinavians: From the Vendel Period to the Tenth Century*, ed. Judith Jesch, Studies in Historical Archaeoethnology 5 (San Marino: Boydell, 2012), 91.

2. Pall E. Olason, ed., *Codex Regius of Gragas*, Corpus Codicum Islandicorum Medii Aevi 3 (Copenhagen: Levin & Munksgaard, 1932), 6.

3. *Gold-Thorir's Saga*, chap. 15; Viðar Hreinsson, ed., *The Complete Sagas of Icelanders, Including 49 Tales*, Viking Age Classics (Reykjavík: Leifur Eiríksson, 1997), 3.354; *Book of Icelanders*, chap. 2; Siân Grønlie, ed., *Íslendingabók =: The Book of Icelanders*, Text Series/Viking Society for Northern Research 18 (London: Viking Society for Northern Research, 2006), 4.

4. Norway was divided into five provinces, each with its own law; Gulathingslag was binding over six counties; Peter Fisher, trans., *Historia Norwegie* (Copenhagen: Museum Tusculanum Press, 2003), 179.

5. Patricia P. Boulhosa, 'Ideas of Law in Medieval Icelandic Legal Texts', in *Legislation and State Formation*, ed. Steinar Imsen, Norgesveldet Occasional Papers 4 (Trondheim: Akademika, 2013), 169.

6. Bryce, *Studies in History and Jurisprudence*, 1.1:271.

7. Thus the term 'Goðic Republic'; Thorsteinn Gundjonsson, *Thingvellir* (Reykjavik: Formprent, 1985), 27.

8. Bryce, *Studies in History and Jurisprudence*, 1.1:279.

9. *Gragas* 1.187-88, 192-93; Sigurður Nordal, *Icelandic Culture* (Ithaca, NY: Cornell University Press, 1990), 80; Helgi Skuli Kjartansson, 'Law Recital According to Old Icelandic Law', *Scripta Icelandica* 60 (2009): 92; Theodore M. Andersson

and William I. Miller, *Law and Literature in Medieval Iceland* (Stanford: Stanford University Press, 1989), 126 n. 15; Andrew Dennis, Peter Foote, and Richard Perkins, trans., *Laws of Early Iceland: Gragas*, vol. 1 (Winnipeg: University of Manitoba Press, 1980), 187.

10. Bryce, *Studies in History and Jurisprudence*, 1.1:275.

11. *Gragas* 1.208-210, 216-17 Bryce, 1.1:275; Gisli Sigurðsson, *The Medieval Icelandic Saga and Oral Tradition* (Harvard University Center for Hellenic Studies eBook), accessed 14 January 2019, https://chs.harvard.edu/CHS/article/display/6824.part-i-oral-tradition-in-iceland-in-the-twelfth-and-thirteenth-centuries-1-from-lawspeaker-to-lawbook.

12. David Friedman, *The Machinery of Freedom*, 2nd ed. (La Salle, IL: Open Court, 2015), 203; Birgir Runolfsson Solvason, 'Ordered Anarchy: Evolution of the Decentralized Legal Order in the Icelandic Commonwealth', *Journal Des Economistes et Des Etudes Humaines* 3 (1992): 1–20.

13. Bryce, *Studies in History and Jurisprudence*, 1.1:276.

14. Bryce, 1.1:297.

15. Helmut Lugmayr, Björg Árnadóttir, and Andrew Cauthery, *The Althing at Thingvellir* (Reykjavík: Iceland Review, 2002), 11.

16. *First Grammatical Treatise*, 224–27.

17. Gisli Sigurðsson, *The Medieval Icelandic Saga and Oral Tradition*.

18. Friedman, *The Machinery of Freedom*, 204; David Friedman, 'Private Creation and Enforcement of Laws', *Journal of Legal Studies* 8 (1979): 401, 406.

19. Bryce, *Studies in History and Jurisprudence*, 1.1:273.

20. Bryce, 1.1:280; Friedman, *The Machinery of Freedom*, 203; William I. Miller, 'Of Outlaws, Horsemeat, and Writing: Uniform Laws and Saga Iceland', *Michigan Law Review* 89 (1991): 2090.

21. Book 4, schol. 156 (150); Adam of Bremen, *History of the Archbishops of Hamburg-Bremen*, trans. Francis Joseph Tschan, Records of Western Civilization (New York: Columbia University Press, 2002), 217.

22. Bryce, *Studies in History and Jurisprudence*, 1.1:287, 292; Jesse L. Byock, *Viking Age Iceland* (London: Penguin, 2001), 309; Stefan Brink, 'Minnunga Maen: The Usage of Old Knowledgeable Men in Legal Cases', in *Minni and Muninn: Memory in Medieval Nordic Culture*, ed. Pernille Hermann, Stephen A. Mitchell, and Agnes S. Arnórsdóttir, Acta Scandinavica 4 (Turnhout: Brepols, 2014), 198.

23. Grønlie, *Íslendingabók*, 53; Axel Olrik, *Viking Civilization* (New York: American Scandinavian Foundation, 1930), 206; Peter Foote, *1117 in Iceland and England*, Dorothea Coke Memorial Lectures (London: Viking Society for Northern Research, 2002), 6; Hannah Burrows, '"In This Country, What Is Found in Books Is to Be Law"', *Quaestio Insularis* 8 (2007): 40.

24. Nordal, *Icelandic Culture*, 40.

25. Dennis, Foote, and Perkins, *Laws of Early Iceland: Gragas*, 1:9; prior to this time, the *Gragas* went by various terms: *Allsherjarlög, Varlög, Islenzklög*; Olason, *Codex Regius of Gragas*, 6; on the precise dating, see Patricia P. Boulhosa, *Icelanders and the Kings of Norway: Mediaeval Sagas and Legal Texts*, Northern World 17 (Leiden: Brill, 2008), 48–51.

26. Byock, *Viking Age Iceland*, 309.

27. MS 1157 in folio from the Old Royal Collection in Copenhagen, now restored to Iceland; Nordal, *Icelandic Culture*, 40.

28. MS 334 in folio in the Arni Magnusson Collection, Copenhagen; Byock, *Viking Age Iceland*, 308–9; on the dating, see Olafur Larusson, ed., *Staðarhólsbók: The Ancient Lawbooks Gragas and Jarnsiða*, Corpus Codicum Islandicorum Medii Aevi 1 (Copenhagen: Levin & Munksgaard, 1936), 9–10.

29. Olason, *Codex Regius of Gragas*, 6.

30. Byock, *Viking Age Iceland*, 309.

31. Jon Viðar Sigurðsson, 'The Education of Sturla Þórðarson', in *Sturla Þórðarson: Skald, Chieftain, and Lawman*, ed. Jon Viðar Sigurðsson and Sverrir Jakobsson, The Northern World 78 (Leiden: Brill, 2017), 26.

32. Patricia P. Boulhosa, 'Narrative, Evidence and the Reception of Jarnsiða', in *Sturla Þórðarson: Skald, Chieftain, and Lawman*, ed. Jón Viðar Sigurðsson and Sverrir Jakobsson, The Northern World: North Europe and the Baltic c. 400–1700 AD. Peoples, Economics and Cultures 78 (Leiden: Brill, 2017), 223; Jorn O. Sunde, 'Daughters of God and Counsellors of the Judges of Men', in *New Approaches to Early Law in Scandinavia*, ed. Stefan Brink and Lisa Collinson, Acta Scandinavica 3 (Turnhout: Brepols, 2014), 138.

33. Sigurður Lindal, *Law and Legislation in the Icelandic Commonwealth* (Stockholm: Stockholm Institute for Scandinavian Law, 2009); Byock, *Viking Age Iceland*, 93.

34. Byock, *Viking Age Iceland*, 95; Bryce, *Studies in History and Jurisprudence*, 1.1:289.

35. Nordal, *Icelandic Culture*, 41.

36. Byock, *Viking Age Iceland*, 308.

37. Nordal, *Icelandic Culture*, 41.

38. Bryce, *Studies in History and Jurisprudence*, 1.1:284–85.

39. Byock, *Viking Age Iceland*, 311.

40. Byock, 310; Lindal, *Law and Legislation in the Icelandic Commonwealth*, 63.

41. Byock, *Viking Age Iceland*, 318.

42. Dennis, Foote, and Perkins, *Laws of Early Iceland: Gragas*, 1:10; Lindal, *Law and Legislation in the Icelandic Commonwealth*, 67; Gisli Sigurðsson, *The Medieval Icelandic Saga and Oral Tradition*; Stefan Brink, 'The Creation of a Scandinavian Provincial Law: How Was It Done?', *Historical Research* 86 (2013): 436; Stefan Brink, 'Reconstruction of Viking and Early Medieval Scandinavian Society', in *Early Law in the North* (forthcoming), 8.

43. Lindal, *Law and Legislation in the Icelandic Commonwealth*, 65.

44. Byock, *Viking Age Iceland*, 311; Dennis, Foote, and Perkins, *Laws of Early Iceland: Gragas*, 1:9–10; Brink, 'Reconstruction of Viking and Early Medieval Scandinavian Society', 14.

45. Byock, *Viking Age Iceland*, 312.

46. Dennis, Foote, and Perkins, *Laws of Early Iceland: Gragas*, 1:11; Miller, 'Of Outlaws, Horsemeat, and Writing', 2091.

47. Miller, 'Of Outlaws, Horsemeat, and Writing', 2091; Lindal, *Law and Legislation in the Icelandic Commonwealth*, 90.

48. Peter Foote, 'Oral and Literary Tradition in Early Scandinavian Law', in *Oral Tradition, Literary Tradition* (Odense: Odense University Press, 1977), 52.

49. Byock, *Viking Age Iceland*, 313; William Ian Miller, *Bloodtaking and Peacemaking: Feud, Law, and Society in Saga Iceland* (Chicago: University of Chicago Press, 1996), 222.

50. Sigurður Lindal, 'The Law Books', in *Icelandic Sagas, Eddas, and Art*, ed. Jónas Kristjánsson (New York: Pierpont Morgan Library, 1982), 41.

51. Byock, *Viking Age Iceland*, 313; Boulhosa, 'Ideas of Law in Medieval Icelandic Legal Texts', 176; Lindal, 'The Law Books', 41.

52. Foote, 'Oral and Literary Tradition in Early Scandinavian Law', 51.

53. Preben M. Sørensen, 'Social Institutions and Belief Systems of Medieval Iceland (c. 870-1400) and Their Relations to Literary Production', in *Old Icelandic Literature and Society*, ed. Margaret Clunies Ross, Cambridge Studies in Medieval Literature 42 (Cambridge: Cambridge University Press, 2000), 22.

54. Laurence M. Larson, trans., *The Earliest Norwegian Laws, Being the Gulathing Law and the Frostathing Law* (New York: Columbia University Press, 1935), 24.

55. J. Storer Clouston, 'Odal Orkney', *Saga-Book* 7 (1911): 88–89.

56. Dennis, Foote, and Perkins, *Laws of Early Iceland: Gragas*, 1:10.

57. Larson, *The Earliest Norwegian Laws, Being the Gulathing Law and the Frostathing Law*, 9; Lester B. Orfield, *The Growth of Scandinavian Law* (Union, N.J: Lawbook Exchange, 2002), 90.

58. Viðar Hreinsson, *The Complete Sagas of Icelanders, Including 49 Tales*, 5.341.

59. Miller, *Bloodtaking and Peacemaking*, 226.

60. Boulhosa, *Icelanders and the Kings of Norway*, 54–55.

61. Alexandra Sanmark, *Viking Law and Order: Places and Rituals of Assembly in the Medieval North* (Edinburgh: Edinburgh University Press, 2017), 10; Ditlev Tamm, 'How Nordic Are the Old Nordic Laws?', in *How Nordic Are the Nordic Medieval Laws: Proceedings from the First Carlsberg Conference on Medieval Legal History*, ed. Per Andersen, Ditlev Tamm, and Helle Vogt, 2nd ed. (Copenhagen: DJØF Pub, 2011), 15.

62. Ann-Marie Long, *Iceland's Relationship with Norway c.870–c.1100*, The Northern World 81 (Leiden: Brill, 2017), 132; Hans Henning Hoff, *Hafliði Másson und die Einflüsse des römischen Rechts in der Grágás*, Ergänzungsbände zum Reallexikon der germanischen Altertumskunde 78 (Boston: De Gruyter, 2011); if the Gulathing even existed at that time; on which, see Long, *Iceland's Relationship with Norway*, 130–31; and, sed contra, Brink, 'Law and Legal Customs in Viking Age Scandinavia', 91; Brink, 'Reconstruction of Viking and Early Medieval Scandinavian Society', 6. Since Norwegian law adapted in Orkney and Shetland already in 872 is essentially Gulathing Law, Brink would seem correct here; Eileen Linklater, 'Udal Law—Past, Present and Future?' (LLB Diss., Glasgow, University of Strathclyde, 2002), (9829970); Jane Ryder, 'Udal Law: An Introduction', *Northern Studies* 25 (1988): 3; Anne I. Riisøy, 'Outlawry', in *New Approaches to Early Law*

in Scandinavia, ed. Stefan Brink and Lisa Collinson, Acta Scandinavica 3 (Turnhout: Brepols, 2014), 104.

63. Birgir Runolfsson Solvason, 'Ordered Anarchy'; Jesse L. Byock, 'Governmental Order in Early Medieval Iceland', *Viator* 17 (1986): 33; Matthias Egeler, 'A Retrospective Methodology for Using Landnamabók as a Source for the Religious History of Iceland?' Some Questions, *Retrospective Methods Network Newsletter* 10 (2015): 78; Höfig Verena, 'A Pre-Modern Nation? Icelanders' Ethnogenesis and Its Mythical Foundations', *Scandinavian Studies* 90 (2018): 125. Riisøy, 'Outlawry', 105 remains convinced of Ari's accuracy.

64. Byock, 'Governmental Order in Early Medieval Iceland', 33; Long, *Iceland's Relationship with Norway*, 70, 73, 127; Grønlie, *Íslendingabók*, xv, xxv–xxvii.

65. Viggo Starcke, *Denmark in World History* (Philadelphia: University of Pennsylvania Press, 1969), 206.

66. Long, *Iceland's Relationship with Norway*, 81–82, 124–25; Grønlie, *Íslendingabók*, xxv.

67. Long, *Iceland's Relationship with Norway*, 116, 122; Grønlie, *Íslendingabók*, xxvii–xxviii.

68. Long, *Iceland's Relationship with Norway*, 134.

69. Boulhosa, 'Ideas of Law in Medieval Icelandic Legal Texts', 172.

70. Jón Hnefill Aðalsteinsson, *Under the Cloak: A Pagan Ritual Turning Point in the Conversion of Iceland*, 2nd ed. (Reykjavík: Háskólaútg, 1999), 180.

71. Byock, *Viking Age Iceland*, 314–15; Jon Viðar Sigurðsson, 'The Education of Sturla Þórðarson', 27.

72. Byock, *Viking Age Iceland*, 318.

73. Byock, 318.

74. Gunnar Jonsson, 'Waldgang und Lebensringzaum (Landesverweisung) im alteren islandischen Recht' (Diss., Hamburg, Hamburg University, 1987), 12; Hermann Baltl, 'Folklore Research and Legal History in the German Language Area', in *Folk Law*, ed. Alison D. Renteln and Alan Dundes, vol. 1, Garland Folklore Casebooks 3 (New York: Garland, 1994), 399.

75. So, too, William Pencak, *The Conflict of Law and Justice in the Icelandic Sagas*, Value Inquiry Book Series 21 (Amsterdam: Rodopi, 1995).

76. Miller, *Bloodtaking and Peacemaking*, 227.

77. Miller, 231.

78. Robert Avis, 'Conflict, Cooperation and Consensus in the Law of Njálls Saga', *Quaestio insularis* 12 (2012): 88.

79. Avis, 97.

80. Avis, 107.

81. Hannah Burrows, 'Cold Cases: Law and Legal Details in the Islendingasogur', *Parergon* 26 (2009): 36; also Bryce, *Studies in History and Jurisprudence*, 1.1:256.

82. Burrows, 'Cold Cases', 37–38, 41; Hannah Burrows, 'Some Þing to Talk About: Assemblies in the Islendingasogur', *Northern Studies* 52 (2015): 65.

83. Burrows, 'Cold Cases', 44–45.

84. Burrows, 50–51.

85. Burrows, 'Some Þing to Talk About', 60–61.

86. Burrows, 'Cold Cases', 53–54; Burrows, 'Some Þing to Talk About', 66; so, too, Boulhosa, *Icelanders and the Kings of Norway*, 47, 53; Brink, 'Law and Legal Customs in Viking Age Scandinavia', 88; and Gunnar Jonsson, 'Waldgang und Lebensringzaum (Landesverweisung) im alteren islandischen Recht', 11.

87. Viðar Hreinsson, *The Complete Sagas of Icelanders, Including 49 Tales*, 5.317.

88. Hermann Pálsson, trans., *Njáll's Saga*, Repr, Penguin Classics (Harmondsworth: Penguin, 1983), 308.

89. Dennis, Foote, and Perkins, *Laws of Early Iceland: Gragas*, 1:140; Hermann Pálsson, *Njáll's Saga*, 302.

90. Brink, 'The Creation of a Scandinavian Provincial Law', 434. Thus, Njálls Saga 70, 'With laws shall our land be built up but with lawlessness laid waste'; Hermann Pálsson, *Njáll's Saga*, 159. Michael Walzer, 'The Legal Codes of Ancient Israel', *Yale Journal of Law & the Humanities* 4 (1992): 348, describes Ancient Israel similarly.

91. Online Medieval and Classical Library Release #15b; http://mcllibrary.org/Heimskringla/ynglinga.html.

92. Hermann Pálsson, *Njáll's Saga*, 301.

93. Miller II, *Oral Tradition in Ancient Israel*, 60–65.

94. Vestein Olason, *The Traditional Ballads of Iceland*, Stofnun Arna Magnussonar a Islandi 22 (Reykjavik: Arni Magnusson Institute, 1982), 96.

95. E.g., 'A Farmer Comes Home from the Thing'; Vestein Olason, 351–52, 354.

96. Jeremy Dodds, trans., *The Poetic Edda* (Toronto: Coach House, 2014).

97. Margaret C. Ross, ed., *Poetry on Christian Subjects*, Skaldic Poetry of the Scandinavian Middle Ages 7 (Turnhout: Brepols, 2007).

98. Eirikr Magnusson and William Morris, trans., *The Tale of Roi the Fool*, In Parenthesis Publications Old Norse Series (Cambridge, Ontario: In parenthesis, 2000).

99. Olrik, *Viking Civilization*, 205–6.

100. Bragi Halldórsson and Knútur S. Hafsteinsson, *Íslendingaþættir: ùrval þrettán þátta med inngangi, skýringum og skrám*, Sigildar sögur 8 (Reykjavík: Mál og Menning, 1999), xxix.

101. Bragi Halldórsson and Knútur S. Hafsteinsson, 194.

102. Bragi Halldórsson and Knútur S. Hafsteinsson, 104–5.

103. Bragi Halldórsson and Knútur S. Hafsteinsson, xxxiii.

104. Bragi Halldórsson and Knútur S. Hafsteinsson, 91.

105. Kari Ellen Gade, ed., *Poetry from the Kings' Sagas 2: From c. 1035 to c. 1300*, Skaldic Poetry of the Scandinavian Middle Ages 2 (Turnhout: Brepols, 2009), 329.

106. Esias Tegner, ed., *Frithiof's Saga*, trans. W. L. Blakely (New York: Leypoldt & Holt, 1867), 10.

107. Bjarni Vilhjalmsson and Oskar Halldorsson, eds., *Islenzkir Malshaettir* (Reykjavik: Almenna, 1966), 212, 300.

108. Gisli Sigurðsson, *The Medieval Icelandic Saga and Oral Tradition*; Brink, 'The Creation of a Scandinavian Provincial Law', 435.

109. Gisli Sigurðsson, 'Medieval Icelandic Studies', *Oral Tradition* 18 (2003): 208.

110. Helgi Skuli Kjartansson, 'Law Recital According to Old Icelandic Law', 89.

111. Helgi Skuli Kjartansson, 89 n. 2.

112. Helgi Skuli Kjartansson, 90.

113. Michael P. McGlynn, 'Orality in the Old Icelandic Grágás: Legal Formulae in the Assembly Procedures Section', *Neophilologus* 93 (2009): 521–23.

114. McGlynn, 527.

115. Hannah Burrows, 'Literary-Legal Relations in Commonwealth-Period Iceland' (Diss., York, University of York, 2007), 18.

116. Grønlie, *Íslendingabók*, 18 n.24.

117. Burrows, 'Literary-Legal Relations in Commonwealth-Period Iceland', 18 n.7.

118. Jón Hnefill Aðalsteinsson, *Under the Cloak*, 35–36, 160.

119. Walter Baetke, trans., *Islands Besiedlung und älteste Geschichte*, Altnordische Dichtung und Prosa 23 (Jena: Eugen Diederichs, 1928).

120. Jón Hnefill Aðalsteinsson, *Under the Cloak*, 36.

121. Jón Hnefill Aðalsteinsson, 163.

122. Jón Hnefill Aðalsteinsson, 164.

123. Jón Hnefill Aðalsteinsson, 172–73.

124. Jón Hnefill Aðalsteinsson, 168–69.

125. Jón Hnefill Aðalsteinsson, 170.

126. Jón Hnefill Aðalsteinsson, 171.

127. Jón Hnefill Aðalsteinsson, 177; also Brink, 'Reconstruction of Viking and Early Medieval Scandinavian Society', 5 n.5.

128. Bertha S. Phillpotts, *Kindred and Clan* (New York: Octagon, 1974), 11.

129. Brink, 'Law and Legal Customs in Viking Age Scandinavia', 91.

130. Phillpotts, *Kindred and Clan*, 22–23, 37.

131. Burrows, 'Literary-Legal Relations in Commonwealth-Period Iceland', 19.

132. Gunnar Jonsson, 'Waldgang und Lebensringzaum (Landesverweisung) im alteren islandischen Recht', 14–15.

133. Jon Viðar Sigurðsson, Frederik Pedersen, and Anders Berge, 'Making and Using the Law in the North, c. 900–1350', in *Making, Using and Resisting the Law in European History*, ed. Gunther Lottes, Eero Medijainen, and Jon Viðar Sigurðsson (Pisa: Plus, 2008), 39.

134. Miller II, *Oral Tradition in Ancient Israel*, 15–18, 20–27.

135. Van den Bergh, 'The Concept of Folk Law in Historical Context', 1994, 19; Van der Toorn, *Scribal Culture*, 13; Westbrook, 'The Laws of Biblical Israel', 111; Bernard S. Jackson, 'Models in Legal History: The Case of Biblical Law', *Journal of Law and Religion* 18 (2002): 8. Bernard S. Jackson, 'Literal Meaning: Semantics and Narrative in Biblical Law and Modern Jurisprudence', *International Journal for the Semiotics of Law* 13 (2000): 439 still embraces Goody and Ong.

136. Foote, 'Oral and Literary Tradition in Early Scandinavian Law', 50, 54.

137. Peter Foote, 'Some Lines in Logrettuþattr', in *Sjötíu Ritgerðir*, ed. Einar Petursson and Jonas Kristjansson, Stofnun Arna Magnussonar a Islandi 12 (Reykjavik: Árni Magnússon Institute for Icelandic Studies, 1977), 199; Foote, 'Oral and Literary Tradition in Early Scandinavian Law', 53.

138. Dennis, Foote, and Perkins, *Laws of Early Iceland: Gragas*, 1:190–91.

139. Foote, 'Some Lines in Logrettuþattr', 200; Foote, 'Oral and Literary Tradition in Early Scandinavian Law', 53.

140. Foote, 'Some Lines in Logrettuþattr', 201–2.

141. Foote, 203.

142. Foote, 204–5; Foote, *1117 in Iceland and England*, 7.

143. Foote, 'Some Lines in Logrettuþattr', 204–5.

144. Foote, *1117 in Iceland and England*, 8.

145. Miller, 'Of Outlaws, Horsemeat, and Writing', 2090.

146. Miller, 2093.

147. Miller, 2092; also Gisli Sigurðsson, *The Medieval Icelandic Saga and Oral Tradition*, 57; and Judy Quinn, 'From Orality to Literacy in Medieval Iceland', in *Old Icelandic Literature and Society*, ed. Margaret Clunies Ross, Cambridge Studies in Medieval Literature 42 (Cambridge: Cambridge University Press, 2000), 34–35.

148. Miller, 'Of Outlaws, Horsemeat, and Writing', 2091.

149. Burrows, '"In This Country, What Is Found in Books Is to Be Law"', 47; Lindal, *Law and Legislation in the Icelandic Commonwealth*, 71–72.

150. Burrows, '"In This Country, What Is Found in Books Is to Be Law"', 49; Birgir Runolfsson Solvason, 'Ordered Anarchy'; Lindal, *Law and Legislation in the Icelandic Commonwealth*, 69–70; Dennis, Foote, and Perkins, *Laws of Early Iceland: Gragas*, 1:191; Quinn, 'From Orality to Literacy in Medieval Iceland', 35. There would be no need to spell out the procedure if this was only a rare 'last resort.'

151. Lindal, *Law and Legislation in the Icelandic Commonwealth*, 77, italics original.

152. Helgi Skuli Kjartansson, 'Law Recital According to Old Icelandic Law', 97; Gisli Sigurðsson, *The Medieval Icelandic Saga and Oral Tradition*.

153. Burrows, '"In This Country, What Is Found in Books Is to Be Law"', 42. Such a practice was attested in Sweden as late as 1206, according to *Diplomatarium suecanum* 131; Inger Larsson, 'The Role of the Swedish Lawman in the Spread of Lay Literacy', in *Along the Oral-Written Continuum*, ed. Slavica Rankovic, Utrecht Studies in Medieval Literacy (Turnhout: Brepols, 2010), 413.

154. Helgi Skuli Kjartansson, 'Law Recital According to Old Icelandic Law', 99; also Burrows, '"In This Country, What Is Found in Books Is to Be Law"', 42.

155. Helgi Skuli Kjartansson, 'Law Recital According to Old Icelandic Law', 99.

156. Burrows, '"In This Country, What Is Found in Books Is to Be Law"', 42–43.

157. Burrows, 42.

158. Lindal, *Law and Legislation in the Icelandic Commonwealth*, 65, 68 n.21.

159. Judith Jesch, 'Murder and Treachery in the Viking Age', in *Crime and Punishment in the Middle Ages*, ed. Timothy Shaw Haskett (Victoria, BC: Humanities Centre, University of Victoria, 1998), 66; Brink, 'Law and Legal Customs in Viking Age Scandinavia', 93–96; it also illustrates how law and cult were intimately linked.

160. Brink, 'Law and Legal Customs in Viking Age Scandinavia', 96–97; Larsson, 'The Role of the Swedish Lawman in the Spread of Lay Literacy', 417–18; Jesch, 'Murder and Treachery in the Viking Age', 67.

161. Helgi Skuli Kjartansson, 'Law Recital According to Old Icelandic Law', 92.

162. E.g., Gragas 1.54; Helgi Skuli Kjartansson, 95; McGlynn, 'Orality in the Old Icelandic Grágás', 527–31; Jon Viðar Sigurðsson, Pedersen, and Berge, 'Making and Using the Law in the North, c. 900-1350', 39.

163. Helgi Skuli Kjartansson, 'Law Recital According to Old Icelandic Law', 95.

164. Hans Fix, 'Poetisches im altislandischen Recht', in *Sprachen und Computer*, ed. Hans Fix, Annely Rothkegel, and Erwin Stegentritt (Dudweiler: AQ-Verlag, 1982), 201; Foote, 'Oral and Literary Tradition in Early Scandinavian Law', 49. Of course these are not proof of "oral tradition," but Helle Vogt and Ditlev Tamm, eds., *The Danish Medieval Laws: The Laws of Scania, Zealand and Jutland*, Medieval Nordic Laws (London: Routledge, 2016), 16–17, they are evidence of aurality, of performance.

165. Fix, 'Poetisches im altislandischen Recht', 194–99.

166. McGlynn, 'Orality in the Old Icelandic Grágás', 531.

167. Elizabeth Jackson, *Old Icelandic Truce Formulas*, Viking Society for Northern Research (London: University College London Press, 2016), 3.

168. Yelena Helgasdóttir, 'When Law Becomes Poetry?' (17th International Saga Conference, Reykholt, Iceland, 2018), http://fornsagnathing2018.hi.is/efnisagrip-fyrirlestra/#Yelena%20SesseljaHelgad%C3%B3ttir.

169. Jackson, *Old Icelandic Truce Formulas*, 3.

170. Jackson, 3–5.

171. Jackson, 5–7.

172. Jon Viðar Sigurðsson, Pedersen, and Berge, 'Making and Using the Law in the North, c. 900-1350', 39.

173. *Book of Icelanders* 1.1.24; Gisli Sigurðsson, *The Medieval Icelandic Saga and Oral Tradition*.

174. Gisli Sigurðsson.

175. Gisli Sigurðsson.

176. Hannah Burrows, 'Rhyme and Reason: Lawspeaker-Poets in Medieval Iceland', *Scandinavian Studies* 81 (2009): 216; Agnes S. Arnórsdóttir, 'Legal Culture and Historical Memory in Medieval and Early Modern Iceland', in *Minni and Muninn: Memory in Medieval Nordic Culture*, ed. Pernille Hermann, Stephen A. Mitchell, and Agnes S. Arnórsdóttir, Acta Scandinavica 4 (Turnhout: Brepols, 2014), 218–19.

177. Burrows, 'Rhyme and Reason', 217.

178. Burrows, 220.

179. Burrows, 227.

180. Burrows, 229–30.

181. Burrows, 231; Gisli Sigurðsson, 'Medieval Icelandic Studies', 207.

182. Gisli Sigurðsson, 'Medieval Icelandic Studies', 207.

183. Hermann Pálsson, *Njáll's Saga*, 85; Miller, *Bloodtaking and Peacemaking*, 226; Orfield, *The Growth of Scandinavian Law*, 91; Nygaard, "Law, Religion," 157.

184. Miller, *Bloodtaking and Peacemaking*, 226.

185. Brink, 'Minnunga Maen', 198.

186. The growing Christian population found themselves outside the law because they could not participate in rites and festivals, while "pagans" found themselves at odds with the law because they wanted to prosecute all Christians for the crimes of a few. Christians in desperation set up their own Lawspeaker, an old goði named Siðu-Hallr (*The Greatest Saga of Óláfr Tryggvason*, 2). Jón Hnefill Aðalsteinsson, *Under the Cloak*, 89–90.

187. Grønlie, *Íslendingabók*, 49–50.

188. Jón Hnefill Aðalsteinsson, *Under the Cloak*, 108, 122–23.

189. Andrea Van Arkel, 'Die Mantel Þorgeir Ljósvetningagoði', in *Maukastella*, ed. Jonas Kristjansson (Reykjavik: Arni Magnusson Institute, 1974), 5–7.

190. Note the emphasis on religious matters in *Ulfjotslog*; Simon Nygaard, "Law, Religion, and Their Role in the Cultivatoin of Cultural Memory in Pre-Christian Icelandic Society," *Scandinavian-Canadian Studies* 28 (2021): 152.

191. Stefan Brink, 'Law', in *Handbook of Pre-Modern Nordic Memory Studies*, ed. Jürg Glauser and Pernille Hermann (Berlin: De Gruyter, 2018), 815.

192. Brink, 'Minnunga Maen', 197; Brink, 'Law', 189.

193. Brink, 'Minnunga Maen', 201; Brink, 'Law', 901.

194. Brink, 'Minnunga Maen', 203–4, 206–7.

195. Brink, 'Law', 901–2.

196. Agnes S. Arnórsdóttir, 'Legal Culture and Historical Memory', 216.

197. Birgir Runolfsson Solvason, 'Ordered Anarchy'.

198. Foote, *1117 in Iceland and England*, 18; cf. Helle Vogt, 'Secundum Consuetudinem et Leges Patrie', in *Custom: The Development and Use of a Legal Concept in the Middle Ages: Proceedings of the Fifth Carlsberg Academy Conference on Medieval Legal History 2008*, ed. Per Andersen and Mia Münster-Swendsen, 1st ed. (Copenhagen: DJØF Pub., 2009), 67.

199. Brink, 'Law and Legal Customs in Viking Age Scandinavia', 105; Brink, 'Reconstruction of Viking and Early Medieval Scandinavian Society', 5, 14; Larsson, 'The Role of the Swedish Lawman in the Spread of Lay Literacy', 419.

200. Larsson, 'The Role of the Swedish Lawman in the Spread of Lay Literacy', 419.

201. Brink, 'Law and Legal Customs in Viking Age Scandinavia', 91; Sanmark, *Viking Law and Order*, 4.

202. Brink, 'Law and Legal Customs in Viking Age Scandinavia', 90–91; Sanmark, *Viking Law and Order*, 9; Olof Sundqvist, *Freyr's Offspring: Rulers and Religion in Ancient Svea Society*, Acta Universitatis Upsaliensis 21 (Uppsala: Uppsala Universitet, 2002), 102.

203. Sundqvist, *Freyr's Offspring*, 102.

204. Thorsteinn Gundjonsson, *Thingvellir*, 32.

205. Clouston, 'Odal Orkney', 92–94; Brian Smith, 'Dull as Ditch Water or Crazily Romantic: Scottish Historians on Norwegian Law in Shetland and Orkney', in *Legislation and State Formation*, ed. Steinar Imsen, Norgesveldet Occasional Papers 4 (Trondheim: Akademika, 2013), 117.

206. Thorsteinn Gundjonsson, *Thingvellir*, 32; Liv Kjørsvik Schei, Gunnie Moberg, and Tróndur Patursson, *The Faroe Islands* (Edinburgh: Birlinn, 2003), 22.

207. Lex Woolf, *From Pictland to Alba*, New Edinburgh History of Scotland 2 (Edinburgh: Edinburgh University Press, 2014), 213.

208. Thorsteinn Gundjonsson, *Thingvellir*, 33.

209. Sven Aggesen, *The Works of Sven Aggesen, Twelfth-Century Danish Historian*, trans. Eric Christiansen, Viking Society for Northern Research Text Series 9 (London: Viking Society for Northern Research, 1992), 78 n.28.

210. Sven Aggesen, 12, 33–35.

211. Frederick T. Wainwright, *The Northern Isles* (New York: Thomas Nelson and Sons, 1964), 155. Oddly, the Northmen who settled in Normandy made no Things; Lucien Musset, Michel Fleury, and François-Xavier Dillmann, *Nordica et normannica: recueil d'études sur la Scandinavie ancienne et médiévale, les expéditions des Vikings et la fondation de la Normandie*, Studia Nordica 1 (Paris: Société des études nordiques, 1997), 255.

212. Cyril James Roy Hart, *The Danelaw* (London: Hambledon, 1992), 31 nn.14, 82, 153; D. M. Hadley, *The Northern Danelaw* (London: Leicester University Press, 2005), 20, 300; and Phillpotts, *Kindred and Clan*, 223: the Danelaw was heavily Scandinavian.

213. Sanmark, *Viking Law and Order*, 172.

214. Sanmark, 176.

215. Brink, 'Law and Legal Customs in Viking Age Scandinavia', 90; Christine Peel, trans., *Guta Lag: The Law of the Gotlanders*, Viking Society for Northern Research Text Series (London: University College London Press, 2009), 14.

216. N. F. Blake, trans., *The Saga of the Jomsvikings*, Icelandic Texts (London: Thomas Nelson and Sons, 1962), 17 n.3.

217. Lawrence G. Berge, 'Hirðskra 1-37, A Translation with Notes' (MA Thesis, Madison, WI, University of Wisconsin, 1968), 10–11.

218. Snorri Sturluson, *Óláfr Haraldsson (The Saint)*, trans. Alison Finlay and Anthony Faulkes, Heimskringla 2 (London: Viking Society for Northern Research, 2014), 73 chap. 80.

219. Tegner, *Frithiof's Saga*, 54, 57–58.

220. Sanmark, *Viking Law and Order*, 106.

221. Sanmark, 108.

222. Thorsteinn Gudjonsson, *Thingvellir*, 28–29.

223. Clouston, 'Odal Orkney', 93.

224. Clouston, 93.

225. Berge, 'Hirðskra 1-37, A Translation with Notes', 11.

226. Snorri Sturluson, *Óláfr Haraldsson (The Saint)*, 74–75 chap. 80.

227. Helgi Skuli Kjartansson, 'Law Recital According to Old Icelandic Law', 91. The entire system of Things is quite similar; Peel, *Guta Lag*, xxvi–xxvii, xxix, xxxii; Brink, 'Law and Legal Customs in Viking Age Scandinavia', 94; Sanmark, *Viking Law and Order*, 10.

228. Larsson, 'The Role of the Swedish Lawman in the Spread of Lay Literacy', 414; Helgi Skuli Kjartansson, 'Law Recital According to Old Icelandic Law', 100.

229. Helgi Skuli Kjartansson, 'Law Recital According to Old Icelandic Law', 100.

230. Sundqvist, *Freyr's Offspring*, 103–5.

231. Sanmark, *Viking Law and Order*, 86.

232. Sanmark, 103.

233. Schei, Moberg, and Patursson, *The Faroe Islands*, 22.

234. Brink, 'Law and Legal Customs in Viking Age Scandinavia', 101.

235. Sanmark, *Viking Law and Order*, 107.

236. Mar Jonsson, 'Uses and Usability of Icelandic Medieval Books of Law', in *Libert Amicorum Ditlev Tam*, ed. Per Andersen et al. (Copenhagen: DJØF, 2011), 158.

237. Mar Jonsson, 159–60.

238. Peel, *Guta Lag*, xxiii.

239. Peel, xxiv–xxv.

240. Peel, xxv.

241. Mar Jonsson, 'Uses and Usability of Icelandic Medieval Books of Law', 153.

242. Mar Jonsson, 161.

243. Peel, *Guta Lag*, xxxiv.

244. Foote, 'Oral and Literary Tradition in Early Scandinavian Law', 48.

245. Foote, *1117 in Iceland and England*, 14; Birgir Runolfsson Solvason, 'Ordered Anarchy'; Miller, *Bloodtaking and Peacemaking*, 223, 228.

246. Miller, *Bloodtaking and Peacemaking*, 228; Lindal, *Law and Legislation in the Icelandic Commonwealth*, 90.

247. Brink, 'Reconstruction of Viking and Early Medieval Scandinavian Society', 15; Riisøy, 'Outlawry', 103; Peel, *Guta Lag*, xxiv, 55.

248. Maurizio Lupoi, 'A European Common Law before Bologna?', in *Law before Gratian*, ed. Per Andersen, Mia Münster-Swendsen, and Helle Vogt, Proceedings of the Carlsberg Academy Conferences on Medieval Legal History 3 (Carlsberg: DJOF, 2007), 7.

249. Bryce, *Studies in History and Jurisprudence*, 1.1:264.

250. Long, *Iceland's Relationship with Norway*, 91.

251. H. Zimmer, *The Irish Element in Mediaeval Culture*, trans. Jane L. Edmands (New York: G. P. Putnam's Sons, 1891), 55–56; Pernille Hermann, 'Who Were the Papar?', in *The Viking Age*, ed. John Sheehan and Donnchadh O Corrain (Dublin: Four Courts, 2010), 146.

252. Kristján Ahronson, *Into the Ocean: Vikings, Irish, and Environmental Change in Iceland and the North*, Toronto Old Norse and Icelandic Series 8 (Toronto: University of Toronto Press, 2015), 68.

253. Aidan MacDonald, 'On "Papar" Names in N. and W. Scotland', *Northern Studies* 9 (1977): 26; Ahronson, *Into the Ocean*, 69–69.

254. MacDonald, 'On "Papar" Names in N. and W. Scotland', 26.

255. Ahronson, *Into the Ocean*, 58–59; Schei, Moberg, and Patursson, *The Faroe Islands*, 67.

256. Ahronson, *Into the Ocean*, 60.

257. Verena, 'A Pre-Modern Nation? Icelanders' Ethnogenesis and Its Mythical Foundations', 125; Angelo Forte, Richard Oram, and Frederik Pedersen, *Viking Empires* (Cambridge: Cambridge University Press, 2005), 133.

258. Kristján Ahronson, 'Testing the Evidence for Northern North Atlantic Papar', in *The Papar in the North Atlantic: Environment and History*, ed. Barbara E Crawford (St. Andrews: University of St. Andrews Press, 2002), 107–8.

259. Ahronson, 116–17, 120.

260. Barbara E. Crawford, *Scandinavian Scotland*, Scotland in the Early Middle Ages 3 (Leicester: Leicester University Press, 1987), 165.

261. Ian Fisher, 'Crosses in the Ocean', in *The Papar in the North Atlantic: Environment and History*, ed. Barbara E Crawford (St. Andrews: University of St. Andrews Press, 2002), 41, 45–46, 49, 52–55.

262. Gudrun Sveinbjarnardottir, 'The Question of the Papar in Iceland', in *The Papar in the North Atlantic: Environment and History*, ed. Barbara E Crawford (St. Andrews: University of St. Andrews Press, 2002), 102.

263. Gudrun Sveinbjarnardottir, 104.

264. Forte, Oram, and Pedersen, *Viking Empires*, 130.

265. Forte, Oram, and Pedersen, 130.

266. Ahronson, *Into the Ocean*, 63–64, 70–73; William P. L. Thomson, *The New History of Orkney*, 3rd ed. (Edinburgh: Birlinn, 2008), 14; Gudrun Sveinbjarnardottir, 'The Question of the Papar in Iceland', 101.

267. MacDonald, 'On "Papar" Names in N. and W. Scotland', 28.

268. Hugh Marwick, 'Antiquarian Notes on Papa Westray', *Proceedings of the Orkney Antiquarian Society* 3 (1924): 36.

269. Gisli Sigurðsson, *Gaelic Influence in Iceland*, Studia Icelandica 46 (Reykjavik: Mennigarsjoðs, 1988), 27.

270. William I. Miller, 'Where's Iceland' (Leiden: Brill, 2016), 87–88.

271. Hermann, 'Who Were the Papar?', 148.

272. MacDonald, 'On "Papar" Names in N. and W. Scotland', 29–30; Crawford, *Scandinavian Scotland*, 166.

273. Verena, 'A Pre-Modern Nation? Icelanders' Ethnogenesis and Its Mythical Foundations', 119; Gisli Sigurðsson, *Gaelic Influence in Iceland*, 24–34.

274. Verena, 'A Pre-Modern Nation? Icelanders' Ethnogenesis and Its Mythical Foundations', 126.

275. Verena, 126 n.17.

276. Verena, 126.

277. W. A. Craigie, 'Gaelic Words and Names in the Icelandic Sagas', *Zeitschrift Für Celtische Philologie* 1 (1897): 444–52.

278. Bo Almqvist, *Viking Ale: Studies on Folklore Contacts between the Northern and the Western Worlds* (Aberystwyth, Wales: Boethius, 1991), 271 n.12; Alfred P. Smyth, *Warlords and Holy Men: Scotland AD 80-1000* (Edinburgh: Edinburgh University Press, 1998), 142–43, 148–49.

279. Forte, Oram, and Pedersen, *Viking Empires*, 132; Smyth, *Warlords and Holy Men*, 156–57.

280. Ahronson, *Into the Ocean*, 63.

281. Bo Almqvist, 'Gaelic/Norse Folklore Contacts', in *Irland und Europa im früheren Mittelalter: Bildung und Literatur = Ireland and Europe in the early Middle Ages: learning and literature*, ed. Próinséas Ní Chatháin and Michael Richter (Stuttgart: Klett-Cotta, 1996), 148–49.

282. Birgir Runolfsson Solvason, 'Ordered Anarchy'.

283. Alfred P. Smyth, *Scandinavian York and Dublin*, vol. 2 (Dublin: Templekieran, 1979), 212, 226; first Norwegian, then Danish; Smyth, *Warlords and Holy Men*, 150–53.

284. Long, *Iceland's Relationship with Norway*, 128; Alfred P. Smyth, *Scandinavian Kings in the British Isles* (Oxford: Oxford University Press, 1977), 124–25; Smyth, *Warlords and Holy Men*, 171–72; Magnus MacLean, *The Literature of the Celts*, Kennikat Press Scholarly Reprints in Irish History and Culture (Port Washington, NY: Kennikat, 1970), 205.

285. Smyth, *Warlords and Holy Men*, 154–55, 161.

286. Smyth, 156; Miller, 'Where's Iceland', 78; James Hunter, *Last of the Free: A Millennial History of the Highlands and Islands of Scotland* (Edinburgh: Mainstream, 1999), 79–80; Gisli Sigurðsson, *Gaelic Influence in Iceland*, 89.

287. Smyth, *Warlords and Holy Men*, 163.

288. Almqvist, *Viking Ale*, 142; Almqvist, 'Gaelic/Norse Folklore Contacts', 145–48, 152–53; W. A. Craigie, 'The Gaels in Iceland', *Proceedings of the Society of Antiquaries of Scotland* 31 (1896): 247–64; Gisli Sigurðsson, *Gaelic Influence in Iceland*, 118–19.

289. Paul B. Taylor, 'Volundarkvida, Þrymskvida, and the Function of Myth', *Neophilologus* 78 (1994): 266.

290. Almqvist, *Viking Ale*, 148; Almqvist, 'Gaelic/Norse Folklore Contacts', 168–70.

291. Crawford, *Scandinavian Scotland*, 212.

292. Wainwright, *The Northern Isles*, 156.

293. Christopher Tolkien, trans., *The Saga of King Heidrek the Wise*, Icelandic Texts (London: Thomas Nelson and Sons, 1960), 10 n.2.

294. Almqvist, 'Gaelic/Norse Folklore Contacts', 156.

295. Tomás Ó Cathasaigh, *Coire Sois, The Cauldron of Knowledge: A Companion to Early Irish Saga* (South Bend: University of Notre Dame Press, 2014), 122; Liam Ronayne, 'Seandlithe Na NGael: An Annotated Bibliography of the Ancient Laws of Ireland', *Irish Jurist* 17 (1982): 132, 137–38; Joseph R. Peden, 'Property Rights in Celtic Irish Law', in *Anarchy and the Law*, ed. Edward P. Stringham (New Brunswick, NJ: Transaction, 2017), 565; D. A. Binchy, 'Linguistic and Legal Archaisms in the Celtic Law-Books', *Transactions of the Philological Society*, 1959, 14; D. A. Binchy, 'The Linguistic and Historical Value of the Irish Law Tracts (1943)', in *Celtic Law Papers*, ed. Dafydd Jenkins (Brussels: Libraire Encyclopedique, 1973), 80–81, 86.

296. Ó Cathasaigh, *Coire Sois*, 124; Francis J. Byrne, *Irish Kings and High-Kings* (New York: St. Martin's, 1973), 14.

297. Ó Cathasaigh, *Coire Sois*, 125; Marylin Gerriets, 'Theft, Penitentials, and the Compilation of the Early Irish Laws', *Celtica* 22 (1991): 29–30; Donnchadh Ó Corrain, 'Nationality and Kingship in Pre-Norman Ireland', in *Nationality and the Pursuit of National Independence*, ed. T. W. Moody, Historical Studies 9 (Belfast: Appletree, 1978), 1–35.

298. Noele Higgins, 'The Lost Legal System: Pre-Common Law Ireland and the Brehon Law', in *Legal Theory Practice and Education* (Athens: Athens Institute for Education and Research, 2011), 4; Peden, 'Property Rights in Celtic Irish Law', 567; John Gilissen, *La Coutume*, Typologie des Sources du Moyen Auge Occidental 41 (Turnhout: Brepols, 1982), 48.

299. Ó Cathasaigh, *Coire Sois*, 125; Binchy, 'The Linguistic and Historical Value of the Irish Law Tracts (1943)', 84–85; John C. Kleefeld, 'From Brouhahas to Brehon Laws', *Law and Humanities* 4 (2010): 22, 46–47.

300. Neil McLeod, 'The Concept of Law in Ancient Irish Jurisprudence', *Irish Jurist* 17 (1982): 361; Eoin Mac Neill and D. A. Binchy, 'Prolegomena to a Study of the "Ancient Laws of Ireland"', *Irish Jurist* n.s. 2 (1967): 111; Binchy, 'Linguistic and Legal Archaisms in the Celtic Law-Books', 15–16; Robin C. Stacey, 'Learning Law in Medieval Iceland', in *Tome: Studies in Medieval Celtic History and Law*, ed. Fiona Edmonds and Paul Russell (Boydell, 2011), 137; Liam Breatnach, *A Companion to the Corpus Iuris Hibernici*, Early Irish Law Series 5 (Dublin: School of Celtic Studies, Dublin Institute for Advanced Studies, 2005), 370.

301. Fergus Kelly, *A Guide to Irish Law*, Early Irish Law 3 (Dublin: Institute for Advanced Studies, 1988), 274, 356–57: 'If you are a king you should know / the prerogative of a ruler / reflection according to rank / contention in the host / cudgels in the ale-house / contracts made in drunkenness / valuation of lands / measurement by poles / augmentations of penalty / theft of the tree-fruit'.

302. Patricia H. Ó Sidodhachain, 'Oral Tradition to Written Word', *Studies: An Irish Quarterly Review* 101 (2012): 329.

303. Stacey, 'Learning Law in Medieval Iceland', 138–39.

304. Robin Chapman Stacey, *Dark Speech: The Performance of Law in Early Ireland*, The Middle Ages Series (Philadelphia: University of Pennsylvania Press, 2007), 47; Binchy, 'The Linguistic and Historical Value of the Irish Law Tracts (1943)', 84.

305. Kelly, *A Guide to Irish Law*, 222, 235 citing *Senchus Mar*, heptad 35 (CIH 31.19-21).

306. Jon Viðar Sigurðsson, Pedersen, and Berge, 'Making and Using the Law in the North, c. 900-1350', 45.

307. Jon Viðar Sigurðsson, Pedersen, and Berge, 46.

308. Agnes S. Arnórsdóttir, 'Cultural Memory and Gender in Iceland from Medieval to Early Modern Times', *Scandinavian Studies* 85 (2013): 381.

309. Agnes S. Arnórsdóttir, 384.

310. Brink, 'The Creation of a Scandinavian Provincial Law', 434. This is also true of early Irish law. Kelly, *A Guide to Irish Law*, 233. Foreign influence of any sort in Icelandic law is denied by Olason, *Codex Regius of Gragas*, 9–10.

311. Elsa Sjöholm, *Sveriges medeltidslagar* (Stockholm, 1988), cited in Brink, 'Reconstruction of Viking and Early Medieval Scandinavian Society', 4; Brink, 'Law and Legal Customs in Viking Age Scandinavia', 88.

312. Brink, 'The Creation of a Scandinavian Provincial Law', 441–42; Brink, 'Law and Legal Customs in Viking Age Scandinavia', 92–93, 99; Sundqvist, *Freyr's Offspring*, 310–11; Sunde, 'Daughters of God and Counsellors of the Judges of Men', 130–36.

313. Peel, *Guta Lag*, xxxvii–xxxviii.

314. Sunde, 'Daughters of God and Counsellors of the Judges of Men', 139.

315. Arnved Nedkvitne, *The Social Consequences of Literacy in Medieval Scandinavia*, Utrecht Studies in Medieval Literacy 11 (Turnhout: Brepols, 2004), 27; Peter Landau, 'The Importance of Classical Canon Law in Scandinavia in the 12th and 13th Centuries', in *How Nordic Are the Nordic Medieval Laws*, ed. Per Andersen, Ditlev Tamm, and Helle Vogt, 2nd ed. (Copenhagen: DJØF Pub, 2011), 24–30. Utrecht Studies in Medieval Literacy 11 (Turnhout: Brepols, 2004).

316. Nedkvitne, *The Social Consequences of Literacy in Medieval Scandinavia*, 27.

317. Landau, 'The Importance of Classical Canon Law in Scandinavia in the 12th and 13th Centuries', 24–25.

318. Nedkvitne, *The Social Consequences of Literacy in Medieval Scandinavia*, 29.

319. Roland Scheel, 'Byzantium—Rome—Denmark—Iceland', in *Transcultural Approaches to Concept of Imperial Rule in the Middle Ages*, ed. Christian Scholl, Torben R. Gebhardt, and Jan Clauß (Frankfurt: Peter Lang, 2017), 281, 294.

320. Scheel, 282–83.

321. Hoff, *Hafliði Másson und die Einflüsse des römischen Rechts in der Grágás*, 380.

322. Signe F. Fuglesang, 'A Critical Survey of Theories on Byzantine Influence in Scandinavia', *Abhandlungen der Geistes- und Sozialwissenschaflichen* 3 (1997): 37.

323. Fuglesang, 53; Elisabeth Piltz, 'Byzantium and Islam in Scandinavia', in *Byzantium and Islam in Scandinavia*, ed. Elisabeth Piltz, Studies in Mediterranean Archaeology 126 (Jonsered, Sweden: Paul Astroms, 1998), 27, 30; Birgit Arrhenius, 'Connections between Scandinavia and the East Roman Empire in the Migration Period', in *From the Baltic to the Black Sea*, ed. David Austin and Leslie Alcock (London: Unwin Hyman, 1990), 118, 134–35.

324. Simon Franklin, *Writing, Society and Culture in Early Rus, c. 950-1300* (Cambridge: Cambridge University Press, 2002), 136–43.

325. Hoff, *Hafliði Másson und die Einflüsse des römischen Rechts in der Grágás*, 39, 42. The alternative view is that 'ermsker' means 'hermits,' perhaps from Southern Italy, or 'from Ermland,' that is, Pomerania; Fuglesang, 'A Critical Survey of Theories on Byzantine Influence in Scandinavia', 36–37.

326. Fuglesang, 'A Critical Survey of Theories on Byzantine Influence in Scandinavia', 35, 38–39, 41, 43, 45, 47, 49, 51.

327. Selma Jonsdottir, *An 11th Century Byzantine Last Judgement in Iceland* (Reykjavik: Almenna, 1959), 11.

328. Selma Jonsdottir, 65, 55.

329. Selma Jonsdottir, 37–47.

330. Selma Jonsdottir, 16–19, 22–24, 27–36.

331. Selma Jonsdottir, 77, 79–84.

332. Admittedly, there is also Latin influence, e.g., in Hertig Fredrik av Normandie, Konráðs saga keisarasonar, Mírmans saga, Thiðreks saga af Bern; Knut Togeby, 'Les Relations Litteraires Entre Le Monde Roman et Le Monde Scandinave', in *Les Relations Litteraires Franco-Scandinaves Au Moyen Age*, ed. Pierre Halleux, Bibliotheque de La Faculte de Philosophie et Lettres de l'Universite de Liege 208 (Paris: Societe d'Edition 'Les Belles Lettres', 1975), 323–28 but these are all late texts.1975

333. Hoff, *Hafliði Másson und die Einflüsse des römischen Rechts in der Grágás*, 39.

334. Alexander M. Bruce, *Scyld and Scef: Expanding the Analogues* (New York: Routledge, 2002), 56.

335. Bruce, 59.

336. Ioannis M. Konidaris, 'The Ubiquity of Canon Law', in *Law and Society in Byzantium: Ninth–Twelfth Centuries*, ed. Angelikē E. Laïu-Thōmadakē and Dieter Simon (Washington, DC: Dumbarton Oaks Research Library and Collection, 1994), 131.

337. J. H. A. Lokin, 'The Significance of Law and Legislation in the Law Books of the Ninth to Eleventh Centuries', in *Law and Society in Byzantium: Ninth–Twelfth Centuries*, ed. Angelikē E. Laïu-Thōmadakē and Dieter Simon (Washington, DC: Dumbarton Oaks Research Library and Collection, 1994), 71.

338. Konidaris, 'The Ubiquity of Canon Law', 133.

339. Lokin, 'The Significance of Law and Legislation in the Law Books of the Ninth to Eleventh Centuries', 80.

340. Lokin, 83.

341. Lokin, 78.

342. *Apologeticus major*, quoted in Gilissen, *La Coutume*, 16; David J. Bederman, *Custom as a Source of Law* (Cambridge: Cambridge University Press, 2010), 17.

343. Hoff, *Hafliði Másson und die Einflüsse des römischen Rechts in der Grágás*, 51.

344. Hoff, 128.

345. Hoff, 174.

346. Hoff, 205, 243.

347. Hoff, 244.

348. Ludwig Burgmann, trans., *Ecloga*, Forschungen zur Byzantischen Rechtsgeschichte 10 (Frankfurt: Lowenklau, 1983), l. 935.

349. Sven Aggesen, *The Works of Sven Aggesen, Twelfth-Century Danish Historian*, 14–15.

350. Konidaris, 'The Ubiquity of Canon Law', 135.

351. Konidaris, 139–40.

352. Konidaris, 150.

353. Bryce, *Studies in History and Jurisprudence*, 1.1:280.

354. Burrows, 'Some Þing to Talk About', 49.

355. Miller II, *Oral Tradition in Ancient Israel*, 35–36, 66–67.

356. Tamm, 'How Nordic Are the Old Nordic Laws?', 9.

357. Stefan Jurasinski, *Ancient Privileges: Beowulf, Law, and the Making of Germanic Antiquity*, Medieval European Studies 6 (Morgantown: West Virginia University Press, 2006), 17.

358. Jurasinski, 19; Baltl, 'Folklore Research and Legal History in the German Language Area', 400.

359. Jurasinski, *Ancient Privileges*, 21 nn.46, 31.

360. Erno Tarkany-Szucs, 'Results and Tasks of Legal Ethnology in Europe', in *Folk Law*, ed. Alison D. Renteln and Alan Dundes, vol. 1, Garland Folklore Casebooks 3 (New York: Garland, 1994), 167; Patrick Wormald, *The Making of English Law*, vol. 1 (Oxford: Blackwell, 1999), 11–12; Brink, 'Law and Legal Customs in Viking Age Scandinavia', 88; Jurasinski, *Ancient Privileges*, 29; Kaius Tuori, *Lawyers and Savages: Ancient History and Legal Realism in the Making of Legal Anthropology* (Milton Park, UK: Routledge, 2015), 33–34.

361. Orfield, *The Growth of Scandinavian Law*, n. 109.

362. Peter Heather, *The Goths*, The Peoples of Europe 9 (Oxford: Blackwell, 2008), 325; Gilissen, *La Coutume*, 42–43; Bederman, *Custom as a Source of Law*, 25–26.

363. Brink, 'Reconstruction of Viking and Early Medieval Scandinavian Society', 3–4; Heike Grahn-Hoek, 'The Thuringi, the Peculiarities of Their Law, and Their Legal Relationship to the *Gentes* of Their Time, Chiefly According to the Lex Thuringorum and Other *Leges Barbarorum* of the Early Middle Ages', in *The Baiuvarii and Thuringi: An Ethnographic Perspective*, ed. Janine Fries-Knoblach, Heiko Steuer, and John Hines, Studies in Historical Archaeoethnology 9 (Woodbridge: Boydell, 2014), 289. Almost all of Late Roman Law had been forgotten: of Justinian's *Corpus Juris Civilis*, the Institutes and Digests were lost, and the Code known but ignored. M. Stuart Madden, 'Paths of Western Law after Justinian', *London Law Review* 2 (2006), 3.

364. Heather, *The Goths*, 325.

365. Grahn-Hoek, 'The Thuringi', 300–303; Sundqvist, *Freyr's Offspring*, 63–78, 223–24.

366. Sanmark, *Viking Law and Order*, 5, 9.

367. Ditlev Tamm, 'How Nordic Are the Old Nordic Laws—Ten Years Later?', in *How Nordic Are the Nordic Medival Laws? Ten Years after: Proceedings of the Tenth Carlsberg Academy Conference on Medieval Legal History 2013*, ed. Per Andersen et al. (Copenhagen: DJØF Publishing, 2014), 5.

368. Starcke, *Denmark in World History*, 78.

369. Sundeep S. Jhutti, *The Getes*, Sino-Platonic Papers 127 (Philadelphia: Department of East Asian Languages and Civilizations, University of Pennsylvania, 2003), 60–61.

370. Ingemar Nordgren, *The Well Spring of the Goths* (New York: iUniverse, 2004), 324.

371. Nordgren, 539.

372. Arne S. Christensen, *Cassiodorus Jordanes and the History of the Goths* (Copenhagen: Museum Tusculanum Press, 2002), 52, 230–31, 233–34, 250–51, 258, 291, 299–300, 316, 345–46. There are some holes one could poke in this argument, particularly at Christensen, 302–3.

373. Jhutti, *The Getes*, 97.

374. Ramon d'Abadal i de Vinyals, 'A propos du Leges Visigothique en Espagne', *Settimane di Studio del centro italiano di studi sul'alto medioevo* 5 (1958): 563.

375. d'Abadal i de Vinyals, 562.

376. d'Abadal i de Vinyals, 566–67; G. Ausenda and Pablo C. Diaz, 'Current Issues and Future Directions in the Study of Visigoths', in *The Visigoths: From the Migration Period to the Seventh Century*, ed. Peter Heather, Studies in Historical Archaeoethnology 4 (San Marino: Boydell, 1999), 509; G. Ausenda, 'Kinship and Marriage among the Visigoths', in *The Visigoths: From the Migration Period to the Seventh Century*, ed. Peter Heather, Studies in Historical Archaeoethnology 4 (San Marino: Boydell, 1999), 129–68; contra E. A. Thompson, *The Goths in Spain* (Oxford: Clarendon, 1969), 134–35; Paul D. King, 'The Character of Visigothic Legislation' (Diss., Cambridge, University of Cambridge, 1967), 2, 6, 9.

377. Paul D. King, *Law and Society in the Visigothic Kingdom*, Cambridge Studies in Medieval Life and Thought, 3.5 (Cambridge: Cambridge University Press, 1972), 7–8; Ausenda, 'Kinship and Marriage among the Visigoths'; I. Wood, 'Social Relations in the Visigothic Kingdom from the Fifth to the Seventh Century', in *The Visigoths: From the Migration Period to the Seventh Century*, ed. Peter Heather, Studies in Historical Archaeoethnology 4 (San Marino: Boydell, 1999), 191. Even in what little is decipherable, 'not a single Germanic word can be found in Euric's code, not even in those norms with Germanic roots'; Pablo C. Diaz, 'Visigothic Political Institutions', in *The Visigoths: From the Migration Period to the Seventh Century*, ed. Peter Heather, Studies in Historical Archaeoethnology 4 (San Marino: Boydell, 1999), 333.

378. Katherine F. Drew, 'The Barbarian Kings as Lawgivers and Judges', in *Life and Thought in the Early Middle Ages*, ed. Robert S. Hoyt (Minneapolis: University of Minnesota Press, 1967), 13–14. The Visigothic law issued in Castilean in 693 as *Fuero Juzgo* withstood six revisions and was transmitted to Texas in the 1700s by Spanish colonizers as *Leyes de los Reinos de las Indias*. Since private rights of individuals under laws of previous sovereignty remain unaffected unless abrogated, it is still binding in Texas; J. E. Ericson and Mary P. Winston, 'Civil Law and Common Law in Early Texas', *East Texas Historical Journal* 2 (1964): 26; Allen C. Steere, 'An Introduction to the Law of Community Property', *Indiana Law Journal* 23 (1947): 34–35.

379. Drew, 'The Barbarian Kings as Lawgivers and Judges', 23.

380. Lupoi, 'A European Common Law before Bologna?', 3; Madden, 'Paths of Western Law after Justinian', 25.

381. Lupoi, 'A European Common Law before Bologna?', 14; Ausenda, 'Kinship and Marriage among the Visigoths', 143.

382. Lupoi, 'A European Common Law before Bologna?', 6.

383. Drew, 'The Barbarian Kings as Lawgivers and Judges', 25; Ausenda, 'Kinship and Marriage among the Visigoths'.

384. Katherine F. Drew, trans., *The Lombard Laws*, 5th ed., Sources of Medieval History 7 (Philadelphia: University of Pennsylvania Press, 1996), 54–55; Drew, 'The Barbarian Kings as Lawgivers and Judges', 25.

385. Giorgio Ausenda and Sam. J. Barnish, 'A Comparative Discussion of Langobardic Feud and Blood-Money Compensation with Parallels from Contemporary Anthropology and from Medieval History', in *The Langobards before the Frankish Conquest*, ed. Giorgio Ausenda, Studies in Historical Archaeoethnology 8 (Woodbridge: Boydell & Brewer, 2009), 313.

386. Drew, 'The Barbarian Kings as Lawgivers and Judges', 26.

387. Patrick Wormald, *Legal Culture in the Early Medieval West* (London: Hambledon, 2004), 3, 27; Herwig Wolfram, *History of the Goths*, trans. Thomas J. Dunlap, 2nd ed. (Berkeley: University of California Press, 1990), 195; Paolo Delogu, 'Kingship and the Shaping of the Lombard Body Politic', in *The Langobards before the Frankish Conquest*, ed. Giorgio Ausenda, Studies in Historical Archaeoethnology 8 (Woodbridge: Boydell & Brewer, 2009), 257.

388. Wormald, *Legal Culture in the Early Medieval West*, 8, 28.

389. Wormald, 11.

390. Wormald, 3.

391. Wormald, 12.

392. Wormald, 14–15.

393. Wormald, 14.

394. Wormald, 15.

395. Wormald, 13.

396. Wormald, 21.

397. Wormald, 22–23, 37; Madden, 'Paths of Western Law after Justinian', 3, 5; Marios Costambeys, 'Kinship, Gender and Property in Lombard Italy', in *The Langobards before the Frankish Conquest*, ed. Giorgio Ausenda, Studies in Historical Archaeoethnology 8 (Woodbridge: Boydell & Brewer, 2009), 93; King, 'The Character of Visigothic Legislation', 18–19, noting a 470 letter of Sidonius Apollinaris.

398. Lupoi, 'A European Common Law before Bologna?', 16; Drew, 'The Barbarian Kings as Lawgivers and Judges', 21.

399. Madden, 'Paths of Western Law after Justinian', 23.

400. Wormald, *Legal Culture in the Early Medieval West*, 24; Drew, *The Lombard Laws*, xix.

401. Madden, 'Paths of Western Law after Justinian', 40; Drew, 'The Barbarian Kings as Lawgivers and Judges', 28; Paul the Deacon, *History of the Lombards*, trans. William D. Foulke (Philadelphia: University of Pennsylvania Press, 2003), 197 note.

402. Ekkehard Kaufmann, 'Rechtssprichwort', in *Handworterbuch zur deutschen Rechtsgeschichte* (Berlin: Erich Schmidt, 2017), 364; Rene Maunier, *Introduction au Folklore juridique* (Paris: Les Editions d'Art et d'Histoire, 1938), 14.

403. Gilissen, *La Coutume*, 65.

404. P. Saintyves, 'Le Folklore juridique', *Etudes de Sociologie et d'Ethnologie juridiques* 12 (1932): 76–77, 89.

405. From which, Antonin Scalia would stand completely at odds; see Bederman, *Custom as a Source of Law*, 77. On the history of customary law in legal realism and otherwise, see Bederman, 14–15, 28–31, 40, 46; Clifford Geertz, 'Off Echoes: Some Comments on Anthropology and Law', *PoLAR* 19 (1996): 33–34.

406. Gilissen, *La Coutume*, 20, 29; Maunier, *Introduction au Folklore juridique*, 9; cf. Peter Kropotkin, *Law and Authority* (London: International, 1886), 7. Kropotkin was under no illusions that customary law was more liberating, but held that with codification, custom as folk habit and routines that perpetuated inequality were confounded; Kropotkin, 9–10.

407. Peter Goodrich, 'Literacy and the Languages of the Early Common Law', *Journal of Law and Society* 14 (1987): 429; T. W. Bennett, *Customary Law in South Africa* (Cape Town: Juta, 2004), 4.

408. Gilissen, *La Coutume*, 25; A. Vilhelm Lundstedt, *Legal Thinking Revisited* (Stockholm: Almqvist & Wiksell international, 1956), 26; G. C. J. J. van den Bergh, 'The Concept of Folk Law in Historical Context', in *Anthropology of Law in the Netherlands: Essays on Legal Pluralism*, ed. Keebet von Benda-Beckmann and A. K. J. M. Strijbosch, Verhandelingen van Het Koninklijk Instituut Voor Taal-, Land- En Volkenkunde 116 (Dordrecht, Netherlands: Foris, 1986), 79.

409. Maunier, *Introduction au Folklore juridique*, 14.

410. Goodrich, 'Literacy and the Languages of the Early Common Law', 437.

411. Oliver Wendell Holmes, *The Fundamental Holmes*, ed. Ronald K. L. Collins (Cambridge: Cambridge University Press, 2010), 139 (1897); Goodrich, 'Literacy and the Languages of the Early Common Law', 430; Gilissen, *La Coutume*, 90–91.

412. Bennett, *Customary Law in South Africa*, 2.

413. Peter Stein, *Regulae Iuris: From Juristic Rules to Legal Maxims* (Edinburgh: Edinburgh University Press, 1966), 5.

414. Karl N. Llewellyn, *Jurisprudence* (Chicago: University of Chicago Press, 1962), 300.

415. Holmes, *The Fundamental Holmes*, 149 (1897); Llewellyn, *Jurisprudence*, 300.

416. Taslim Olawale Elias, 'The Problem of Reducing Customary Laws to Writing', in *Folk Law*, ed. Alison D. Renteln and Alan Dundes, vol. 1, Garland Folklore Casebooks 3 (New York: Garland, 1994), 320; Helge Dedek, 'School of Life: Learned Law and the Scholastic Habitus', in *Law and Private Life in the Middle Ages*, ed. Per Andersen, Mia Münster-Swendsen, and Helle Vogt (Copenhagen: DJØF, 2011), 116; see Albie Sachs, *The Strange Alchemy of Life and Law* (Oxford: Oxford University Press, 2011), 146 for a modern equivalent.

417. Owen Barfield, 'Poetic Diction and Legal Fiction', in *The Importance of Language*, ed. Max Black (Englewood Cliffs, NJ: Prentice-Hall, 1969), 58–59.

418. Stein, *Regulae Iuris*, 156.

419. Barfield, 'Poetic Diction and Legal Fiction', 64, quoting Frederic William Maitland.

420. Willam H. Stoddard, 'Law and Institutions in the Shire', *Mythlore*, no. 70 (Autumn 1992): 7, describing the fictional world of J. R. R. Tolkien's Shire!; See Llewellyn, *Jurisprudence*, 299 for the real world.

421. Holmes, *The Fundamental Holmes*, 140 (1897).

422. J. Van der Ploeg, 'Studies in Hebrew Law', *Catholic Biblical Quarterly* 12 (1950): 257. The derivation of the word, its apparent plural form, even its vocalization, is quite problematic; Bruno Volkwein, 'Masoretisches `edut, `edwot, `edot', *Biblische Zeitschrift* 13 (1968): 38–39; Georg Fohrer, *Studien zur alttestamentlichen Theologie und Geschichte* (Berlin: De Gruyter, 1969), 341.

423. Gilissen, *La Coutume*, 31; Maunier, *Introduction au Folklore juridique*, 15.

424. Alf Ross, *On Law and Justice* (London: Stevens & Sons, 1958), 92.

425. Stoddard, 'Law and Institutions in the Shire', 6.

426. Saintyves, 'Le Folklore juridique', 102–3; Kaufmann, 'Rechtssprichwort', 365; Dedek, 'School of Life: Learned Law and the Scholastic Habitus', 105–7; contra Kenneth Pennington, 'Learned Law, Droit Savant, Gelehrtes Recht', *Syracuse Journal of International Law and Commerce* 20 (1994): 205–15.

427. Brendan Tobin and Rodrigo de la Cruz, 'Customary Law, Traditional Knowledge and Intellectual Property' (Geneva: World Intellectual Property Organization Secretariat, 2013), www.wipo.int/export/sites/www/tk/en/resources/pdf/overview_customary_law.pdf.

428. Elias, 'The Problem of Reducing Customary Laws to Writing', 321.

429. René David, 'Sources of Law', in *International Encyclopedia of Comparative Law* (Tübingen: Mohr Siebeck, 1984), 99.

430. Tobin and de la Cruz, 'Customary Law, Traditional Knowledge and Intellectual Property'.

431. Borislav T. Blagojevic, 'The Comparative Method in the Study of Customary Law as a Historical Category', in *Mélanges de droit comparé: en l'honneur du doyen Åke Malmström*, ed. Stig Strömholm, ACTA Instituti Upsaliensis Iurisprudentiae Comparativae 14 (Stockholm: Norstedt, 1972), 35.

432. Holmes, *The Fundamental Holmes*, 147 (1897).

433. Llewellyn, *Jurisprudence*, 300. Moreover, it is not unusual for some customary law to be kept secret 'Customary Law and Traditional Knowledge', Background Briefs (Geneva: World Intellectual Property Organization, 2016), 2.

434. Nygaard, "Law, Religion," 152.

435. Ross, *On Law and Justice*, 95; Holmes, *The Fundamental Holmes*, 141 (1897).

436. David, 'Sources of Law', 97.

437. Tobin and de la Cruz, 'Customary Law, Traditional Knowledge and Intellectual Property'.

438. Bederman, *Custom as a Source of Law*, 178; Stein, *Regulae Iuris*, 13.

439. Stein, *Regulae Iuris*, 16.

440. Roscoe Pound, *An Introduction to the Philosophy of Law*, Rev. ed. (New Haven: Yale University Press, 1982), 65–66.

Chapter Three

Oral-Written Customary Law in Ancient Israel

We can now turn at last to Ancient Israel. The goal in this section is to discuss both the actual legal system, oral and written, of Israel and Judah prior to the Babylonian conquest of the latter, as well as the laws of the Pentateuch, in particular the so-called Covenant Code in Exod 20:22–23:19. Because of the serious problems with finding accurate legal information in the Icelandic sagas, narratives of the Hebrew Bible will be "mined" for insights into Israelite law only cautiously.[1] The book of Proverbs will be explored for reasons to be iterated below.

As in Iceland and the Gothic world, the legal system of Judah and Israel was customary law (Gen 34:2; 2 Sam 13:12; 2 Kgs 11:14).[2] The word מִשְׁפָּט regularly translates "custom" or even "customary law" (Deut 25:1; 1 Sam 2:13; Jer 32:8);[3] in 2 Kgs 1:7 it is the way in which Elijah used to dress (Exod 26:30; 1 Kgs 6:38; 18:28; 2 Kgs 17:26; Ezek 43:11; Ps 119:132).[4] Textual depictions of judicial process "conspicuously omit any reference to the application of written rules" (e.g., Exod 21:18–19; Deut 16:18–20).[5] The שֹׁטְרִים in the latter text ("appoint judges and *officers* in all your towns") are not scribes, as the Septuagint has it (γραμματεις) based on its etymology, but merely officials—forms of the word occur in this sense on an inscribed bowl from Hazor in northern Israel and the Dead Sea Scroll 4QMyst[a] 1.4.[6] Even in late texts, criminal justice is based on actual decisions, not by code but precedent (Lev 24:10–12; Num 15:32).[7] King David grants judgement for a woman of Tekoa in 2 Sam 14:5–7 that not only does not appeal to statutory law, "it is diametrically opposed to a known rule" in Num 35:31–33.[8] The same is true for the trial of Naboth in 1 Kings 21: no law codes or commandments are invoked.[9] As Bernard Jackson writes, "The use of such codes by judges in courts . . . remains singularly devoid of evidence."[10]

Further proof that the legal system must have been something other than what we have in the Pentateuch lies in the fact that the Law of Moses is missing key areas of law.[11] It refers to divorce, and modifies it, but never sets out its basics. It provides no legislation on how to marry in the first place.[12] A legal institution known as the גואל, "Redeemer," is referred to but never explained.[13] There is no law by which one could call a disloyal messenger to account.[14] Birth or war-captive grounds for slavery are never laid out in the Covenant Code, nor is theft of anything other than an animal considered.[15] All of this was known by custom.[16]

This means the Israelite legal system was oral,[17] based in a body of oral lore shared and developed by acknowledged experts who intentionally transmitted and manipulated its contents.[18] Instructions for judges in Deut 16:18 say nothing about consultation of codes.[19] The only legal document we have from the Pre-Exilic period, the Yavneh Yam Inscription, invokes no laws.[20] That the Hebrew Bible regularly depicts law *recitation* from written texts (e.g., Exod 24:3–7; Deut 31:9–11; Josh 8:30–35) relates not to the functioning legal system but to the performance of a display document, exactly as at the Icelandic Althing.[21]

PERFORMANCE OF LAW

To begin to reconstruct performance schemas for Pre-Exilic Israelite law, we may begin with space. Assemblies like Things would have played an important role in legal performance (Num 1:16; 14:10; 16:2; Josh 24:22; Judg 20:7–11; 1 Kgs 12:3; Prov 5:14; Hammurabi, 5).[22] The place of assembly most commonly designated is the gate.[23] The physical features of Ancient Near Eastern gate complexes dispose them well for such assemblies. In fact, modifications to gate design in the Iron II period provided the one large open space for otherwise densely crowded towns and cities.[24] The gate is consistently the locus of litigation, especially civil litigation, across the Former Prophets (e.g., 2 Sam 15:2–6; 19:8–9; 2 Kgs 7:1)—Amos (5:10), Isaiah (29:21), Proverbs (e.g., 22:22–23; 31:23), Psalms (e.g., 55:12; 121; 127:5), Ruth (e.g., 4:1–2), and Job,[25] as well as at the Bronze Age Canaanite city of Ugarit (e.g., KTU 1.17 v.6–8).[26] Criminal proceedings are held at the gate in Exod 32:26; Deut 21:18–21; 22:13–24; and Josh 20:4, as in the Old Hittite Laws (*COS* 1.76 §50; 2.19 §187–88, 199).[27]

Can we be sure this is also the location of "legislative" assembly, in the sense of the Icelandic Things? Gates are designated locations for public address (Jer 17:19; 19:2; 2 Chron 32:6; Prov 31:31; Neh 8:1–2; also Code of Hammurabi 58 [*COS* 2.131]; "Man and his god" *COS* 1.179.106–115).[28]

Elders "sit" (a legal term; Exod 18:13; Isa 28:6) in the gate (*Atrahasis* COS 1.130.2.38–41),[29] discussing affairs of state (Gen 34:20–24; 1 Kings 22, on which see below).[30] Excavated gates at Dan, Bethsaida, and Tel Mevorakh have raised platforms that could have functioned like a Law Rock for assembly leaders.[31]

Yet perhaps we need to look at places other than gates. Occasionally, assemblies in locations other than gates are mentioned. Several assemblies at the "Tent of Meeting" are remarkably "secular" and legislative in nature (Exod 18:21–25; Num 8:9; 11:16; 19:4; 27:1–6; Josh 19:51).

Threshing floors sometimes serve for judicial proceedings (1 Kgs 22:10; Laws of Eshnunna 19; Ugaritic text KTU 1.17 ii.5–8; perhaps Ruth 3:10–14), economic disputes (PIS 1124, 1134; MDP 375.6; Papyrus Tebtunis 375).[32] Smaller village moots would not have had the option of a gateworks,[33] and threshing floors had to be high ground, open to the breezes, usually circular or semi-circular, naturally suited for assembly.[34] Like Nordic Things, threshing floors appear throughout antiquity as ritual locales (Harpocration, *Lexicon of the Ten Orators*, s.v. "Haloa"; Eustathius, *On Homer's Iliad*, 9.530).[35]

An indeterminate רְחוֹב, plaza, serves for public assize in Deut 13:16; 2 Sam 21:12; Neh 8:1, 3, 16; 2 Chron 29:4. In 1 Kgs 22:10, the same space is called a gate, threshing floor, and רְחוֹב.

Or it may be necessary to begin with terminology rather than narrative. The text uses terms קהל, מוֹעֵד, and עֵדָה interchangeably for what look like Things (e.g., Sir 7:7; 44:15; 46:7) and does not clarify whether these are representative assemblies or gatherings of the entire community—a blurring typical of Icelandic Things.[36] Rost concludes different terminology was used by the different sources that went into the composition of the Pentateuch: the so-called "Deuteronomic Source" prefers קְהֵל and the "Priestly Writer" עֵדָה.[37] Nevertheless, the hiphil of קהל appears in Lev 8:3; Num 8:9; 10:7; 20:8 in legislative, juridical contexts.[38] The term מוֹעֵד describes a representative assembly in Num 2:2 (Isa 14:13; 33:20).[39] The Things depicted in Numbers 1 and 16, as well as in Joshua 23 and 24, appear to be about 250 people, which must be representative since it is hardly the entire congregation envisioned as 600,000 people. Cognates to קהל are used for such assemblies in related languages.[40] Images of divine and human assemblies with comparable terms from Ugarit and Phoenicia confirm the representative council image (e.g., KTU 1.2 ii.14 from Ugarit; the prophet narrative preserved in the Deir Alla inscription, 1.19; and the reference in the Egyptian Tale of Wen-Amon to *mw-ʿd*, equivalent to Ugaritic *m'd* and Hebrew עֵדָה [41]. (מוֹעֵד the word continues to serve for Things in Elephantine (AP 15.22, 26; 82.5; BMAP 2.7; 7.21).[42]

If קְהֵל indicates a Thing, several are located in the text. Judg 20:1–2 places one at Mizpah (1 Sam 7:5, 11).[43] Although Mizpah (Tell en-Nasbeh) "bears

little resemblance to the large administrative centers such as Lachish III/IV or
Megiddo VA/IVB, IVA, and III,"[44] a two-gate system built in the 9th century,
standing until the 5th, provided a long rectangular open area of 500 m².[45] A
thousand people could have assembled without unnecessary crowding.[46] Jerusalem Things appear in 1 Kgs 8:1–2, 65; and 1 Kgs 12:21.

2 Sam 20:14 describes Sheba rebelling against David on behalf of Northern
tribes and fleeing to Abel Beth-Maacah, whereupon its Beerites "assemble"
(קהל) inside. When Joab arrives to attack the town, an elderly woman accuses
him of trying to destroy "a city and a mother in Israel" and tells him that
people used to "inquire" there. Alt read this inquiry legally, rather than oracular, in the light of the use of קהל, and understands the "mother" to be the city.[47]
Area A at the northern end of the 9th century lower city contains a paved
area with a raised dais at one end, possibly an open court enclosed by meter-
wide walls.[48] The excavators of Abel Beth-Maacah, noting the discovery of
425 animal astragals in an Iron II amphora on the dais instead consider the
inquiry oracular, and the wise woman to be the "mother in Israel" like Deborah, whom Joab would destroy along with the city.[49] Of course, Deborah,
too, functions legally,[50] and the translation seems awkward since Joab is not
threatening the woman directly.

Geographic names are also formed from the root קהל, and along the lines of
"Thing," these might indicate the presence of Things at those places: Kehe-
lathah of Num 33:22–23 (LXX Makellath) and Makheloth (Num 33:25–26),
although there is nothing in the text to suggest such a function.

It is tempting to push the parallels with the Althing further, to speculate
about law recitation in ancient Israel.[51] Von Rad and Noth postulated an
annual covenant renewal ceremony at Shechem that involved such recitation on the basis of Deut 27:14–15 and Joshua 24.[52] Although Shechem may,
indeed, have hosted a Thing, as we have seen, Clements long ago showed no
evidence supports a covenant renewal ceremony,[53] especially at Shechem.[54]

LEGAL PERFORMERS

The legal performers active in ancient Israelite Things, if they correspond
to any figures in the Hebrew Bible, are the so-called "elders" (Josh 8:33;
24:1; Judg 9:2–6, 23–24; 1 Sam 16:4; 23:11–12; 30:26–31; Job 12:12; Prov
20:29).[55] Joshua 24 uses "elders" and "men of Israel" interchangeably, and
since the number of elders in a town whenever one is given is in the seven-
ties, these would be those with the right to speak in assembly.[56] City elders
also function as assembled representatives in Amarna Letters (EA 100, lines
11–15) and at Alalakh (AT 271.6, 8, 16; 322.4).[57] A letter from Ishme-Dagan

of Assyria to Yasmah-Adad refers to (Hanaean?) "elders" gathered in "assembly" (ARM 4.50–53, no.29, rev. 22–23) as elders did at Emar (ASJ 14.44).[58]

The קְרוּאֵי הָעֵדָה of Num 1:16; 16:2 play the assembled representative role, as do the "Sons of the City" at Ugarit (e.g., PRU vol. 4, p. 154, no. RS 17.146, lines 19ff., 36ff.; PRU vol. 4, p. 158, no RS 18.115, obv. Line 6, rev. 2, 22, 29). Although there are none in the Covenant Code, even the שׁוֹפֵט judge, if we draw on the Punic parallel *šūfeṭ,* can be a representative in a *colloquium* (Livy 28.38; roughly a Thing) or *senatum* (Livy 30.7; equivalent to an Althing). If the narratives can be believed (e.g., Naboth's blasphemy trial), the Israelite king had no role in such an assembly.[59]

Alongside such individuals were acknowledged experts responsible for the sharing, transmission, and development of the law, although the elders may also have played this role (Exod 21:28–29; 22:1–3).[60] An Ugaritic letter from the King of Amqi (PRU 4. 219 = RS 17.424C+397B, lines 24–27) refers to such "memory men" (see above): "Ask the fathers of Ugarit if [anyone in the past] collected *miksu* from a merchant who is at the [king's] feet."[61] Mark Leuchter and other scholars describe the role of the "landed gentry" (Heb. עַם הָאָרֶץ) in the time of King Josiah as such preservers of old traditions, rememberers of law and masters of legal maneuvers like Njáll and Skapti.[62]

There are also the חֻקְקִים, a word forms of which are suggestive of engraving in Isa 49:16; Ezek 4:1; 23:14; Prov 8:27; but of governing in Judg 5:9, 14–15; and of working at law in Isa 10:1.[63] One should not envision two roots, one from Proto-Semitic *ḤQQ* and one from *ḤQQ*, nor can the basic meaning derive from engraving laws on clay,[64] since the legal meaning is present already in Gen 49:10 and the governing meaning in Judges 5 and Deut 33:21. The key seems to be not the writing implement but the scepter (Num 21:18; Ps 60:9), ceremonial instrument of judges (like a gavel) in *Iliad* 18.505–506, or even "Fasces," given the plural, symbolizing jurisdiction for the Etruscans and Rome (Livy, *Ab urbe condita,* 1:8).[65] Likewise in Egypt, the god Thoth, who pronounces judgements in the name of the Pharaoh (Papyrus Leiden 1; Pyramid Texts 252),[66] is in the New Kingdom called "Lord of the divine script" [*mdw*] ("The Stories of Setne Khamwas"),[67] a word that also means "staff,"[68] which Hodge believes indicates a baton designating authority to pronounce law.[69]

I am not convinced, however, that פְּלִלִים of Exod 21:22 refers to lawmen who have authority to state what law applies in what situation, distinct from the authority of a שׁוֹפֵט or דַּיָּן judge (for the latter, 1 Sam 24:16; Ps 68:8).[70] The root פלל outside Hebrew only occurs in Akkadian texts from Karum Kanesh.[71] Its use there, in Gen 48:11; Deut 32:31; Ezek 16:52; and Job 31:11, 28 all suggest "estimation" or "assessment,"[72] in a pseudo-plural, and not any sort of individuals.[73]

Although its vision of court proceedings is likely that of the Post-Exilic period, the book of Job contains three imagined judicial scenes in the speeches of Job. In Job 9:33, Job wishes there were (or laments that there is not) a מוֹכִיחַ, an agent of "binding arbitration" in a court setting (9:32).[74] The physical sign of this arbitration is his placing of his hands on both of the disputing parties (v. 34).[75] The same courtroom context obtains in 16:19–21, where the "arbitration" of v. 21 is imagined as performed by a [שָׂהֲדִי], testa-tor.[76] The term is Aramaic, inserted as a parallel to the Hebrew word [עֵדִי] or witness.[77] The book of Job regularly presents pairs of Hebrew and Aramaic terms in this manner, and the same parallel occurs in Gen 31:47 where Laban, speaking Aramaic since he is Aramean, refers to the Hebrew "witness" (עֵד) as "testimony," שָׂהֲדוּתָא.[78] In the third scene, the imagined individual is now a גוֹאֵל, "redeemer," and while the context of these corrupt verses might sug-gest a person who is "more than a witness and greater than an arbiter,"[79] the scene is obviously a parallel to that envisioned in the other two passages. The גוֹאֵל, however, is a well-known Israelite legal personage, and although he has a range of roles, from blood avenger to fiscal surety (Lev 25:25, 48; Num 35:15; Deut 19:6; 2 Sam 14:11), one of those is as public defender or Duty Counsel (Prov 23:10–11; Isa 41:10–14; Ps 119:154).[80] All of these entail a male kinsman who functions as an advocate, but not a trained class of legal scholars nor a lawgiver like the Elders.

Nevertheless, Deut 31:10–13 does mandate an annual recitation of the Torah, and the second person singular pronouns of vv 9 and 11 suggest a single individual was expected to perform this recitation.[81] Such public recita-tions appear in Josh 8:30–35 and 2 Kgs 23:1–2. Views have differed on how historically accurate these recitations are: Holladay accepted their existence in the First Temple Period, Nelson considered them fanciful, and Newsom believes they represent a Second Temple practice, where scrolls acted as both *aides memoires* and as "physical signifier of the authority of God."[82] Never-theless, she admits the Post-Exilic scene of Torah recitation in Nehemiah 8 is entirely different, liturgical with ritual responses (v 6) and gestures (v 7) and listeners who, unlike the other passages, do *not* understand what is being recited.[83] So either two *different* recitation practices obtained in the Second Temple Period, or that envisioned in Deuteronomy and the Former Proph-ets is First Temple or imaginary. Finally, perhaps the requirement in Deut 17:18–19 that the king "write out his own copy of this Torah" is a late rein-terpretation (presumably by the so-called Deuteronomist, but that is beyond the scope of this study) of an earlier requirement for the king to annually or cyclically *recite* the Torah.[84]

LEGAL PERFORMANCE PRACTICES

Although covenant renewal ceremonies are unlikely, we are on surer ground noting other ritualized practices of law.[85] The legal act of raising the hand to take an oath is attested in Isa 13:2 and Prov 1:24.[86] The ear, symbolic of obedient listening of the slave, was pierced in submission to the owner when a slave was no longer redeemable (Exod 21:6; Deut 15:17; Job 40:24–28).[87] Spreading a mantle over someone extends protective patronage like a bird spreading its wings (Ezek 16:8; Ruth 3:9; Deut 32:11; Jer 48:40; 49:22; Job 39:26; Exod 25:20; 37:9; 1 Kgs 6:27; 8:7; 2 Chron 3:13; 5:8).[88]

The verbal contents of Israelite customary law would have been short aphorisms like Gen 9:6, often with chiasms and other performative features.[89] The law in Deut 19:16–21 seems to witness two independently circulating oral dicta for the same legal situation: "Then you shall do to him as he meant to do to his brother" and "Life for life, eye for eye, tooth for tooth, hand for hand, foot for foot"—the former reappearing in Judg 1:6–7 and 15:4–11 and Prov 24:29 (where it is contested); the latter, in 1 Kgs 20:39–43 and 2 Kgs 10:24.[90]

On the other hand, we have seen already with Iceland and elsewhere that legal acts are often sacral acts, that lawmen are ritual functionaries, and we should assume the same for Israel. Thus, in Exod 21:6, the slave who does not wish to be manumitted is brought both to the "door"—perhaps city gate—and "to God." In several places, אֱלֹהִים, God, has traditionally been understood to refer to human judges (Exod 22:7–8, 26–27; Deut 1:17).[91] More probably, such cases are being brought to *both* human jurisdiction and by that very act, "to God."

None of this eliminates the role of writing in the customary law of ancient Israel and Judah. Iron Age legal memoranda, perhaps on ostraca or wax tablets like those found in the Uluburun shipwreck, would have been memory aids for official lawmen as well as the private possessions of individuals.[92]

THE FUNCTION OF LAWBOOKS

Those written artifacts of law are not identical to the laws and "law codes" of the Hebrew Bible. Like *Grágás,* biblical "law codes" are not codes at all.[93] They are scientific treatises or hornbooks with much theoretical, even theological, reflection and glossing.[94] They were never legislative and never meant to prescribe law or to serve as lawbooks for judges (or in their cultic laws, for liturgists).[95] Their *sitz im leben* is rather the education system, pedagogical—as befits what is called "curriculum" (Heb. תּוֹרָה; see Isa 1:10;

28:9).[96] For this reason, the Covenant Code formally resembles Ancient Near Eastern omen lists.[97]

Debate over the existence of schools in Pre-Exilic Israel and Judah has by and large turned quite skeptical. Already in 1974, Norman Whybray examined the purported evidence and dismissed it thoroughly. In the 1990s, the epigraphic evidence used by Emile Pueche and Graham Davies to support scribal schools,[98] Stuart Weeks was able to discount.[99]

On the other hand, James Crenshaw notes that the officials in Judah who read and wrote Aramaic in the 8th and 7th centuries would have required years of study.[100] Isa 28:9–13 looks like a mockery of a school.[101] Much has changed in the light of recent archaeological discoveries. Even discounting those whose nature is debated, the synchronic consistency of Hebrew paleography, sophisticated, consistent, and meticulous morphology, consistent orthography, and the use of the complicated Egyptian hieratic numeral system all attest to sophisticated knowledge of trained professionals.[102]

Moreover, the aforementioned debate is about *scribal* schools, while the "schools" of law in Iceland such as the one "hosted" by Njáll were *oral*. Non-scribal schools of law like those we described for Iceland could have existed in Iron II Israel and Judah and the counter evidence of Whybray and Weeks would not be relevant.[103]

As such "curriculum," the Covenant Code, for instance, consists of moot or actual cases and questions spun out to their theoretical conclusion, and then varied.[104] The variation provides parameters for extrapolating further legal principles.[105] Minor issues therefore receive extensive treatment and minute distinctions, while other important areas of the law are simply ignored. What remains is often contradictory (e.g., Exod 13:12 vs. 34:19), at other times redundant (Exod 23:19 = 34:26),[106] structured but, like *Grágás,* a turgid, puzzling, unwieldy structure.[107] What remains is not customary decisions, but something formulated like decisions that are based on custom.[108] Even where this remainder appears capable of being interpreted in a statutory manner, we need not conclude it ever was.[109]

As we have seen with Iceland, there is no contradiction between the existence of books like these so-called codes and a customary law system that was primarily oral.[110] In fact, attributing a legislative role to paradigmatic cases drawn out to varied applications "reveal[s] a consciousness of judicial precedent as a valid source of law."[111] Even the Deuteronomic reform, when King Josiah "finds a lawbook" in the Temple and embarks on a campaign of orthodoxy, shows no sign of moving Peter Foote/*Hafliðaskrá*-style to written law only, as the written lawbook serves no function after its private reading to Josiah [112]

On the other hand, two factors must be noted. First, some of the material in the Covenant Code (e.g., 22:17ff) and elsewhere is an authentic part of Iron

Age Israelite law.[113] Just as with *Grágás,* remnants of the oral law survive into the late texts.[114] Indeed, some of the old material in the biblical laws may have always been written, serving as we have seen written artifacts of law function in oral-and-written societies.[115] For example, the phrase, "For he is his money" tacked on the end of Exod 21:20–21, suggesting a slave is chattel property, contradicts the legal provisions that precede it. It is a proverbial piece of anterior law (see below on Proverbs), a legal catchphrase embedded here into "teaching."[116] The same holds for "life for life, eye for eye, tooth for tooth, hand for hand, foot for foot," inserted three times (Exod 21:23–25; Lev 24:20; Deut 19:21) and in each case contradicting the punishment stated at that place. Rather than see these as late Priestly insertions, their diction suggests a legal maxim from customary law.[117] Exod 21:12–14 seems to first present a traditional legal dictum, then play out two different hypothetical scenarios with different parties involved to allow for future legal reasoning to extrapolate new cases, the procedures and principles already set.

This material is, however, descriptive rather than proscriptive.[118] And more importantly, we may have no good way of knowing which portions of the Covenant Code, for instance, once served as written artefacts of, say, 10th-century Israelite law,[119] especially since markers of performance might only be evidence of, for instance, 7th-century performance of written law.[120] For, as we have seen, in a legal system such as this, the resultant "codes" are mishmashes of various layers from different periods.[121] Editors, primarily Post-Exilic editors, picked from the riches of the customary law of the Pre-Exilic community according to their own strategies, choosing to put certain laws alongside the narratives of the Pentateuch and vice versa.[122]

Moreover, although the book of Deuteronomy revises the Covenant Code and the so-called Holiness Code of Leviticus revises Deuteronomy—of that, there is little doubt—there is no systematic harmonization of the three.[123] They cover a significantly different range of activities and at the same time "pluralize the law. Old laws are not canceled, but rather new laws or revised versions of old ones are added," exactly, as Walzer shows, as with Mesopotamian law codes.[124] This is, as we have seen, characteristic of customary law: "Law is old; new law is a contradiction in terms; for either new law is derived explicitly or implicitly from the old, or it conflicts with the old, in which case it is not lawful."[125]

The second factor has just been alluded to: that material in the Covenant Code and elsewhere in the Pentateuch is now in writing does not mean that it was not orally performed. Some may have been performed within the legal system, falling into the category described in the preceding paragraph. Other sections may have been performed in the pedagogical context of Israelite legal education.[126] In neither case would this be limited to any single form of laws— for instance, apodictic.[127] Casuistic laws in the Covenant Code look much the same as parts of *Grágás* (e.g., the section "*Um hross reiðir*").[128]

In both cases, signs of oral performance include rhyme, meter, alliteration, and temporal and geographic deictic language.[129] Examples of such poetry in the Covenant Code include Exod 21:18 "בְּאֶבֶן אוֹ בְאֶגְרֹף"; 22:4 "בְּעִירֹה וּבִעֵר"; 22:8."[130] "עַל־שֶׂה עַל־שַׂלְמָה"; 22:9 "אוֹ־נִשְׁבַּר אוֹ־נִשְׁבָּה"; 23:5 "מֵעֲזֹב לוֹ עָזֹב תַּעֲזֹב עִמּוֹ" So, too, we find the regular use of cognate infinitives—double infinitives with infinitive absolute, commonly (but often mistakenly) translated as "emphatic." Exod 22:22 has a remarkable *three sets* of such pairs; they can hardly be all translated emphatically, but read aloud, they are assonant and memorable.

Several of these excerpts are quite obscure, barely translatable. Thus, what is the "אֶגְרֹף" in Exod 21:18? Is the verb in Exod 22:4 "to burn" or "to graze"?[131] And is Exod 23:5 corrupt as the *BHS* footnote suggests? I would argue instead that these archaic (note the pargogic *nun* in Exod 22:8), un-grammatical phrases are legal relicts, old maxims or idioms like "metes and bounds" or "assault and battery" that have become fixed.[132] They form hooks for real or imaginary cases to be hung on.[133]

Stock phrasing is used at the end of the first three laws in Deut 22:13–30, vv 21, 22, and 24.[134] The stock phrase יַחְדָּו לַמִּשְׁפָּט is used as a legal summons in Isa 41:1 and Job 9:32.[135]

Deictic language appears regularly. Direct speech that is to be said in legal proceedings appears in Num 5:19, 21–22; 18:26–29; 30–32; Deut 21:20; 22:16–17; and 26:3, 13. The word "today" plays a deictic role in Deut 13:18; 15:5, 15; 19:9; 20:3; 26:3. In the latter two, we have both direct speech and "today."

In addition, as in Iceland, recitation of stories was part of the teaching and possibly recitation of the law—stories like the daughters of Zelophehad (Num 27:1–11; 36), "those impure at Passover" (Num 9:6–12), and the "man who cursed God's name" (Lev 24:10–23).[136]

Both of these two factors combine to make it difficult and unnecessary to try to pry laws out of the Covenant Code that were "originally oral."[137] All of the laws were oral, and all of them obviously also written. This is not a matter of stages, if our focus is on the 8th and 7th centuries. As Westbrook writes, "Written sources and oral traditions reinforced each other."[138]

BORROWINGS FROM FOREIGN LAW

As with Icelandic law, it is also certainly true and has long been recognized that biblical law, especially the Covenant Code, is indebted to wider Ancient

Near Eastern law, especially as exemplified in the Code of Hammurabi. As we have seen, one should expect that Israelite law also borrowed from the law of neighboring peoples. Nevertheless, the nature of the dependence of biblical and Israelite law on Ancient Near Eastern law has been much debated.

Before entering into that debate, the nature of Ancient Near Eastern law should be described, and here the focus is on Mesopotamian and Hittite law of ancient Anatolia. Although the societies from which we have law "codes" are very different from ancient Israel in terms of administrative complexity and the duration of such complexity, in terms of the extent and duration of literacy, and in terms of the sheer volume of texts, nevertheless the law "codes" are no more codes than those of the Bible, and the legal system appears to have been largely customary.[139]

As Niels Peter Lemche writes, "Written law did not play any role in Western Asia."[140] The legal systems of Mesopotamia were oral, confirmed by the paucity of juridical sources over the long history of the region.[141] With regard to the Code of Hammurabi, the fact that it has been found in some forty copies, many centuries later than Hammurabi, means it was eventually, at least, not used as a legal code.[142] Certainly, even in Hammurabi's reign, the Code must have had oral supplementation: there is insufficient criminal law here[143] and no legislative material.[144] Legal literature of Hammurabi's own Old Babylonian period shows all sorts of conflicts that the Code ignores and never refers to the Code.[145] It refers to custom or to the *dīnat sharrim*, "decision of the king," and often does exactly opposite of what the Code requires.[146] Hammurabi himself, in a letter to a commander stationed on the Hittite border (AbB 13.10.3.9–44) appeals not to his own Code but to "the binding rule applied as from olden time."[147] On the other hand, at least in its immediate historical context the Code may have corresponded to the enforced laws. Hammurabi's son and successor Samsu-Iluna explicitly abrogates LH 180, which required the families of *nadītum* priestesses to support them financially in the Sippar cloister.[148]

Nevertheless, the main role the law codes played was as school texts, "scientific treatises on the law."[149] Their format is much the same as Babylonian omen series, medical, and astronomical texts.[150] Each law starts with a singular "borderline" case, real or hypothetical, from which other laws and legal principles were derived.[151] This took place gradually; as redaction is evident in LH 9–13:13 was added directly on to 11, and then 12 added later.[152] This happened as "the ancient Babylonian student . . . worked out and applied his legal principles."[153] This is of crucial importance, as it means the point of the "laws" was always ultimately to inculcate certain dispositions, certain tendencies, precedents, "wisdom."[154]

Herein lies the connection, as we have seen, to actual Iron Age Israelite customary law. We can envision a linguistic relict, anything from an idiom of two words to a full legal maxim, upon which a real or moot case is hung or added to a case.[155] From that case, principles can be derived, and these are then applied to new cases "in the gates." The principle is what carries forward, however, far more than the exemplary case itself: "When a case is done, the rule just applied returns from its brief excursion into detail, and reverts to its normal condition of generality."[156]

The resultant "codes," however, are descriptive, not proscriptive.[157] At the same time, those codes preserve signs of performance,[158] indicative—as in Iceland, and as in Greece (Sophocles, *Antigone*, 23.8.27–30; Hermippus, *Frag.* 88 Wehli; Strabo, 12.2.9; Aelian, *Varia Hist.* 2.29; Plutarch, *Solon* 3; Pseudo-Aristotle, *Problemata* 19.28.919–20a)[159]—of oral legal pedagogy and possibly of some sort of legal performance akin to the Lawspeaker's ritual recitation.[160] Finally, we cannot exclude the role played by the "codes" as tokens of power, present as objects for display or whose ritual reading functioned "magically."[161] As Bernard Jackson insists, the function of the written law should not be limited to any one of these purposes.[162]

Although its influence on Israelite law is negligible, a word should be said about Egyptian law. Much of what we have is deeds and mortgages, along with a good deal of criminal investigations and "police" documents.[163] Written law does seem to have played a role in Egyptian society, but prior to the end of the New Kingdom there was no codified law and the legal system was largely common law.[164]

The parallels between biblical law and Ancient Near Eastern law are well established.[165] Those between the Covenant Code and the Code of Hammurabi (1750 BC) are the most extensive, but parallels have also been thoroughly illustrated with and between Middle Assyrian Laws (1076 BC; e.g., MAL A.8 with Deut 25:11–12; MAL A.50 with Exod 21:22–25), Hittite Laws (1650 BC; e.g., HL 1–4 with Deut 22:23–27; HL 17–18 with Exod 21:22; HL 21, 25, 256 with Deut 22:13–21), the Laws of Eshnunna (1770 BC; e.g., LE 53 with Exod 21:35), the Laws of Lipit-Ishtar (ca. 1930 BC), and the Sumerian Laws of Ur-Nammu.[166] The Ur-Nammu laws are from the Third Dynasty of Ur, ca. 2100 BC, and the oldest copy (RIM E3/1.1.1.20) is from that time, but this was not published until 2011 (AD); up to that point, the law was known from multiple Old Babylonian copies from Nippur, Ur, and Sippar.[167] Beyond this list of the main cuneiform legal texts, there are countless others: the Laws of the Rented Oxen (1800) Sumerian Laws Exercise Tablet (1800), Sumerian Laws Handbook of Forms (1700), various Hittite edicts, and so forth.[168]

It seems to me that there are broadly speaking three possible lines of explanation of Israel's absorption of Ancient Near Eastern law.[169] Those can be designated: coincidental (Daube, Jackson), literary (Otto, Malul, Wright, Van Seters), and existential (Westbrook), although I will argue that Otto's literary dependence and Westbrook's existential continuum can be fit together to represent what I judge accurately represents the ancient situation.

David Daube and his student Bernard Jackson argue that both Israel and Mesopotamian cultures reflect typologically similar legal regimes on an evolutionary scale, and that this accounts for the similarities of their laws.[170] Besides the many problems outlined early in this study with such evolutionary typologies, if they *were* valid one would expect the Laws of Gortyn (5th century) and Zaleukos (ca. 660 BC) to be similar to Israel's, and they are not.[171]

David Wright and John Van Seters argue for directly *literary* dependence of the Covenant Code on the Code of Hammurabi.[172] For Van Seters, the Covenant Code was copied from Hammurabi's Code by Jews in the Babylonian Exile in the 6th century. He argues that the Covenant Code regulates the life of the Exilic community, that Exod 23:13 "every place you invoke my name" means in Babylon in Exile, and that "animals of one's enemy" in 23:4–5 has to be in Babylon because why would foreign animals roam Israel?

However, these two items are Van Seters's only examples of things in the Covenant Code that fit the Diaspora best.[173] There is really not the slightest hint that the audience is anywhere but Canaan. How plausible is it that the Exiles read copies of the Code, in any case? Van Seters notes that Nabonidus was obsessed with early documents, strongly antiquarian.[174] Yet although there are dozens of copies of the Code of Hammurabi from multiple periods after the Old Babylonian,[175] from the Neo-Babylonian period we have only four copies, and from the Persian only one. Neo-Babylonian laws (COS 2.133:360–61) are totally different from the Code of Hammurabi and the Covenant Code: they have no prologue or epilogue, and the protasis is not "if . . ." but *amêlu* SA, "a man who. . . ."

The Neo-Assyrian period has produced sixteen copies of the Code of Hammurabi, and this is the period where David Wright thinks borrowing took place.[176] Wright has done the most of any scholar to lay out the parallels with the Covenant Code,[177] "There is a thicker web of correspondences, mainly in the casuistic laws but also in the apodictic laws and now even in the appendix to the Covenant Code."[178] He shows the clear correspondence between Hammurabi 117–27 and Exod 21:2–22:14.[179]

But, to be clear, Wright envisions the Covenant Code as a "unitary composition that creatively reworked laws and motifs from LH [Hammurabi]."[180] "The whole of the Covenant Code is based on LH."[181] The Covenant Code is a literary creation, one that has not only no connection to actual Israelite practiced law but no place in Israelite legal education either. It is not the product of customary law at all, and none of it ever served in legal performance.

In some essays,[182] Wright never even mentions parallels between the Covenant Code and Hittite or Sumerian laws, even when those are closer than parallels with Hammurabi.[183] The Eshnunna laws are much closer to the Covenant Code than Hammurabi is in both the "oxen goring each other" laws and on burglary, and the Hittite Laws seem to supply the structure of the goring oxen law.[184,185] Wright admits that a "handful of casuistic laws have correlations with laws in other known law collections but not found in LH," but denies these are relevant because "one can confidently conclude that the Covenant Code used LH, one cannot claim with certainty that the Covenant Code used any of these other known collections because of problems in their attestation . . . the Covenant Code could not have used the Hittite Laws."[186] That last point is obvious, but nowhere does Wright address Westbrook's explanation for the parallels in spite of this lack of direct links: that it is not a matter of written laws at all but a common law tradition (see below).[187] And the fact remains that we do not know if Israelite authors ever read the Code of Hammurabi, so it remains just as likely that they read Middle Assyrian laws.[188]

Moreover, unfortunately, Wright's excellent work outlining the parallels of Hammurabi and the Covenant Code goes too far, "matches" too much, with "special pleading forcing laws into categories that make them match or seizing upon the most tangential resemblance as evidence of influence."[189] Some are merely parallels in terminology based on very common words,[190] while significant differences in, say, person of address, are dismissed as irrelevant.[191] Wright neglects the essential half of the comparative task that enumerates *differences* as well as parallels.[192]

He denies his matches are special pleading.[193] Yet the Covenant Code does *not* follow the ordering of the Code of Hammurabi the way Wright claims: Exod 21:5–9 is not found in Hammurabi, which Wright does not explain, and vv 13, 15, and 18–19 are in the wrong places if they are supposed to match Hammurabi's Code.[194] Even some of the matches Wright can point to only work with certain recensions of the Hammurabi Code, which seems a bit too convenient.[195]

In addition, Wright considers some laws in Deuteronomy, such as Deut 15:12, to date to a period in Israel's history prior to the Covenant Code's adoption of Hammurabi.[196] Why, then, would Deut 15:12 look so much like Hammurabi 117, especially if Exod 21:2, 7 draws on Hammurabi and not on Deuteronomy? Wright offers no explanation for the resemblances between Deuteronomy and Hammurabi, except where he follows Georg Braulik in considering portions of Deuteronomy (e.g., chap. 19) as late Post-Exilic.[197]

Finally, neither Wright nor Van Seters offer an explanation for those parts of the Code of Hammurabi that have no counterpart in the Covenant Code,[198] or for why the resultant text of the Covenant Code has such "striking inconsistencies of form and content."[199]

Yet Wright may be correct in one respect. As Eckart Otto, Hans Ulrich Steymans, Bernard Levinson, and I have shown elsewhere, the Assyrian period was one of great literary influence on Israelite culture and literature.[200] To the model of "diffusion" I will outline below one might easily add "literary influence at the *redactional* stage: that is, the points at which the biblical texts were assembled and edited," exactly as we saw from canon law influence in *Grágás*.[201]

Raymond Westbrook explains the parallels between Ancient Near Eastern law texts as the result of "legal synchronism," legal tradition influencing Common Law over millennia.[202] This "very conservative tradition stretching over thousands of years"[203] began in Sumer and spread across Western Asia.[204] It may have entered Canaan via the cuneiform scribal schools of Late Bronze Age Hazor and Megiddo,[205] but since it was the same common law tradition in the 10th century as in the 8th, as well, this need not be specified.[206] Others have argued that this common legal tradition extended even further in time and space, contributing the uncharacteristic (for Greece) laws about mistreatment of orphans and aged parents in Hesiod's *Works and Days* 327–34 (echoing Exod 22:17, 21; Lev 20:9).[207]

Westbrook's detractors have noted that a single legal culture over such a vast chronological range stretches the imagination.[208] Even if one limited its scope to the Akkadian-speaking world, the array of rising and falling kingdoms, ethnic groups, and migrations make it highly unlikely.[209] This characterization of Westbrook, however, is not entirely accurate. What Westbrook envisions is a combination of legal preservation like we have seen with Visigothic remnants in modern Texas along with the clear prestige the Code of Hammurabi in particular had, down into the Neo-Assyrian period.[210]

It may nevertheless be an inapt way to describe the situation, but where Westbrook is entirely correct is in his explanation of the nature of Ancient Near Eastern "law codes," a definition I have adopted above. Westbrook, like Lemche, rightly sees actual Ancient Near Eastern law as common law, as customary law. He also identifies the Covenant Code as a similar pedagogical text, again a view I fully agree with based on the comparative evidence discussed above.

In spite of this, the adoption of foreign elements into the Israelite legal tradition and into the Covenant Code and other Pentateuchal legal texts is probably a literary matter, as Wright and others argue, for the following reasons. This borrowing ought not to be divorced from the wider issue of parallels between the various non-Israelite laws.[211] Considering a law like Exodus 21:22–25, "When men have a fight and they injure a pregnant woman so that she suffers a miscarriage," one must ask: how often does that actually happen? Yet this unusual situation appears in Exodus 21 and in the Code of Hammurabi *and* in the Middle Assyrian laws *and* in Sumerian laws centuries earlier and in the Hittite laws.[212] Since we cannot assume a single legal system covering all these societies, we must see here a literary phenomenon, a matter of textual borrowing or oral tradition borrowing oral tradition. Moreover, as J. J. Finkelstein wrote some time ago, "It is possibly the very rarity of such an accidental occurrence that was the cause of its first incorporation into the body of law cases that were part of the curriculum in the scribal schools."[213]

Much foreign law incorporation probably did take place in the Neo-Assyrian period, as argued above.[214] Wright's Elsa Sjöholm–like total dependence model does not work, however. Canaanite law, given the albeit minimal evidence from Hazor,[215] shows continuity with the cuneiform traditions that warrant us considering earlier periods of influence as well.[216] In the same way as Gothic law shows up in modern Texas, as we have seen (note 399 above), not because the same legal system covered both the Visigoths and Texas, but because memorable stories or cases pass down in customary law, just as such stories or phrases found in laws from Ur-Nammu and Eshnunna could survive in someone's legal traditions down to the Iron II period in order to influence Israel and Judah—Aramaic laws, for instance, about which we know quite little. But given the intense Aramean contact with Israel and Judah, that possibility is distinct. And what was the law of Moab, or Edom? As Jackson writes, "The ancient Near East in itself is an amazing field of cross currents."[217] It is not so much that we have no way of knowing how the laws could have come to Israel, but the contrary: there are simply too many opportunities for that to have happened for us to be definite.[218]

The use of foreign material in the Israelite laws is similar to the use of canon law in *Grágás*. As Hans Henning Hoff showed for that relationship, both content and phraseology are borrowed. Moreover, as scholars have long illustrated, the Pentateuch's departures from cuneiform law precisely in the borrowed passages are among the most informative of the ethical values behind the biblical "curriculum."[219] As Samuel Jackson has shown in his exhaustive study of all the Ancient Near Eastern laws, the correspondence is in what was seen to be an offence, especially criminal law.[220] The legal pedagogical regimes differ by regularly treating the exact unlikely situation quite differently.[221]

Consider the famed "ox that gores" in Exod 21:28–32, set as the first of three cases of indirect damages (vv 28–36), where the basis for liability is ownership. The possible scenarios listed are the same, and in the same order, as in Hammurabi's Code, laws 250–51, and also found in the Eshnunna Laws,

54. Distinctly different in the biblical example is the requirement that the ox be stoned to death and not eaten. Since Frazer, this has been cited as an example of animals being punished like humans for crimes. Israel does not, however, punish animals for crimes, and stoning is nowhere the punishment for homicide in the Old Testament; it is the punishment for ritual defilement of the community. As Marilyn Katz has shown, following Van Selms, this case resembles the unknown murderer in Deut 21:1–9: "If someone slain is found . . . lying in the field, and it is not known who killed him, then your elders and your judges shall go out and shall measure the distance to the cities that are around the slain one. And then the nearest city to the slain one, the elders of that city shall take a heifer of the herd . . . and the elders of that city shall bring the heifer down to a wadi . . .; then there they shall break the neck of the heifer in the wadi."[222] In Israelite ethics, homicide brings bloodguilt; if they do not know "upon whom," it is on everyone. Blame for misdeeds accrues to the whole of the local society, thus crime is a misdemeanor.[223]

NOTES

1. Bernard S. Jackson, *Wisdom-Laws: A Study of the* Mishpatim *of Exodus 21:1–22:16* (Oxford: Oxford University Press, 2006), 433, is comfortable using the narratives; Hector Avalos, 'Legal and Social Institutions in Canaan and Ancient Israel', in *Civilizations of the Ancient Near East*, ed. Jack Sasson (Peabody, Mass.: Hendrickson, 1995), 616, cautions against it.

2. Alt, *Essays on Old Testament History and Religion*, 116; Carlos Sánchez del Rio, 'Teoria del Derecho en Israel', *Relaciones Internacionales* 28 (2019): 102; Raymond Westbrook, *Studies in Biblical and Cuneiform Law*, Cahiers de La Revue Biblique 26 (Paris: Gabalda, 1988), 4; Bernard S. Jackson, 'Modelling Biblical Law', *Chicago-Kent Law Review* 70 (1995): 1763.

3. J. Van der Ploeg, 'Šāpaṭ et Mišpāṭ', in *Lijst van de voornaamste geschriften van Prof. Dr. B. D. Eerdmans*, ed. Joh. De Groot and F. Dykema, Oudtestamentische Studiën 2 (Leiden: Brill, 1943), 151–52.

4. L. L. Morris, 'Judgment and Custom', *Australian Biblical Review* 7 (1959): 72; Van der Ploeg, 'Studies in Hebrew Law', 250; Hans W. Hertzberg, 'Die Entwicklung der Begriffes משפט im AT', *Zeitschrift für die Alttestamentliche Wissenschaft* 30 (1923): 265–66. It is formed by a *mem*-object added to שפט, which 'comprises all the phases of a primitive "trial"'; Van der Ploeg, 'Studies in Hebrew Law', 248–49.

5. Bernard S. Jackson, 'Exodus 21:18–19 and the Origins of the Casuistic Form', *Israel Law Review* 33 (1999): 816; Meyer, *Das Apodiktische Recht*, 62.

6. David J. A. Clines, ed., *The Concise Dictionary of Classical Hebrew* (Sheffield: Sheffield Phoenix Press, 2009), 457; see already David Zvi Hoffmann, *Das Buch Deuteronomium* (Berlin: Poppelauer, 1913), 273.

7. Zeev W. Falk, *Hebrew Law in Biblical Times* (Jerusalem: Wahrmann, 1964), 29; Sophie Démare-Lafont, 'Les lois dans le monde cuneiforme', in *Writing Laws in Antiquity*, Beihefte zur Zeitschrift für altorientalische und biblische Rechtsgeschichte 19 (Wiesbaden: Harrassowitz, 2017), 24, on *stare decisis* in Mesopotamia.

8. Dale Patrick, *Old Testament Law* (Eugene, OR: Wipf & Stock, 2011), 195.

9. Patrick, 196.

10. Jackson, 'Law in the Ninth Century', 373.

11. Julian Morgenstern, 'The Book of the Covenant, Part II', *Hebrew Union College Annual* 7 (1930): 32; Martin Noth, *A History of Pentateuchal Traditions* (Englewood Cliffs, NJ: Prentice-Hall, 1972), 18.

12. Carolyn Pressler, 'Sexual Legislation', in *The Oxford Encyclopedia of the Bible and Law*, ed. Brent A. Strawn (Oxford: Oxford University Press, 2019), 290.

13. Noted already by Johann D. Michaelis, *Commentaries on the Laws of Moses*, trans. A. Smith, vol. 1 (London: F. C. and J. Rivington, 1814), 10, 474.

14. David Daube, *Law and Wisdom in the Bible* (West Conshohocken, PA: Templeton, 2010), 87.

15. David Daube, 'The Self-Understood in Legal History', *Green Bag* 2 (1999): 414.

16. Daube, 418–19.

17. Eliezer Schweid, *The Philosophy of the Bible as Foundation of Jewish Culture. Philosophy of Biblical Law*, Reference Library of Jewish Intellectual History (Boston: Academic Studies Press, 2008), 108; Jackson, *Wisdom-Laws*, 68.

18. Martin Noth, *The Laws in the Pentateuch* (Philadelphia: Fortress, 1968), 14, 18.

19. Jackson, 'Models in Legal History: The Case of Biblical Law', 15–16.

20. It is possible that the garrison was Egyptian, the governor either Egyptian or a Greek mercenary, so Judahite law may not have applied; U. Rüterswörden, "Das Deuteronomium im Lichte epigraphischer Zeugnisse," in *Sprachen—Bilder—Klänge: Dimensionen der Theologie im Alten Testament und in seinem Umfeld*, ed. C. Karrer-Grube et al., AOAT 359 (Münster: Ugarit-Verlag, 2009), 251.

21. James W. Watts, *Reading Law*, The Biblical Seminar 59 (Sheffield: Sheffield Academic Press, 1999), 22–23 notes the parallel but entirely misses its significance, insisting it proves written law was the basis of the Israelite legal system.

22. Michaelis, *Commentaries on the Laws of Moses*, 1:229.

23. Rolf P. Knierim, 'Customs, Judges, and Legislators in Ancient Israel', in *Early Jewish and Christian Exegesis: Studies in Memory of William Hugh Brownlee*, ed. Craig A. Evans and William F. Stinespring, Scholars Press Homage Series 10 (Atlanta: Scholars, 1987), 5.

24. Daniel A. Frese, 'The Civic Forum in Ancient Israel' (Diss., San Diego, University of California, San Diego, 2012), 204–5; Daniel A. Frese, *The City Gate in Ancient Israel and Her Neighbors: The Form, Function, and Symbolism of the Civic Forum in the Southern Levant*, Culture and History of the Ancient Near East 108 (Leiden: Brill, 2020), 131.

25. Hillary Nyika, 'The Traditional Israelite Legal Setting', in *Wisdom, Science, and the Scriptures: Essays in Honor of Ernest Lucas*, ed. Stephen Finamore and John Weaver (Eugene, OR: Pickwick, 2014), 34–35.

26. Frese, *The City Gate in Ancient Israel*, 152.

27. Nyika, 'The Traditional Israelite Legal Setting', 36; Frese, *The City Gate in Ancient Israel*, 153.

28. Frese, 'The Civic Forum in Ancient Israel', 209–10.

29. Frese, 223.

30. Frese, *The City Gate in Ancient Israel*, 158.

31. Frese, 'The Civic Forum in Ancient Israel', 228–30.

32. Maurice M. Aranov, 'The Biblical Threshing-Floor in the Light of the Ancient Near Eastern Evidence' (Diss., New York, New York University, 1977), 158.

33. Victor H. Matthews, 'Entrance Ways and Threshing Floors', *Fides et Historia* 19 (1987): 29.

34. Aranov, 'Biblical Threshing-Floor', 168.

35. Aranov, 127.

36. C. Umhau Wolf, 'Traces of Primitive Democracy in Ancient Israel', *Journal of Near Eastern Studies* 6 (1947): 100; V. Wagner, 'Die Gerichtsverfassung Israels nach der Weisheitsliteratur des Alten Testaments', *Biblische Zeitschrift* 56 (2012): 97; Leonhard Rost, *Die Vorstufen von Kirche und Synagoge im Alten Testament* (Darmstadt: Wissenschaftliche Buchgesellschaft, 1967), 9–11, 79, 83; Hanoch Reviv, *The Elders in Ancient Israel* (Jerusalem: Magnes, 1989), 60–61.

37. Rost, *Die Vorstufen von Kirche und Synagoge im Alten Testament*, 31–32, 41, 84–85, 88.

38. Baruch A. Levine, ed., *Numbers 1–20: A New Translation with Introduction and Commentary*, The Anchor Bible 4 (New York: Doubleday, 1993), 139.

39. Levine, 412.

40. David H. Müller, 'Himjarische Studien', *ZDMG* 30 (1876): 685.

41. Levine, *Numbers 1 - 20*, 130–31, 412.

42. A. E. Cowley, trans., *Aramaic Papyri of the Fifth Century B.C.*, Ancient Texts and Translations (Eugene, OR: Wipf & Stock, 2005), 45, 49, 200–201.

43. Susan Niditch, *Judges: A Commentary*, The Old Testament Library (Louisville: Westminster John Knox, 2008), 202.

44. Jeffrey R. Zorn, 'Tell En-Nasbeh: A Re-Evaluation of the Architecture and Stratigraphy of the Early Bronze Age, Iron Age and Later Periods' (Diss., Berkeley, University of California, Berkeley, 1993), 1.158.

45. Jeffrey R. Zorn, 'An Inner and Outer Gate Complex at Tell En-Nasbeh', *Bulletin of the American Schools of Oriental Research* 307 (1997): 53, 56, 63–64.

46. G. Keith Still, 'Crowd Dynamics' (Diss., University of Warwick, 2000), http://www.gkstill.com/CV/PhD/CrowdDynamics.html.

47. Alt, *Essays on Old Testament History and Religion*, 130 n.47.

48. Nava Panitz-Cohen and Naama Yahalom-Mack, 'The Wise Woman of Abel Beth Maacah', *Biblical Archaeology Review*, October 2019, 33.

49. Robert A. Mullins, 'A City and a Mother in Israel', *Bible Study Magazine*, April 2019, 45; Panitz-Cohen and Yahalom-Mack, 'The Wise Woman of Abel Beth

Maacah', 30; Panitz-Cohen and Yahalom-Mack, 31 notes that cities are indeed often called mothers (e.g., Josh 17:11).

50. Their argument that 'Wise Women' designate a particular oracular role (Panitz-Cohen and Yahalom-Mack, 'The Wise Woman of Abel Beth Maacah', 31) blurs the difference of the Wise Woman of Tekoa, Deborah, Micah's Levite [sic], and this woman. Panitz-Cohen and Yahalom-Mack, 31 states that 'many scholars think that "mother" is used in the sense of an oracle or augur,' but offer no references.

51. Rudolf Smend, *Yahweh War and Tribal Confederation* (Nashville: Abingdon, 1970), 45, debates this possibility; Watts, *Reading Law*, 28–29, does so on shakier grounds: the placement of the law in narrative and the law's mnemonic devices.

52. Gerhard Von Rad, *The Problem of the Hexateuch and Other Essays* (New York: McGraw-Hill, 1984), 36–39.

53. R. E. Clements, *Prophecy and Tradition* (Atlanta: John Knox, 1975), 10–11.

54. Otto Eissfeldt, 'Lade und Stierbild', *Zeitschrift für die alttestamentliche Wissenschaft* 58 (1940–41): 193 n.3.

55. Wagner, 'Die Gerichtsverfassung Israel nach der Weisheitliteratur des alten Testaments', 96; Avalos, 'Legal and Social Institutions in Canaan and Ancient Israel', 622; Tikva Frymer-Kenski, 'Israel', in *A History of Ancient Near Eastern Law*, ed. Raymond Westbrook, vol. 2, Handbook of Oriental Studies. Section 1, The Near and Middle East 72 (Leiden: Brill, 2003), 988; Reviv, *The Elders in Ancient Israel*, 38–39; Alt, *Essays on Old Testament History and Religion*, 116.

56. Wolf, 'Traces of Primitive Democracy in Ancient Israel', 99.

57. Rowe Ignacio Marquez, 'Alalakh', in *A History of Ancient Near Eastern Law*, ed. Raymond Westbrook, vol. 2, Handbook of Oriental Studies. Section 1, The Near and Middle East 72 (Leiden: Brill, 2003), 695.

58. Raymond Westbrook, 'Emar and Vicinity', in *A History of Ancient Near Eastern Law*, ed. Raymond Westbrook, vol. 2, Handbook of Oriental Studies. Section 1, The Near and Middle East 72 (Leiden: Brill, 2003), 659.

59. Wagner, 'Die Gerichtsverfassung Israels nach der Weisheitsliteratur des Alten Testaments', 96.

60. Reviv, *The Elders in Ancient Israel*, 68.

61. Reviv, 142. For Greece, see SEG 30.380; 33.275; 34.296; Laws of Gortyn 9.31–33; and discussion in Rosalind Thomas, 'Written in Stone? Liberty, Equality, Orality and the Codification of Law', *Bulletin of the Institute of Classical Studies* 40 (1995): 66–68.

62. Mark Leuchter, 'The Sociolinguistic and Rhetorical Implications of the Source Citations in Kings', in *Soundings in Kings: Perspectives and Methods in Contemporary Scholarship*, ed. Mark Leuchter and Klaus-Peter Adam (Minneapolis: Fortress, 2010), 125, 202.

63. Falk, *Hebrew Law in Biblical Times*, 28.

64. As per Charles A. Briggs, *The Higher Criticism of the Hexateuch*, 3rd ed. (New York: Charles Scribner's Sons, 1897), 248.

65. Van der Ploeg, 'Studies in Hebrew Law', 251.

66. Carleton T. Hodge, 'Thoth and Oral Tradition', in *General and Amerindian Ethnolinguistics*, ed. Mary Ritchie Key and Stanley S. Newman, Contributions to the Sociology of Language 55 (Berlin: Mouton de Gruyter, 1989), 407, 409–10.

67. M. Lichtheim, *Ancient Egyptian Literature* (Berkeley: The Univerisity of California Press, 1975), 3.125–51.

68. Alan H. Gardiner, *Ancient Egyptian Onomastica* (Oxford: Oxford University Press, 1947), 510, S43.

69. Hodge, 'Thoth and Oral Tradition', 411.

70. E. A. Speiser, 'The Stem *PLL* in Hebrew', *Journal of Biblical Literature* 82 (1963): 302.

71. Speiser, 301.

72. Speiser, 303–4.

73. Klaas R. Veenhof, 'Hebrew *Pelilim* and Old Assyrian *Palalum*', in *Biblical Hebrew in Context: Essays in Semitics and Old Testament Texts in Honour of Professor Jan P. Lettinga* (Leiden: Brill, 2018), 22–27; Michaelis, *Commentaries on the Laws of Moses*, 1:47.

74. Norman C. Habel, ed., *The Book of Job: Commentary*, Cambridge Bible Commentary 16 (Cambridge: Cambridge University Press, 1975), 55.

75. Edoard Dhorme, *A Commentary on the Book of Job* (Nashville: Nelson, 1926), 144.

76. Habel, *The Book of Job*, 91.

77. Ramon Auge, *Job*, La Biblia de Montserrat 9 (Montserrat: Monestir de Montserrat, 1959), 157.

78. Dhorme, *A Commentary on the Book of Job*, 239.

79. Habel, *The Book of Job*, 104.

80. Dhorme, *A Commentary on the Book of Job*, 283; Morris Jastrow, *The Book of Job* (Philadelphia: Lippincott, 1920), 265; Ramir Auge, *Job*, La Biblia de Montserrat 9 (Montserrat: Monestir de Montserrat, 1959), 176–77.

81. Carol A. Newsom, 'Scenes of Reading', in *Reading for Faith and Learning: Essays on Scripture, Community, & Libraries in Honor of M. Patrick Graham*, ed. John B. Weaver (Abilene: Abilene Christian University Press, 2017), 20–21.

82. Newsom, 21–24.

83. Newsom, 25–27.

84. Already in the early rabbinic period, there was considerable debate over whether he actually wrote out a physical copy of the law; Hoffmann, *Das Buch Deuteronomium*, 321–26.

85. Cf. Nygaard, 'Law, Religion,' 162.

86. Ake Viberg, *Symbols of Law*, Coniectanea Biblica Old Testament Series 34 (Stockholm: Almqvist & Wiksell International, 1992), 31.

87. Viberg, 86.

88. Viberg, 143.

89. Bernard S. Jackson, *Studies in the Semiotics of Biblical Law*, Journal for the Study of the Old Testament Supplements 314 (Sheffield: Sheffield Academic Press, 2000), 215.

90. Jackson, 'Models in Legal History: The Case of Biblical Law', 18.

91. David W. Amram, 'Summons', *University of Pennsylvania Law Review* 68 (1920 1919): 51–52.

92. Patrick, *Old Testament Law*, 24; William Morrow, 'Legal Interactions: The *MISPATIM* and the Laws of Hammurabi', *Bibliotheca Orientalis* 70 (2013): 328.

93. Raymond Westbrook, 'What Is the Covenant Code?', in *Theory and Method in Biblical and Cuneiform Law: Revision, Interpolation and Development*, ed. Bernard M. Levinson, Journal for the Study of the Old Testament 181 (Sheffield: Sheffield Academic Press, 1994), 34; Jonathan Burnside, *God, Justice and Society: Aspects of Law and Legality in the Bible* (Oxford: Oxford University Press, 2011); and potentially Bernard M. Levinson, *'The Right Chorale': Studies in Biblical Law and Interpretation*, Forschung zum alten Testament 54 (Tubingen: Mohr Siebeck, 2008).

94. Levinson, *'The Right Chorale': Studies in Biblical Law and Interpretation*, 31; Westbrook, *Studies in Biblical and Cuneiform Law*, 2; cf. Llewellyn, *Jurisprudence*, 302.

95. Noth, *A History of Pentateuchal Traditions*, 14; John H. Walton, 'Understanding Torah: Ancient Legal Text, Covenant Stipulation, and Christian Scripture' (Institute for Biblical Research, Boston, 2017).

96. Levinson, *'The Right Chorale': Studies in Biblical Law and Interpretation*, 31; Westbrook, *Studies in Biblical and Cuneiform Law*, 3; Joseph Blenkinsopp, *Wisdom and Law in the Old Testament*, Oxford Bible Series 10 (Oxford: Oxford University Press, 1995), 84; Patrick, *Old Testament Law*, 200; Veenhof, 'Hebrew *Pelilim* and Old Assyrian *Palalum*', 14; Other suggested etymologies include Gesenius's "point" > "instruct," adopted by Smend, Kuenen, Kittel, Duhm, Pedersen, Eichrodt, and Alt; Wellhausen's "throw [oracularly]," accepted by Mowinckel, Lods, and Kohler; and Albright's Akkadian loanword *tērtu*; all eliminated by Gunnar Östborn, Tora *in the Old Testament* (Lund: Hakan Ohlssons, 1945), 4, 6–7, 9–13, 16–18. תּוֹרָה in every case denotes oral law; Van der Ploeg, 'Studies in Hebrew Law', 253. It refers broadly to the entire corpus of the law; Briggs, *The Higher Criticism of the Hexateuch*, 255, at least until P; Östborn, Tora *in the Old Testament*, 64.

97. Raymond Westbrook, 'Biblical and Cuneiform Law Codes (1985)', in *Law from the Tigris to the Tiber: The Writings of Raymond Westbrook*, ed. Bruce Wells and F. Rachel Magdalene, vol. 1 (Winona Lake: Eisenbrauns, 2009), 8–11; Van der Toorn, *Scribal Culture*, 121–22: 'If white fungi fill a man's house: the owner of that house will become poor. If fungus is seen on a south wall: the mistress of that house will die.'

98. Emile Puech, 'Les écoles dans l'israël préexilique', in *Congress Volume Jerusalem*, Vetus Testament Supplement 40 (Leiden: Brill, 1996), 189–203; Graham I. Davies, 'Were There Schools in Ancient Israel?', in *Wisdom in Ancient Israel*, ed. John Day, Robert P. Gordon, and H. G. M. Williamson (Cambridge: Cambridge University Press, 1995), 210–11.

99. Stuart Weeks, *Early Israelite Wisdom* (New York: Oxford University Press, 1994), 132–56.

100. James L. Crenshaw, *Education in Ancient Israel* (New York: Doubleday, 1998), 88.

101. Crenshaw, 91.

102. Miller II, *Oral Tradition in Ancient Israel*, 46; David M. Carr, 'The Tel Zayit Abecedary in (Social) Context', in *Literate Culture and Tenth-Century Canaan: The Tel Zayit Abecedary in Context*, ed. Ron E. Tappy and P. Kyle McCarter (Winona Lake, Ind: Eisenbrauns, 2008), 114, 120; Christopher A. Rollston, *Writing and Literacy in the World of Ancient Israel: Epigraphic Evidence from the Iron Age*, Archaeology and Biblical Studies 11 (Atlanta: Society of Biblical Literature, 2010), 91–92, 95–96, 108–9, 113; Christopher A. Rollston, 'Scribal Curriculum during the First Temple Period', in *Contextualizing Israel's Sacred Writings*, ed. Brian B. Schmidt, Society of Biblical Literature: Ancient Israel and Its Literature 22 (Atlanta: SBL, 2015), 83–89.

103. Crenshaw, *Education in Ancient Israel*, 107–13; Rollston, 'Scribal Curriculum during the First Temple Period', 81.

104. Veenhof, 'Hebrew *Pelilim* and Old Assyrian *Palalum*', 13; Knierim, 'Customs, Judges, and Legislators in Ancient Israel', 8; Jackson, 'Exodus 21:18–19 and the Origins of the Casuistic Form', 816–17; Van der Toorn, *Scribal Culture*, 135; Sara J. Milstein, 'Making a Case: The Repurposing of "Israelite Legal Fictions" as Post-Deuteronomic Law', in *Supplementation and the Study of the Hebrew Bible*, ed. Saul M. Olyan and Jacob L. Wright, Brown Judaic Studies 361 (Providence: Brown Judaic Studies, 2018), 162–63, 172.

105. Burnside, *God, Justice and Society*, 19; Veenhof, 'Hebrew *Pelilim* and Old Assyrian *Palalum*', 13; Pressler, 'Sexual Legislation', 291; Jackson, 'Literal Meaning', 444; Jackson, 'Modelling Biblical Law', 1767.

106. Brevard S. Childs, *Exodus*, Old Testament Library (Louisville: Westminister John Knox, 1975), 613.

107. Childs, 459, 614.

108. Knierim, 'Customs, Judges, and Legislators in Ancient Israel', 9; Milstein, 'Making a Case', 170–71.

109. Jackson, 'Exodus 21:18–19 and the Origins of the Casuistic Form', 820.

110. Meir Malul, 'Review of *Studies in Biblical and Cuneiform Law* by Raymond Westbrook (Paris: Gabalda, 1988)' *Orientalia* n.s. 59 (1990): 86, does not understand how both could co-exist.

111. Raymond Westbrook and Bruce Wells, *Everyday Law in Biblical Israel: An Introduction* (Louisville: Westminster John Knox, 2009), 13; cf. Pound, *An Introduction to the Philosophy of Law*, 69.

112. Patrick, *Old Testament Law*, 201. Does D mean to repeal the laws of Exodus it contradicts? Or is merely that in customary law, an 'overruling' claims not to change law but to declare the earlier cases erroneous? Stein, *Regulae Iuris*, 6. Certainly that was true in Rome, where *lex* could not alter *ius* where the latter was settled by custom, while one *lex* could be abrogated without difficulty in later *lex*; Stein, 14.

113. Jackson, 'Modelling Biblical Law', 1760; Childs, *Exodus*, 456–57.

114. Viberg, *Symbols of Law*, 17.

115. Milstein, 'Making a Case', 167.

116. Mayer Sulzberger, *The Status of Labor in Ancient Israel* (Philadelphia: Dropsie College for Hebrew and Cognate Learning Press, 1923), 9.

117. Sulzberger, 10.

118. Westbrook, *Studies in Biblical and Cuneiform Law*, 5.

119. Knight, 'Tradition-History-Criticism: The Development of the Covenant Code', 111; Alt, *Essays on Old Testament History and Religion*, 110.

120. Clemens Locher, *Die Ehre einer Frau in Israel: exegetische und rechtsvergleichende Studien zu Deuteronomium 22, 13–21* (Göttingen: Vandenhoeck & Ruprecht, 1986), 91. And why limit ourselves to Exodus? The law in Deut 21:1–9 is also found at Ugarit, in an Akkadian letter from the King of Carchemish to Ammishtamru, Rs 20.22 (*Ugaritica* 5, pp. 94–97; Westbrook, 'The Laws of Biblical Israel', 109.

121. The argument to the contrary in Westbrook, 'What Is the Covenant Code?' is based on pure analogy to Mesopotamia and logical non sequitur. See discussion in Bernard M. Levinson, 'The Case for Revision and Interpolation within the Biblical Legal Corpora', in *Theory and Method in Biblical and Cuneiform Law: Revision, Interpolation and Development*, ed. Bernard M. Levinson, Journal for the Study of the Old Testament 181 (Sheffield: Sheffield Academic Press, 1994), 39; Samuel Greengus, 'Some Issues Relating to the Comparability of Laws and the Coherence of the Legal Tradition', in *Theory and Method in Biblical and Cuneiform Law: Revision, Interpolation and Development*, ed. Bernard M. Levinson, Journal for the Study of the Old Testament 181 (Sheffield: Sheffield Academic Press, 1994), 77.

122. Edward Greenstein, 'The Relation between Law and Narrative in the Pentateuch' (Law and Literature: Mutual Negotiations, Tel Aviv, 2001).

123. Walzer, 'The Legal Codes of Ancient Israel', 335. As Briggs, *The Higher Criticism of the Hexateuch*, 246, showed long ago, תוצמ seems to be the term D uses for דרירמ it revises.

124. Walzer, 'The Legal Codes of Ancient Israel', 346, 335–37; Samuel Greengus, 'Legal and Social Institutions of Ancient Mesopotamia', in *Civilizations of the Ancient Near East*, ed. Jack Sasson (Peabody, Mass.: Hendrickson, 1995), 472; Milstein, 'Making a Case', 175.

125. Stein, *Regulae Iuris*, 5; Bennett, *Customary Law in South Africa*, 2.

126. Milstein, 'Making a Case', 162.

127. Jackson, *Wisdom-Laws*, 66; Bernard S. Jackson, 'The Original Oral Law', in *Jewish Ways of Reading the Bible*, ed. George J. Brooke, Journal of Semitic Studies Supplement 11 (Oxford: Oxford University Press, 2000), 5–6.

128. Byock, *Viking Age Iceland*, 315.

129. Jackson, *Wisdom-Laws*, 434.

130. Noted already by Michaelis, *Commentaries on the Laws of Moses*, 1:47.

131. Christoph Dohmen, *Exodus 19–40*, Herders Theologischer Kommentar zum Alten Testament (Freiburg: Herder, 2012), 146.

132. Jonathan Roper, 'Ronald or Donald: Vernacular Theorizing on Language' (International Society for Folk Narrative Research, Miami, 2016); Stein, *Regulae Iuris*, 107. See John E. Harvey, *Retelling the Torah*, vol. Journal for the Study of the Old Testament Supplement 403 (Sheffield: Sheffield Academic Press, 2004) for their reappearance in the Deuteronomistic History.

133. Stein, *Regulae Iuris*, 105.

134. Jack Lundbom, *Deuteronomy: A Commentary* (Grand Rapids: Eerdmans, 2013), 628.

135. Amram, 'Summons', 52.

136. Frymer-Kenski, 'Israel', 979; we might also consider places and topographic features serving as mnemonics for certain laws; Bennett, *Customary Law in South Africa*, 4.

137. Jackson, *Wisdom-Laws*, 69.

138. Westbrook, 'The Laws of Biblical Israel', 111.

139. Westbrook, *Studies in Biblical and Cuneiform Law*, 4; Raymond Westbrook, 'The Character of Ancient Near Eastern Law', in *A History of Ancient Near Eastern Law*, ed. Raymond Westbrook, vol. 1, Handbook of Oriental Studies. Section 1, The Near and Middle East 72 (Leiden: Brill, 2003), 21.

140. Lemche, 'Justice in Western Asia in Antiquity', 1696.

141. Sophie Démare-Lafont, 'L'ecriture du droit en Mesopotamie', in *Loi et Justice dans la Litterature du Proche-Orient ancien*, ed. Olivier Artus, Beihefte zur Zeitschrift für altorientalische und biblische Rechtsgeschichte 20 (Wiesbaden: Harrassowitz, 2013), 69, 72; F. Rachel Magdalene, 'Legal Science Then and Now: Theory and Method in the Work of Raymond Westbrook', *Maarav* 18 (2011): 59, attributes this paucity instead to "subsidiarity" in Mesopotamian law.

142. Westbrook, 'Biblical and Cuneiform Law Codes (1985)', 12, 14–17; Démare-Lafont, 'L'ecriture du droit en Mesopotamie', 70; and already, J. J. Finkelstein, *The Ox That Gored*, Transactions of the American Philosophical Society, 71.2 (Philadelphia: The American Philosophical Society, 1981), 15; Magdalene, 'Legal Science Then and Now', 56–57.

143. Lemche, 'Justice in Western Asia in Antiquity', 1699.

144. Westbrook, *Studies in Biblical and Cuneiform Law*, 5; Greengus, 'Legal and Social Institutions of Ancient Mesopotamia', 471.

145. Lemche, 'Justice in Western Asia in Antiquity', 1698; Westbrook, 'The Character of Ancient Near Eastern Law', 19; Milstein, 'Making a Case', 163.

146. Greengus, 'Some Issues Relating to the Comparability of Laws and the Coherence of the Legal Tradition', 82, noting OB letter AbB 3.1 by Samsu-Iluna; Raymond Westbrook, 'Cuneiform Law Codes and the Origins of Legislation (1989)', in *Law from the Tigris to the Tiber: The Writings of Raymond Westbrook*, ed. Bruce Wells and F. Rachel Magdalene, vol. 1 (Winona Lake: Eisenbrauns, 2009), 87–90; Raymond Westbrook, 'Judges in Cuneiform Sources', in *Law from the Tigris to the Tiber: The Writings of Raymond Westbrook*, ed. Bruce Wells and F. Rachel Magdalene, vol. 2 (Winona Lake: Eisenbrauns, 2009), 200–201.

147. Westbrook, 'The Character of Ancient Near Eastern Law', 14.

148. C. Janssen, 'Samsu-Iluna and the Hungry *Naditums*', *Northern Akkad Project Reports* 5 (1991): 3–40. I am grateful to Sandra Jacobs for bringing this to my attention.

149. Westbrook, *Studies in Biblical and Cuneiform Law*, 2, following on F. R. Kraus in 1960; Raymond Westbrook, 'Codification and Canonization (2000)', in *Law from the Tigris to the Tiber: The Writings of Raymond Westbrook*, ed. Bruce Wells and F. Rachel Magdalene, vol. 1 (Winona Lake: Eisenbrauns, 2009), 121–22;

Milstein, *Tracking the Master Scribe*, 12. On the nature of Mesopotamian schools and their curricula, see Niek Veldhuis, 'The Cuneiform Tablet as an Educational Tool', *Dutch Studies on Near Eastern Languages and Literatures* 2 (1996): 11–26; and Jonathan Stokl, 'Schoolboy Ezekiel: Remarks on the Transmission of Learning', *Die Welt Des Orients* 45 (2019): 54–55.

150. Westbrook, 'Biblical and Cuneiform Law Codes (1985)', 8–11; Westbrook, 'Codification and Canonization (2000)', 126; Démare-Lafont, 'Les lois dans le monde cuneiforme', 22.

151. Westbrook, *Studies in Biblical and Cuneiform Law*, 4; Van der Toorn, *Scribal Culture*, 135; Magdalene, 'Legal Science Then and Now', 49; Milstein, 'Making a Case', 166–67; *miṣvot* can mean "tests"; W. T. Gerber, *Hebraischen Verba Denominativa* (Leipzig: J. C. Hinrichs'sche, 1896), 124.

152. I. Tzvi Abusch, *Essays on Babylonian and Biblical Literature and Religion*, Harvard Semitic Museum Publications 65 (Leiden: Brill, 2020), 344.

153. Abusch, 345.

154. Myrto Theocharous, 'Response to John Walton, Understanding Torah: Ancient Legal Text, Covenant Stipulation, and Christian Scripture' (Institute for Biblical Research, Boston, 2017).

155. Stein, *Regulae Iuris*, 105.

156. Bennett, *Customary Law in South Africa*, 3.

157. Westbrook, *Studies in Biblical and Cuneiform Law*, 5; Milstein, 'Making a Case', 163.

158. Démare-Lafont, 'L'ecriture du droit en Mesopotamie', 73, with illustration of Hammurabi's Code.

159. Thomas, 'Written in Stone', 63–64; Eric A. Havelock, *The Literate Revolution in Greece and Its Cultural Consequences*, Princeton Series of Collected Essays (Princeton: Princeton University Press, 1982), 130–31; References in Athenaeus's *Deipnosophistae*, 619b, and Strabo, *Geographica*, 12.2.9, to singing the Laws of Charondas by a nomōidos, "Lawsinger," and in Claudius Aelianus's *Varia Historia*, 2.39, to children of Crete learning laws with music are taken by Michael Gagarin, *Writing Greek Law* (Cambridge: Cambridge University Press, 2008), 34–35 to refer not to laws at all but either to *nomoi* as "melodies" or "general rules such as those in Hesiod's *Works and Days*," because he finds it "nearly impossible to imagine someone putting, say, the Gortyn laws" to a melody. But no melody is mentioned, only to singing, which could easily be recitative or parlando. Gagarin also insists these are not oral laws, since they already existed in writing by this time. But, of course, that is precisely the oral-and-written phenomenon we see worldwide: oral performance of written texts, with modification happening both in the performance and in the subsequent re-writing. Gagarin retains a Great Divide between orality and literacy. It would be nice to add "8th century BC" tablets discovered in the early 19th century at Corinth supposedly dealing with music, which mentioned "priests sang the nomoi." J. G. Murhard, 'Discovery of Ancient Greek Tablets Relative to Music', *The Harmonicon: A Journal of Music* 4 (1825): 74. A text so at variance with the known chronology of Greek music was already deemed suspect by William C. Stafford's 1830 *History of Music*, p. 131 footnote. It has been dismissed as "a lengthy 'text'

with an even lengthier pseudo-scholarly 'commentary'"; Mark Evan Bonds, *Music as Thought: Listening to the Symphony in the Age of Beethoven* (Princeton, N.J: Princeton University Press, 2006), 96. I have found no indication of what happened to these tablets, and the current Archaeological Mission to Corinth also has no idea (personal communication).

160. Démare-Lafont, 'L'ecriture du droit en Mesopotamie', 74.

161. Greengus, 'Legal and Social Institutions of Ancient Mesopotamia', 472; William M. Schniedewind, 'Scripturalization in Ancient Judah', in *Contextualizing Israel's Sacred Writings*, ed. Brian B. Schmidt, Society of Biblical Literature: Ancient Israel and Its Literature 22 (Atlanta: SBL, 2015), 306.

162. Jackson, *Wisdom-Laws*, 70–71.

163. Sandra L. Lippert, 'Ancient Egypt', *Journal of Ancient Civilizations*, 2019, 89.

164. Lippert, 90; Russ VerSteeg, *Law in the Ancient World* (Durham, N.C.: Carolina Academic Press, 2002), 129.

165. Albrecht Goetze, 'Mesopotamian Laws and the Historian', in *Folk Law*, ed. Alison D. Renteln and Alan Dundes, vol. 1, Garland Folklore Casebooks 3 (New York: Garland, 1994), 492.

166. Burnside, *God, Justice and Society*, 6; Van der Toorn, *Scribal Culture*, 136.

167. Miguel Civil, 'The Law Collection of Ur-Nammu', in *Cuneiform Royal Inscriptions and Related Texts in the Schøyen Collection*, ed. A. R. George and Miguel Civil, Cornell University Studies in Assyriology and Sumerology 17 (Bethesda: CDL, 2011), 221, 226.

168. Samuel A. Jackson, *A Comparison of Ancient Near Eastern Law Collections Prior to the First Millennium BC*, Gorgias Dissertations 35 (Piscataway, NJ: Gorgias, 2008), 38–43.

169. Cf. Morrow, 'Legal Interactions: The *MISPATIM* and the Laws of Hammurabi', 310–11.

170. David Daube, *Collected Works of David Daube*, ed. Calum M. Carmichael, vol. 5.1, Studies in Comparative Legal History (Berkeley: Robbins, 1992), 318; Jackson, 'Evolution and Foreign Influence in Ancient Law'.

171. See, e.g., http://www.locriantica.it/english/figures/zaleukos.htm.

172. Malul does, as well; Me'ir Malul, *The Comparative Method in Ancient Near Eastern and Biblical Legal Studies*, Alter Orient und Altes Testament 227 (Kevelaer: Butzon & Bercker, 1990), 152, 159, but is less explicit about the mechanics of the dependence.

173. John. Van Seters, *A Law Book for the Diaspora: Revision in the Study of the Covenant Code* (Oxford: Oxford University Press, 2003), 174.

174. John Van Seters, 'Revision in the Study of the Covenant Code and a Response to My Critics', *Scandinavian Journal of the Old Testament* 21 (2007): 5–28.

175. Martha T. Roth, *Law Collections from Mesopotamia and Asia Minor*, Writings from the Ancient World 6 (Atlanta: Scholars, 1997), 73.

176. David P. Wright, 'Origin, Development, and Content of the Covenant Code', in *The Book of Exodus: Composition, Reception, and Interpretation*, ed. Thomas B.

Dozeman, Craig A. Evans, and Joel N. Lohr, Supplements to Vetus Testamentum 164 (Leiden: Brill, 2014), 242–43.

177. David P. Wright, 'How Exodus Revises the Laws of Hammurabi', *The Torah. Com* (blog), 2019, thetorah.com/how-exodus-revises-the-laws-of-hammurabi; David P. Wright, 'Laws of Hammurabi', *Maarav* 10 (2003): 72–87.

178. Wright, 'Origin, Development, and Content of the Covenant Code', 224.

179. Wright, 227, fig. 1.

180. Wright, 228.

181. David P. Wright, *Inventing God's Law: How the Covenant Code of the Bible Used and Revised the Laws of Hammurabi* (Oxford: Oxford University Press, 2009), 110.

182. E.g., Wright, 'Origin, Development, and Content of the Covenant Code'.

183. Westbrook, 'The Laws of Biblical Israel', 107; Bruce Wells, 'The Covenant Code and Near Eastern Legal Traditions: A Response to David Wright', *Maarav* 13 (2006): 95–96; Westbrook and Wells, *Everyday Law in Biblical Israel*, 24–25.

184. Raymond Westbrook, 'Biblical and Cuneiform Law Codes', in *Folk Law*, ed. Alison D. Renteln and Alan Dundes, vol. 1, Garland Folklore Casebooks 3 (New York: Garland, 1994), 502; Wells, 'The Covenant Code and Near Eastern Legal Traditions: A Response to David Wright', 105, 109; Westbrook and Wells, *Everyday Law in Biblical Israel*, 28, 86. Sara Milstein notes structural parallels between Sumerian Legal Fictions (what Martha Roth called "model court cases") and Deuteronomy 21–22, 24–25, that are stronger than those between the Bible and LH; Milstein, 'Making a Case', 169.

185. Milstein, 'Making a Case', 169.

186. Wright, *Inventing God's Law*, 110.

187. Wells, 'The Covenant Code and Near Eastern Legal Traditions: A Response to David Wright', 16, 28.

188. Wells, 87.

189. Westbrook, 'The Laws of Biblical Israel', 107; Morrow, 'Legal Interactions: The *MISPATIM* and the Laws of Hammurabi', 314; Me'ir Malul, 'Review of *Inventing God's Law* by David P. Wright (Oxford: Oxford University Press, 2009)', *Strata* 29 (2011): 156–57; see data already in Jackson, 'Evolution and Foreign Influence in Ancient Law', 373.

190. Bruce Wells, 'Review of *Inventing God's Law* by David P. Wright (Oxford: Oxford University Press, 2009)', *The Journal of Religion* 90 (2010): 559.

191. Morrow, 'Legal Interactions: The *MISPATIM* and the Laws of Hammurabi', 314.

192. Morrow, 321.

193. Wright, *Inventing God's Law*, 24.

194. Wells, 'The Covenant Code and Near Eastern Legal Traditions: A Response to David Wright', 112–13; Malul, 'Review of *Inventing God's Law* by David P. Wright (Oxford: Oxford University Press, 2009)', 157.

195. Malul, 'Review of *Inventing God's Law* by David P. Wright (Oxford: Oxford University Press, 2009)', 157.

196. David P. Wright, 'Intertextuality in the Laws of Hammurabi, the Covenant Code, and Deuteronomy, and the Date of the Covenant Code' (International Organization for the Study of the Old Testament, Helsinki, 2010).

197. Wright.

198. Wells, 'Review of *Inventing God's Law* by David P. Wright (Oxford: Oxford University Press, 2009)', 559.

199. Alt, *Essays on Old Testament History and Religion*, 106–7.

200. Robert D. Miller II, *Covenant and Grace in the Old Testament: Assyrian Propaganda and Israelite Faith*, Perspectives on Hebrew Scriptures and Its Contexts 16 (Piscataway, NJ: Gorgias, 2012), 121–45.

201. Burnside, *God, Justice and Society*, 7.

202. Westbrook, *Studies in Biblical and Cuneiform Law*, 7; Westbrook, 'The Character of Ancient Near Eastern Law', 24; following Alt, *Essays on Old Testament History and Religion*, 118.

203. Westbrook, *Studies in Biblical and Cuneiform Law*, 7.

204. Westbrook, 2.

205. Westbrook, 3.

206. Magdalene, 'Legal Science Then and Now', 39.

207. Ruth Scodel, 'Prophetic Hesiod' (Orality and Literacy VI, Ann Arbor, 2012).

208. Jackson, 'Modelling Biblical Law', 1756.

209. Finkelstein, *The Ox That Gored*, 19.

210. Westbrook, 'The Character of Ancient Near Eastern Law', 4; Sophie Démare-Lafont, 'Ancient Near Eastern Laws', in *Theory and Method in Biblical and Cuneiform Law: Revision, Interpolation and Development*, ed. Bernard M. Levinson, Journal for the Study of the Old Testament 181 (Sheffield: Sheffield Academic Press, 1994), 107; Sandra Jacobs, *The Body as Property: Physical Disfigurement in Biblical Law*, Library of Hebrew Bible/Old Testament Studies 582 (London: Continuum, 2015), 75–76.

211. Milstein, 'Making a Case', 164–65, 168.

212. Van der Toorn, *Scribal Culture*, 136–37.

213. Finkelstein, *The Ox That Gored*, 21.

214. Wright, 'Intertextuality in the Laws of Hammurabi, the Covenant Code, and Deuteronomy, and the Date of the Covenant Code'.

215. William W. Hallo and Hayim Tadmor, 'A Lawsuit from Hazor', *Israel Exploration Journal* 27 (1977): esp. 2, 4, 6, 8, 11.

216. Ugaritic legal texts are frustratingly limited to contracts, mortgages, and other economic documents, plus a few royal edicts totally unlike Hammurabi or the Covenant Code; Dennis Pardee and Robert Hawley, 'Les textes juridiques en langue ougaritique', in *Trois Millenaires de formulaires juridiques*, ed. Sophie Démare-Lafont and André Lemaire, Haute Etudes Orientales--Moyen et Proche-Orient, 4.48 (Geneva: Droz, 2010), 125–40.

217. Jackson, 'Evolution and Foreign Influence in Ancient Law', 382.

218. In this, we are still with Finkelstein, *The Ox That Gored*, 20.

219. Finkelstein, 5, 29; Jackson, 'Modelling Biblical Law', 1755.

220. Jackson, *A Comparison of Ancient Near Eastern Law Collections Prior to the First Millennium BC*, 244.

221. Jackson, 247.

222. Marilyn A. Katz, 'Ox-Slaughter and Goring Oxen', *Yale Journal of Law & the Humanities* 4 (1992): 249–78.

223. Kropotkin, *Law and Authority*, 14.

Chapter Four

Oral Law and Proverbs

We have already seen how proverb-like legal maxims embedded within the legal material of the Pentateuch may reflect the actual oral workings of Israelite customary law, either contemporaneous with the pedagogical texts in which they are now found or earlier than those texts.[1] Berend Gemser argued in 1953 that these proverbs should not be considered *later* glosses added to existing laws,[2] suggesting proverbial wisdom might have been the framework for the Israelite customary legal system.[3]

I would emend this suggestion further to eliminate sequencing of the Torah and the book of Proverbs altogether, arguing that both draw on customary law, much of which circulated in proverbs. Thus, Prov 6:1–5, which advises against going surety for someone you do not know, 4QInstruction turns into a binding law. Ben Sirah, however, reverses the meaning, assuming only the needy ask to borrow so one *should* lend, without interest. If we had only Ben Sirah and 4QInstruction, without Proverbs, we would know the two were related but debate the relationship, where both actually depend on a *tertium quid*. In the case of the Torah and the book of Proverbs, we often lack the ancient source common to both.[4]

And while we are in this particular text, v 2 with its two reflexive *niphal* verbs, easily rememberable, is probably neither a consequential clause following from the conditions in v 1 nor a second conditional clause but a self-contained unit pasted at this point. The confusing v 3 that follows ends with four words that evidently give the means by which citizens can save themselves—an untranslatable archaic relict.

The rôle of legal proverbs or brocards in customary law is well known,[5] especially in Africa, where they form an integral part of the customary legal system.[6] They are often of an older age than the law they purport to support, and many are of foreign origin.[7] They regularly become embedded into legal

literature.[8] Some of these are not "hooks to hang cases on," but rather proverbs about legal topics. Legal proverbs fall into multiple categories: modes of
administering justice, rules of logic, fundamental legal principles, maxims for
the laws of evidence, and so forth.[9] Often they are alliterative, pararhyming,
or assonant: *Circuitus est evitandus*; *Malus usus est abolendus*; *Cursus curiae
est lex curiae*; *Aliud est celare, aliud tacere*.[10] Usually anonymous, some are
attributed to famous jurists: *Non capitur qui jus Publicum sequitur* (Ulpian,
d. 223)[11]; *Creditor qui permittit rem venire pignus dimittit* (Gaius, d. 180).[12]

In the specific ethnographic analogies we have examined, there is a proverb
("The independent in the seat of the dependent and the dependent in the seat
of the independent") inserted into the early 8th-century Irish *Crith Gablach*
law (par. 6). In Irish law, such brocards (*roscada*) are "often held together by
alliteration and sometimes cast in a primitive type of verse,"[13] and they need
not be short. A ten-line archaic legal poem, almost each line two syllables and
full of alliteration, was also inserted as an appendix to the *Crith Gablach*.[14]

Formal and contextual similarities between the biblical book of Proverbs
and legal prohibitions in the Pentateuch (initially, apodictic laws) have been
elucidated since the 1960s.[15] This is natural since as we have seen, customary law does not distinguish between the properly legal and propriety. Some
scholars have noted links between Proverbs and the Torah's poverty laws,
with parallels in Egyptian wisdom literature illustrating the broader customary law context.[16] Specific parallels abound between Proverbs and Deuteronomy in particular (e.g., Prov 1:11; 20:10 with Deut 25:13–16; Prov 20:22
with Deut 19:19; Prov. 22:28; 23:10 with Deut 19:14; 27:17).[17] Prov 24:23
reappears in Prov 28:21, and both bear some relationship to Deut 16:19.
Nyika argues Deuteronomy depends on Proverbs,[18] but it is more likely that
both depend on proverbial wisdom circulating in Israelite customary law, to
which Prov 18:5 also relates. The proof of this interconnection is that Lev
19:15 presents the same topic with entirely different wording.[19] This body of
proverbial customary law or customary legal proverbs is drawn upon by both
the books of Micah and Hosea.[20]

We are not looking for proverbs that function solely legally, however, as
Archer Taylor, "the twentieth-century doyen of international paremiology,"[21]
wrote long ago. "No single application of a proverb exhausts its meaning.
Except in a vague paraphrase there is no defining a proverb."[22]

Sara Milstein suggests several Proverbs that might belong to Israelite
legal education: Prov 12:17; 14:5, 25; 16:10, 29; 17:8, 14; 18:5, 17; 19:5,
9, 28; 20:8; 21:6, 28; 23:33; 24:23–25, 28; 25:2; 26:17, 21; 29:9, 12, 14,
26; 31:8–9, 23, "to name but a few."[23] Hillary Nyika adds Prov 17:23, 26;
21:14–15; 23:10–11; 25:7–8; 28:8; 30:13–14.[24] Skladny notes a concentra-
tion of legal proverbs in Prov 10–22:16, but also 25:2 and 26:26.[25] Wagner's

more cautious list focusses on "anti-monarchic" legal wisdom in Prov 16:10, 12; and 20:8, 26.[26]

In the book of proverbs, many advise against litigation (Prov 3:30; 6: 16, 19; 25:7–10; 29:9; also economic topics at 6:1–5; 11:15; 17:18; 20:16; 22:26–27).[27] Others clearly have lawmen as their target audience, but the content is again not legal: "Open your mouth, judge righteously, defend the rights of the poor and needy" (Prov 31:9; also 18:5; 22:22–23).[28] There are proverbs of legal procedure: Prov 6:16–19; 19:28; 21:28; 25:18—all of which note the dangers of false witnesses.[29] Prov 24:23–25 provides more extensive instructions for judges (using a stock pair of verbs, יִקְּבֻהוּ יִזְעָמוּהוּ, appearing together also in the Balaam story), as do 18:17; 19:19; 29:24. Thus, Proverbs contains not only proverbial snippets of law but of legal procedure (as does Ben Sirah 7–8), just like the Latin legal maxims discussed above; and we find the same in ancient Egypt, such as the Hyksos-period "Ashmolean Washing Board" text.[30]

Contemporary Book of Proverbs study is quite resistant to such analysis of individual proverbs or units of proverbs, especially when a context is proposed *other* than the current Book of Proverbs.[31] But as Suzanna Millar has shown, neither immediate nor distant literary context need replace social context.[32] Proverbs remain proverbs, similar to folk proverbs cross-culturally, quoted by judges, kings, and prophets, self-referential as proverbs, with the formal, structural, stylistic features of individual discourses.[33] Within the book of Proverbs, the same A-line appears later on with a different B-line; Prov 24:23 becomes the A-line of Prov 28:21. "Whoever digs a pit may fall into it" appears in Prov 26:27; Ps 57:6; Qoh 10:8; and Sir 27:26. Finally, it makes no difference whether these proverbs were composed in writing, since, as we have seen, there is no oral-to-written evolution in literature, and we are not interested in the *origins* of specific proverbs at all.[34] Millar's insight opens up avenues for studying individual proverbs and, to return to the start of this study, their *several* performative schemas.

Contemporary paremiology looks at the pragmatic functions of proverbs, the way a proverb "works" only if its performer and the recipient understand it as a formulation of a social function.[35] Much of the work on legal proverbs, especially in Africa (cited above) is restricted to their use in lawsuits and legal argument, as speech acts, how they "often and effectively contribute to the linguistic forming of argumentative structures."[36]

There is more to study, however. Even in Africa, proverbs may be used "to draw the attention of other jury members to a judicial norm."[37] "Proverbs in ancient legal texts reveal specific functionality . . . passed on through oral tradition, reflected and preserved in written form through the use of proverbs—legal rules and principles are portrayed."[38] This is because

there is one additional voice in the performance of a proverb, additional
to the performer and the receiver: "The effect of a proverb grounds on
... the voice of 'the third party,'"[39] the authority of the proverb itself. In
this case, it is the legal authority of custom to which the proverb attests.[40]
Performance of proverbs thus foregrounds the act of quotation, building its
authority on the unseen third party of "ancient" custom.[41] The performance
of proverbs, therefore, borders on the ritual; as Lotte Tarkka writes, "When
the authority of proverbial speech was shown to have its origin in mythic
time ... language gained a ritual dimension ... repeatedly legitimized in
performance."[42]

Moreover, legal proverbs in a customary law society take on an even more
hallowed performativity. As Peter Stein writes, the application to a legal
principle of "a maxim was for a common lawyer akin to attributing it to
natural reason for a Roman lawyer. In each case, no further justification was
needed."[43]

As Jacqueline Vayntrub has shown, "Nearly every instance of the term
mashal . . . refers to a composition that is orally performed by characters in
the narrative."[44] "*Mashal* indicates a type of formal, rhythmic speech performed by characters" (e.g., 1 Samuel 24; Ezekiel; Isa 14:4; Mic 2:4; Hab
2:6).[45] Vayntrub does not see any reason for these depicted performances
to be taken as realistic or representative of "ultimately inaccessible ancient
performance."[46] Yet such depicted performances are, in fact, of great value
for reconstrucuting ancient performance, a literate but *aural* audience's
perception of an oral situation that—in multiple Germanic examples, for
instance—is identical to real ancient oral practice.[47] And, of course, ethnographic analogy and Ancient Near Eastern texts assist our access to such
performances.

Since, however, performances are often particular to genres,[48] it may be
necessary to subdivide legal Proverbs on the basis of formal, semantic elements, suggestive of discrete performative schemas. Udo Rüterswörden has
attempted such a division, but into three categories based largely on verb use,[49]
and there is nothing to suggest this division is not arbitrary or that it has any
bearing on performance.

It would be helpful to have Ancient Near Eastern texts depicting the "performance" of legal proverbs. Legal proverbs abound in the Ancient Near
East. Some, again, are advice to judges (e.g., from Mesopotamia, UET 6/2
259[50] and VAT 8807 rev. 4.11–14;[51] from Egypt, "Maxims of Ptahhotep,"
13.1–2 §28; 15.5 §36;[52] Papyrus Millingen / "Instruction of Amenemhet,"
1.5 (*AEL* 1.136); and Papyrus Insiger #14 14.16 [*AEL* 3.196]). Collection 13
in Alster's first volume of Sumerian proverbs reads like an ancient Egyptian
Blackstone's Police Manual.[53]

However, some Ancient Near Eastern proverbs give judicial procedure: from the "Instruction of Ankhsheshonq," 16.25, "Do not disdain a small document, a small fire, a small soldier"; 26.3–6, "[There is] . . . [for throwing] a man out. There is a stick for bringing him in. There is imprisonment for giving life. There is release for killing" (*AEL* 3.179). Still others are properly brocards, legal instructions in proverbial form—such as "Instruction of Amenemope," 16.2–9, "If you find a large debt against a poor man, Make it into three parts; Release two of them and let one remain: You will find it a path of life; You will pass the night in sound sleep; in the morning you will find it like good news."[54] Note, the instructions are not directed at the lender, but at an official who has the authority to annul the debt.

That these proverbs, too, functioned in law independently of the literary texts from which we know them is proven by the quotation of one of the 24th-century "Maxims of Ptahhotep" in an autobiographical text from the 15th-century tomb of Rekhmire at Thebes (col. 14), introduced by "Lo, it is said that," in the context of the transcript of Pharaoh's speech detailing the legal proceedings of a court case (cols. 1–21).[55]

The transfer is not only from "wisdom literature" *to* law, however; Aramaic legal proverbs from Elephantine (AP [Cowley] 217.156) appear in the 5th-century Aramaic *Story of Ahikar*, as Jonas Greenfield showed in the 1970s.[56] The transference is from free-floating proverb into wisdom literature, customary law, and legal pedagogical literature, with no inherent sequence to those points of contact and no reason to believe the proverb could not subsequently move out of one into another.[57]

NOTES

1. Phillip R. Callaway, 'Deut 21:18–21: Proverbial Wisdom and Law', *Journal of Biblical Literature* 103 (1984): 348, albeit espousing an evolutionary view of law.

2. Berend Gemser, 'The Importance of the Motive Clause in the Old Testament Law', *Supplements to Vetus Testamentum* 1 (1953): 64–66.

3. Gemser, 64–66; John M. Thompson, *The Form and Function of Proverbs in Ancient Israel* (The Hague: Mouton, 1974), 76.

4. I am grateful to Prof. Bradley Gregory for this analogy.

5. Saintyves, 'Le Folklore juridique', 92; Stein, *Regulae Iuris*, 154–55; Gilissen, *La Coutume*, 63; Outi Lauhakangas, *The Matti Kuusi International Type System of Proverbs*, Folklore Fellows' Communications 275 (Helsinki: Suomalainen Tiedeakatemia, 2001), 33.

6. J. C. Chakanza, *Wisdom of the People: 2000 Chinyanja Proverbs*, Kachere Books 13 (Blantyre, Malawi: Christian Literature Association in Malawi, 2000), paras 142, 145, 187, 425, 487, 537; Ernest Gray, 'Some Proverbs of the Nyanja

People', *African Studies* 3 (1944): 106–10; J. Olowo Ojoade, 'Proverbial Evidences of African Legal Customs', *International Folklore Review* 6 (1988): 26–35.

7. J. H. Hillebrand, *Deutsche Rechtssprichwörter gesammelt und erläutert* (Zurich: Meyer und Zelle, 1868), 1–2.

8. Saintyves, 'Le Folklore juridique', 95.

9. Herbert Broom, *A Selection of Legal Maxims*, 8th ed. (Philadelphia: T and J W Johnson, 1882).

10. Respectively, circuity is to be avoided; an evil custom is to be abolished; practice of the Court is law of the Court; it is one thing to conceal, another to be silent.

11. To insist on a rule of public law is not to overreach.

12. A creditor who permits the sale of the thing pledged loses his security. These are collected in Broom; for examples of their use, see Stein, *Regulae Iuris*, 161–62.

13. Binchy, 'Linguistic and Legal Archaisms in the Celtic Law-Books', 15.

14. CIH 570.34–571.16; Kelly, *A Guide to Irish Law*, 274, 356–57#7 (Appendix 1 No. 42).

15. Erhard S. Gerstenberger, *Wesen und Herkunft des 'apodiktischen Rechts'* (1965; Repr. Eugene, OR: Wipf & Stock, 2009), 129; Westbrook and Wells, *Everyday Law in Biblical Israel*, 82; Daube, *Law and Wisdom in the Bible*, 97; Blenkinsopp, *Wisdom and Law in the Old Testament*, 97, 151; see, however, the helpful corrective in Daube, *Law and Wisdom in the Bible*, 89.

16. Katharine J. Dell, *The Book of Proverbs in Social and Theological Context* (Cambridge: Cambridge University Press, 2006), 159.

17. Thompson, *The Form and Function of Proverbs in Ancient Israel*, 77–78; Dell, *The Book of Proverbs in Social and Theological Context*, 168–73; Shamir Yona, 'The Influence of Legal Style on the Style of the Aphorisms', in *Birkat Shalom*, ed. Chaim Cohen (Winona Lake: Eisenbrauns, 2008), 416–19; Bernd U. Schipper, '"Teach Them Diligently to Your Son!" The Book of Proverbs and Deuteronomy', in *Reading Proverbs Intertextually*, ed. Katherine Dell and Will Kynes (New York: T & T Clark, 2019), 21–34.

18. Nyika, 'The Traditional Israelite Legal Setting', 42–49.

19. I am grateful to my student World Kim for pointing this out to me.

20. Hans Walter Wolff, *Micah the Prophet* (Philadelphia: Fortress Press, 1981), 23–25, 41, 52, 67, 137, 144; Choon-Leong Seow, 'Hosea 14:10 and the Foolish People Motif', *Catholic Biblical Quarterly* 44 (1982): 212–24.

21. Wolfgang Mieder, 'Origin of Proverbs', in *Introduction to Paremiology*, ed. Hrisztalina Hrisztova-Gotthardt and Melita A. Varga (Berlin: De Gruyter, 2015), 28.

22. Archer Taylor, *The Proverb* (Cambridge, Mass.: Harvard University Press, 1931), 10.

23. Milstein, 'Making a Case', 171 n.35.

24. Nyika, 'The Traditional Israelite Legal Setting', 42–49.

25. Udo Skladny, *Die ältesten Spruchsammlungen in Israel* (Göttingen: Vandenhoeck & Ruprecht, 1962), 39, 48.

26. Wagner, 'Die Gerichtsverfassung Israels nach der Weisheitsliteratur des alten Testaments', 98.

27. The same sentiment, expressed with some of the same metaphors, is in the Ramesside Ostracon Petrie 11, lines verso 3–4; Alan H. Gardiner, 'A New Moralizing Text', *Wiener Zeitschrift Fur Die Kunde Des Morgenlandes* 54 (1957): 44; and the Babylonian 'Counsels of Wisdom,' 31–35; W. G. Lambert, *Babylonian Wisdom Literature* (Winona Lake: Eisenbrauns, 1996), 101.

28. Compare Sylvia Powels, 'Samaritan Proverbs', *Abr-Nahrain* 28 (1990): para. 18.

29. Cf. Powels, para. 26.

30. John Barns, 'A New Wisdom Text from a Writing-Board in Oxford', *Journal of Egyptian Archaeology* 54 (1968): 76.

31. William P. Brown, *Wisdom's Wonder: Character, Creation, and Crisis in the Bible's Wisdom Literature* (Grand Rapids: Eerdmans, 2014); Knut Martin Heim, *Poetic imagination in proverbs: variant repetitions and the nature of poetry*, Bulletin for Biblical Research Supplements 4 (Winona Lake: Eisenbrauns, 2013); Vayntrub, *Beyond Orality*, 90.

32. Suzanna Millar, 'A Proverb in a Collection Is Dead?' (Reframing Wisdom, London, 2019); Lotte Tarkka, 'The Poetics of Quotation', in *Genre—Text—Interpretation*, ed. Kaarina Koski and Frog, Studia Fennica Folkloristica / Suomalaisen Kirjallisuuden Seura 22 (Helsinki: Finnish Literature Society, 2016), 175, 178.

33. Also, Neal R. Norrick, 'Subject Area, Terminology, Proverb Definitions, Proverb Features', in *Introduction to Paremiology*, ed. Hrisztalina Hrisztova-Gotthardt and Melita A. Varga (Berlin: De Gruyter, 2015), 7.

34. Mieder, 'Origin of Proverbs', 28; Taylor, *The Proverb*, 9, 35.

35. Hrisztalina Hrisztova-Gotthardt and Melita A. Varga, *Introduction to Paremiology* (Berlin: De Gruyter, 2015), 135.

36. Hrisztova-Gotthardt and Varga, 145; Outi Lauhakangas, 'Use of Proverbs and Narrative Thought', *Folklore: Electronic Journal of Folklore* 35 (2007): 81, https://doi.org/10.7592/FEJF2007.35.lauhakangas.

37. Kwesi Yankah, 'Proverb Rhetoric and African Judicial Process', *Journal of American Folklore*, 1986, 288, 292–94.

38. Hrisztova-Gotthardt and Varga, *Introduction to Paremiology*, 135 n.60.

39. Lauhakangas, 'Use of Proverbs and Narrative Thought', 82.

40. Lauhakangas, 83.

41. Tarkka, 'The Poetics of Quotation', 175, 180.

42. Tarkka, 187.

43. Stein, *Regulae Iuris*, 160.

44. Vayntrub, *Beyond Orality*, 80.

45. Vayntrub, 80–81.

46. Vayntrub, 81, 86.

47. John D. Niles, 'The Myth of the Anglo-Saxon Oral Poet', *Western Folklore* 62 (2003): 12, 37; Mark Amodio, *Writing the Oral Tradition* (Notre Dame: Notre Dame University Press, 2004), 39.

48. Richard Bauman, 'Performance', in *A Companion to Folklore*, ed. Regina F. Bendix and Galit Hasan-Rokem, Blackwell Companions to Anthropology 15 (Oxford: Wiley-Blackwell, 2012), 103; see Hittite evidence in Monika Schuol,

Hethitische Kultmusik: eine Untersuchung der Instrumental- und Vokalmusik anhand hethitischer Ritualtexte und von archäologischen Zeugnissen, Orient-Archäologie 14 (Rahden: Marie Leidorf, 2004), 141.

49. Udo Rüterswörden, 'Das kasuistische Recht die Weisheit', in *Ex oriente Lux: Studien zur Theologie des Alten Testaments*, ed. Angelika Berlejung and Raik Heckl, Arbeiten zur Bibel und ihrer Geschichte 39 (Leipzig: Evangelische Verlagsanstalt, 2012), 326–28.

50. Bendt Alster, *Proverbs of Ancient Sumer*, vol. 1 (Bethesda: CDL, 1997), 310.

51. Lambert, *Babylonian Wisdom Literature*, 219 pl. 55–57.

52. William Kelly Simpson, ed., *The Literature of Ancient Egypt: An Anthology of Stories, Instructions, Stelae, Autobiographies, and Poetry*, 3rd ed. (New Haven: Yale University Press, 2003), 142, 144.

53. Alster, *Proverbs of Ancient Sumer*, 1:207.

54. Simpson, *The Literature of Ancient Egypt*, 234–35.

55. Norman de Garis Davies, *The Tomb of Rekh-Mi-Re' at Thebes*, Publications of the Metropolitan Museum of Art Egyptian Expedition (New York: Plantin, 1943), 86–87, 87 n.45.

56. Yona, 'The Influence of Legal Style on the Style of the Aphorisms', 413–15.

57. Rüterswörden, 'Das kasuistische Recht die Weisheit', 330. As Taylor, *The Proverb*, 59–60, already knew, Prov 15:1 somehow appears in Aeschylus, and we have no way to know how many hands it passed through in between.

Conclusion

Perhaps our best reconstruction of legal performance for ancient Israel and Judah would draw from the ethnographic analogy we began with: an Althing—dare we say at Shechem? summoned by shofar blast?—attracting artisans, arabbers, and merchants, juggling troupes and drinking booths, but most especially the elders from the kingdom. Legal points are decided, exemptions granted. If there was a Lawspeaker, a poet-lawman, he delivered no judgments and had no power of enforcing a decision.[1]

Throughout the kingdom, advising village moots in gates and threshing-floors and tutoring their students, were the חֹקְקִים, expert memory men skilled at law and at oratory. That law was customary, with all we have seen that definition entails: a body of oral lore based on tradition rather than active legislation, not a set of preserved formally adopted rules, but manipulated tradition; perhaps written legal memoranda collected and eventually preserving authentic early elements; small narratives and proverbs. The law was in the process of being privately codified, using a variety of informants, and collected in ever larger and ever more diverse corpora. Our best glimpse at what a "piece" of that law might have looked like could be a text like Prov 26:17, "Like somebody who takes a passing dog by the ears is one who meddles in the grievance of another," marked at its heart with a mnemonic "עֹבֵר מִתְעַבֵּר."

NOTE

1. Bryce, *Studies in History and Jurisprudence*, 1.1:276.

Bibliography

N.b., Names of Icelandic authors are alphabetized according to first name, except when they have a surname.

Abadie, Philippe. *L'histoire d'Israël entre mémoire et relecture*. Lectio divina 229. Paris: Cerf, 2009.

Abusch, Tzvi. *Essays on Babylonian and Biblical Literature and Religion*. Harvard Semitic Museum Publications 65. Leiden: Brill, 2020.

———. "The First Incantation in Maqlû and the Second Šuilla Prayer to Nergal." Cambridge, 2017.

Adam of Bremen. *History of the Archbishops of Hamburg-Bremen*. Translated by Francis Joseph Tschan. Records of Western Civilization. New York: Columbia University Press, 2002.

Afanasjeva, V. "Mündliche überlieferte Dichtung ('Oral Poetry') und schriftliche Literatur in Mesopotamien." In *Wirtschaft und Gesellschaft im alten Vorderasien*, edited by J. Harmatta and G. Komoroczy, 121–36. Nachdruck aus den Acta Antiqua Academiae Scientarum Hungaricae, 12.1–4. Budapest: Akademiai Kiado, 1976.

Agnes S. Arnórsdóttir. "Cultural Memory and Gender in Iceland from Medieval to Early Modern Times." *Scandinavian Studies* 85 (2013): 378–99.

———. "Legal Culture and Historical Memory in Medieval and Early Modern Iceland." In *Minni and Muninn: Memory in Medieval Nordic Culture*, edited by Pernille Hermann, Stephen A. Mitchell, and Agnes S. Arnórsdóttir, 211–30. Acta Scandinavica 4. Turnhout: Brepols, 2014.

Ahlström, Gösta W. "Oral and Written Transmission." *Harvard Theological Review* 59 (1966): 69–81.

Ahronson, Kristján. *Into the Ocean: Vikings, Irish, and Environmental Change in Iceland and the North*. Toronto Old Norse and Icelandic Series 8. Toronto: University of Toronto Press, 2015.

————. "Testing the Evidence for Northern North Atlantic Papar." In *The Papar in the North Atlantic: Environment and History*, edited by Barbara E Crawford, 107–20. St. Andrews: University of St. Andrews Press, 2002.

Almqvist, Bo. "Gaelic/Norse Folklore Contacts." In *Irland und Europa im früheren Mittelalter: Bildung und Literatur = Ireland and Europe in the early Middle Ages: learning and literature*, edited by Próinséas Ní Chatháin and Michael Richter, 139–73. Stuttgart: Klett-Cotta, 1996.

————. *Viking Ale: Studies on Folklore Contacts between the Northern and the Western Worlds*. Aberystwyth, Wales: Boethius, 1991.

Alster, Bendt. *Proverbs of Ancient Sumer*. Vol. 1. Bethesda: CDL, 1997.

Alt, Albrecht. *Essays on Old Testament History and Religion*. Anchor Books. Garden City: Doubleday, 1968.

Amit, Yairah. *History and Ideology: Introduction to Historiography in the Hebrew Bible*. Sheffield: Sheffield Academic Press, 2001.

Amodio, Mark. *Writing the Oral Tradition*. Notre Dame: Notre Dame University Press, 2004.

Amram, David W. "Summons." *University of Pennsylvania Law Review* 68 (1919–1920): 50–67.

Andersen, Per. "The Power of the Law." In *The Power of Book: Medial Approaches to Medieval Nordic Legal Manuscripts*, edited by Lena Rohrbach, 55–74. Berliner Beiträge Zur Skandinavistik 19. Berlin: Nordeuropa Institut, Humboldt-Universität, 2014.

Andersson, Theodore M., and William I. Miller. *Law and Literature in Medieval Iceland*. Stanford: Stanford University Press, 1989.

Aranov, Maurice M. "The Biblical Threshing-Floor in the Light of the Ancient Near Eastern Evidence." Diss., New York University, 1977.

Arav, Rami. "Do Biblical Laws Reflect a Tribal Society?" *The Torah. Com* (blog), September 13, 2019. https://www.thetorah.com/article/do-biblical-laws-reflect-a-tribal-society.

Armann Jakobsson. "The Trollish Acts of Thorgrimr the Witch." *Saga-Book* 32 (2008): 39–66.

Armistead, Samuel G. "Epic and Ballad." *Olifant* 8 (1981): 376–88.

Arnold, Bill T. "The Weidner Chronicle and the Idea of History in Israel and Mesopotamia." In *Faith, Tradition, and History*, edited by Alan R. Millard, James K. Hoffmeier, and David W. Baker, 129–48. Winona Lake: Eisenbrauns, 1994.

Arrhenius, Birgit. "Connections between Scandinavia and the East Roman Empire in the Migration Period." In *From the Baltic to the Black Sea*, edited by David Austin and Leslie Alcock, 118–37. London: Unwin Hyman, 1990.

Asdis Egilsdottir. "From Orality to Literacy." In *Reykholt Som Makt-Og Lærdoms-senter*, edited by Else Mundal, 215–28. Snorrastofa 3. Reykholt, Iceland: Snorrastofa, 2006.

Auge, Ramir. *Job*. La Biblia de Montserrat 9. Montserrat: Monestir de Montserrat, 1959.

Ausenda, G. "Kinship and Marriage among the Visigoths." In *The Visigoths: From the Migration Period to the Seventh Century*, edited by Peter Heather, 129–68. Studies in Historical Archaeoethnology 4. San Marino: Boydell, 1999.

Ausenda, G., and Pablo C. Diaz. "Current Issues and Future Directions in the Study of Visigoths." In *The Visigoths: From the Migration Period to the Seventh Century*, edited by Peter Heather, 473–530. Studies in Historical Archaeoethnology 4. San Marino: Boydell, 1999.

Ausenda, Giorgio, and Sam. J. Barnish. "A Comparative Discussion of Langobardic Feud and Blood-Money Compensation with Parallels from Contemporary Anthropology and from Medieval History." In *The Langobards before the Frankish Conquest*, edited by Giorgio Ausenda, 309–40. Studies in Historical Archaeoethnology 8. Woodbridge: Boydell & Brewer, 2009.

Avalos, Hector. "Legal and Social Institutions in Canaan and Ancient Israel." In *Civilizations of the Ancient Near East*, edited by Jack Sasson, 1:615ff. Peabody, Mass.: Hendrickson, 1995.

Avis, Robert. "Conflict, Cooperation and Consensus in the Law of Njálls Saga," *Quaestio Insularis* 12 (2012): 85–109.

Baetke, Walter, trans. *Island Beseidlung Und Alteste Geschichte*. Altnordische Dichtung Und Prosa 23. Jena: Eugen Diederichs, 1928.

Baltl, Hermann. "Folklore Research and Legal History in the German Language Area." In *Folk Law*, edited by Alison D. Renteln and Alan Dundes, 1:397–406. Garland Folklore Casebooks 3. New York: Garland, 1994.

Barfield, Owen. "Poetic Diction and Legal Fiction." In *The Importance of Language*, edited by Max Black. Englewood Cliffs, NJ: Prentice-Hall, 1969.

Barnish, Sam J., and Federico Marazzi. *The Ostrogoths from the Migration Period to the Sixth Century*. Rochester: Boydell, 2007.

Barns, John. "A New Wisdom Text from a Writing-Board in Oxford." *Journal of Egyptian Archaeology* 54 (1968): 71–76.

Barstad, Hans M. "Eduard Nielsen's *Oral Tradition* Sixty Years After." *Scandinavian Journal of the Old Testament* 27 (2013): 8–21.

———. *History and the Hebrew Bible: Studies in Ancient Israelite and Ancient Near Eastern Historiography*. Forschungen zum Alten Testament 61. Tübingen: Mohr Siebeck, 2008.

Bartusch, Mark W. *Understanding Dan: An Exegetical Study of a Biblical City, Tribe and Ancestor*. London: Sheffield Academic Press, 2003.

Bauman, Richard. *Let Your Words Be Few*. 8. Cambridge: Cambridge University Press, 1983.

———. "Performance." In *A Companion to Folklore*, edited by Regina F. Bendix and Galit Hasan-Rokem. Blackwell Companions to Anthropology 15. Oxford: Wiley-Blackwell, 2012.

Beckman, Gary. "The Limits of Credulity." *Journal of the American Oriental Society* 125 (2005): 343–52.

Bederman, David J. *Custom as a Source of Law*. Cambridge: Cambridge University Press, 2010.

Beggs, Gordon J. "Proverbial Practice: Legal Ethics from Old Testament Wisdom." *Wake Forest Law Review* 30 (1995): 831–45.

Bellefontaine, Elizabeth. "Customary Law and Chieftainship: Judicial Aspects of 2 Samuel 14.4–21." *Journal for the Study of the Old Testament* 38 (1987): 47–72.

Ben Zvi, Ehud. "Clio Today and Ancient Israelite History." In *"Not Even God Can Alter the Past": Reflections on 16 Years of the European Seminar in Historical Methodology*. European Seminar in Historical Methodology 10. London: T & T Clark, 2015.

Bennett, T. W. *Customary Law in South Africa*. Cape Town: Juta, 2004.

Berge, Lawrence G. "Hirðskra 1–37, A Translation with Notes." MA Thesis, University of Wisconsin, 1968.

Bergh, G. C. J. J. van den. "The Concept of Folk Law in Historical Context." In *Anthropology of Law in the Netherlands: Essays on Legal Pluralism*, edited by Keebet von Benda-Beckmann and A. K. J. M. Strijbosch, 67–89. Verhandelingen van Het Koninklijk Instituut Voor Taal-, Land- En Volkenkunde 116. Dordrecht, Netherlands: Foris, 1986.

———. "The Concept of Folk Law in Historical Context." In *Folk Law*, edited by Alison D. Renteln and Alan Dundes, 1:5–32. Garland Folklore Casebooks 3. New York: Garland, 1994.

Bergman, Jan. "Commentary." In *Science of Religion: Studies in Methodology*, edited by Lauri Honko, 15–21. Religion and Reason 13. The Hague: Mouton, 1979.

Beyerlin, Walter. "Gattung und Herkunft des Rahmens im Richterbuch." In *Tradition und situation*, 1–29. Göttingen: Vandenhoeck & Ruprecht, 1963.

———. "Geschichte und heilsgeschichtliche Traditionsbildung im Alten Testament." *Vetus Testamentum* 13 (1963): 1–25.

Binchy, D. A. "The Linguistic and Historical Value of the Irish Law Tracts (1943)." In *Celtic Law Papers*, edited by Dafydd Jenkins, 71–107. Brussels: Libraire Encyclopedique, 1973.

———. "Linguistic and Legal Archaisms in the Celtic Law-Books." *Transactions of the Philological Society*, 1959, 14–24.

Birgir Runolfsson Solvason. "Ordered Anarchy: Evolution of the Decentralized Legal Order in the Icelandic Commonwealth." *Journal des economistes et des etudes humaines* 3 (1992): 1–20.

Birkeland, Harris. *Zum Hebraischen Traditionswesen*. Avhandlinger Utgitt av det Norse Videnskaps-Akademi, 1938: 1. Oslo: Norse Videnskaps-Akademi, 1938.

Bjarni Vilhjalmsson and Oskar Halldorsson, eds. *Islenzkir Malshaettir*. Reykjavik: Almenna, 1966.

Blagojevic, Borislav T. "The Comparative Method in the Study of Customary Law as a Historical Category." In *Mélanges de droit comparé: en l'honneur du doyen Åke Malmström*, edited by Stig Strömholm. ACTA Instituti Upsaliensis Iurisprudentiae Comparativae 14. Stockholm: Norstedt, 1972.

Blake, N. F., trans. *The Saga of the Jomsvikings*. Icelandic Texts. London: Thomas Nelson and Sons, 1962.

Blenkinsopp, Joseph. *Wisdom and Law in the Old Testament*. Oxford Bible Series 10. Oxford: Oxford University Press, 1995.

Boganeva, Elena. "The Variations of the Image of the Tower of Babel and the Associated Etiologies in the Belarusian Folk Bible." In *Variation in Folklore and Language*, edited by Piret Voolaid and Saša Babič, 33–48. Cambridge: Cambridge Scholars Press, 2019.

Bonds, Mark Evan. *Music as Thought: Listening to the Symphony in the Age of Beethoven.* Princeton, N.J.: Princeton University Press, 2006.

Bos, Jacques. "Historical Research after the Demise of the Grand Narratives." *Historical Methods: A Journal of Quantitative and Interdisciplinary History* 42 (2009): 155–58.

Bos, James M. "The 'Literalization' of the Biblical Prophecy of Doom." In *Contextualizing Israel's Sacred Writings*, edited by Brian B. Schmidt, 263–80. Society of Biblical Literature: Ancient Israel and Its Literature 22. Atlanta: SBL, 2015.

Botha, J. Eugene. "Exploring Gesture and Nonverbal Communication in the Bible and Ancient World." *Neotestamentica* 30 (1996): 1–19.

Boulhosa, Patricia P. *Icelanders and the Kings of Norway: Mediaeval Sagas and Legal Texts.* Northern World 17. Leiden: Brill, 2008.

———. "Ideas of Law in Medieval Icelandic Legal Texts." In *Legislation and State Formation*, edited by Steinar Imsen, 169–82. Norgesveldet Occasional Papers 4. Trondheim: Akademika, 2013.

———. "Layout and the Structure of the Text on Konungsbók." In *The Power of Book: Medial Approaches to Medieval Nordic Legal Manuscripts*, edited by Lena Rohrbach, 75–97. Berliner Beiträge zur Skandinavistik 19. Berlin: Nordeuropa Institut, Humboldt-Universität, 2014.

———. "Narrative, Evidence and the Reception of Járnsíða." In *Sturla Þórðarson: Skald, Chieftain, and Lawman*, edited by Jón Viðar Sigurdsson and Sverrir Jakobsson, 223–32. The Northern World: North Europe and the Baltic c. 400–1700 AD: Peoples, Economics and Cultures 78. Leiden: Brill, 2017.

Bragi Halldórsson and Knútur S. Hafsteinsson. *Íslendingaþættir: úrval þrettán þátta med inngangi, skýringum og skrám.* Sigildar sögur 8. Reykjavík: Mál og Menning, 1999.

———. *On Jewish Music.* Rev. ed. Frankfurt: Peter Lang, 2011.

Breatnach, Liam. *A Companion to the Corpus Iuris Hibernici.* Early Irish Law Series 5. Dublin: School of Celtic Studies, Dublin Institute for Advanced Studies, 2005.

Bremmer Jr., Rolf H. "The Orality of Old Frisian Law Texts," *Amsterdamer Beiträge zur älteren Germanistik* 73 (2014): 1–48.

Brettler, Marc Z. "Method in the Application of Biblical Source Material to Historical Writing." In *Understanding the History of Ancient Israel*, edited by H. G. M. Williamson, 305–36. Proceedings of the British Academy 143. Oxford: Oxford University Press, 2007.

Briggs, Charles A. *The Higher Criticism of the Hexateuch.* 3rd ed. New York: Charles Scribner's Sons, 1897.

Brink, Stefan. "Law." In *Handbook of Pre-Modern Nordic Memory Studies*, edited by Jürg Glauser and Pernille Hermann, 185–97. Berlin: De Gruyter, 2018.

————. "Law and Legal Customs in Viking Age Scandinavia." In *The Scandinavians: From the Vendel Period to the Tenth Century*, edited by Judith Jesch, 87–127. Studies in Historical Archaeoethnology 5. San Marino: Boydell, 2012.

————. "Minnunga Maen: The Usage of Old Knowledgeable Men in Legal Cases." In *Minni and Muninn: Memory in Medieval Nordic Culture*, edited by Pernille Hermann, Stephen A. Mitchell, and Agnes S. Arnórsdóttir, 197–210. Acta Scandinavica 4. Turnhout: Brepols, 2014.

————. "Reconstruction of Viking and Early Medieval Scandinavian Society." In *Early Law in the North*, 1–15, forthcoming.

————. "The Creation of a Scandinavian Provincial Law: How Was It Done?" *Historical Research* 86 (2013): 432–42.

————. "The Origins of the Swedish Medieval Laws." In *How Nordic Are the Nordic Medieval Laws? Ten Years after: Proceedings of the Tenth Carlsberg Academy Conference on Medieval Legal History 2013*, edited by Per Andersen, Kirsi Salonen, Helle I. M. Sigh, and Helle Vogt. Copenhagen: DJØF Publishing, 2014.

Broom, Herbert. *A Selection of Legal Maxims*. 8th ed. Philadelphia: T. and J. W. Johnson, 1882.

Brown, William P. *Wisdom's Wonder: Character, Creation, and Crisis in the Bible's Wisdom Literature*. Grand Rapids: Eerdmans, 2014.

Bruce, Alexander M. *Scyld and Scef: Expanding the Analogues*. New York: Routledge, 2002.

Bryce, James. *Studies in History and Jurisprudence*. Vol. 1.1. New York: Oxford University Press, 1901.

Bühler, Karl. "The Psychophysics of Expression of Wilhelm Wundt (1933)." In *The Language of Gestures*, 30–54. The Hague: Mouton, 1973.

Burgmann, Ludwig, trans. *Ecloga*. Forschungen zur Byzantinischen Rechtsgeschichte 10. Frankfurt: Lowenklau, 1983.

Burnside, Jonathan. *God, Justice and Society: Aspects of Law and Legality in the Bible*. Oxford: Oxford University Press, 2011.

Burrows, Hannah. "Cold Cases: Law and Legal Details in the Islendingasogur." *Parergon* 26 (2009): 35–55.

————. "'In This Country, What Is Found in Books Is to Be Law.'" *Quaestio Insularis* 8 (2007): 36–50.

————. "Literary-Legal Relations in Commonwealth-Period Iceland." Diss., University of York, 2007.

————. "Rhyme and Reason: Lawspeaker-Poets in Medieval Iceland." *Scandinavian Studies* 81 (2009): 215–38.

————. "Some Þing to Talk About: Assemblies in the Islendingasogur." *Northern Studies* 52 (2015): 47–75.

Burrows, Millar. "Ancient Israel." In *The Idea of History in the Ancient Near East*, 101–31. New Haven: Yale University Press, 1955.

Bushnaq, Inea. *Arab Folk-Tales*. Cairo: The American University in Cairo Press, 1987.

Byock, Jesse L. "Governmental Order in Early Medieval Iceland." *Viator* 17 (1986): 19–34.

———. *Viking Age Iceland*. London: Penguin, 2001.

Byrne, Francis J. *Irish Kings and High-Kings*. New York: St. Martin's, 1973.

Callaway, Phillip R. "Deut 21:18–21: Proverbial Wisdom and Law." *Journal of Biblical Literature* 103 (1984): 341–52.

Cardozo, Benjamin N. *The Nature of the Judicial Process*. New Haven: Yale University Press, 1921.

Carr, David M. *The Formation of the Hebrew Bible: A New Reconstruction*. New York: Oxford University Press, 2011.

———. "The Many Uses of 'Intertextuality' in Biblical Studies." Helsinki: International Organization for the Study of the Old Testament, 2010.

———. "Orality, Textuality, and Memory." In *Contextualizing Israel's Sacred Writings*, edited by Brian B. Schmidt, 161–73. Society of Biblical Literature: Ancient Israel and Its Literature 22. Atlanta: SBL, 2015.

———. "The Tel Zayit Abecedary in (Social) Context." In *Literate Culture and Tenth-Century Canaan: The Tel Zayit Abecedary in Context*, edited by Ron E. Tappy and P. Kyle McCarter, 113–30. Winona Lake, Ind: Eisenbrauns, 2008.

———. "Torah on the Heart." *Oral Tradition* 25 (2010): 17–39.

———. *Writing on the Tablet of the Heart: Origins of Scripture and Literature*. Oxford: Oxford University Press, 2005.

Carr, Edward Hallett. *What Is History?: The George Macaulay Trevelyan Lectures Delivered in the University of Cambridge, January–March 1961*. New York: Random House, 1961.

Carter, Jane B. "Ancestor Cult and the Occasion of Homeric Performance." In *A Companion to Ancient Epic*, edited by John Miles Foley, 285–312. Malden, Mass.: Blackwell, 2005.

Casanowicz, Immanuel M. *Paronomasia in the Old Testament*. Boston: J. S. Cushing, 1894.

Cassuto, Philippe. "La Bible: le lu, l'écrit et autres points." In *Oralité & écriture dans la Bible & le Coran*, edited by Philippe Cassuto and Pierre Larcher, 11–40. Marseille: Presses Universitaires de Provence, 2014.

Chakanza, J. C. *Wisdom of the People: 2000 Chinyanja Proverbs*. Kachere Books 13. Blantyre, Malawi: Christian Literature Association in Malawi, 2000.

Chauvin, Victor. *Bibliographie des ouvrages arabes ou relatifs aux Arabes*. Liege: Vaillant-Carmanne, 1901.

Chi, Ai Nguyen. "Les traces de l'oralité en Gen 39." In *Narrativité, oralité et performance*, edited by Alain Gignac, 106–24. Collection Terra Nova 4. Leuven: Peeters, 2018.

Christensen, Arne S. *Cassiodorus Jordanes and the History of the Goths*. Copenhagen: Museum Tusculanum Press, 2002.

Civil, Miguel. "The Law Collection of Ur-Nammu." In *Cuneiform Royal Inscriptions and Related Texts in the Schøyen Collection*, edited by A. R. George and Miguel Civil, 221–86. Cornell University Studies in Assyriology and Sumerology 17. Bethesda: CDL, 2011.

Clements, R. E. *Prophecy and Tradition*. Atlanta: John Knox, 1975.

Clifton, Bruno J. "Family and Identity in the Book of Judges." Diss., Cambridge University, 2018.

Clines, David J. A., ed. *The Concise Dictionary of Classical Hebrew*. Sheffield: Sheffield Phoenix Press, 2009.

Clouston, J. Storer. "Odal Orkney." *Saga-Book* 7 (1911): 85–98.

Colbert, David. *The Birth of the Ballad*. Skrifter Utgivna Av Svenskt Visarkiv 10. Stockholm: Svenskt Visarkiv, 1989.

Coogan, Michael D. "Literacy and the Formation of Biblical Literature." In *Realia Dei*, edited by Prescott H. Williams and Theodore Hiebert, 47–61. Atlanta: Scholars, 1999.

Costambeys, Marios. "Kinship, Gender and Property in Lombard Italy." In *The Langobards before the Frankish Conquest*, edited by Giorgio Ausenda, 69–94. Studies in Historical Archaeoethnology 8. Woodbridge: Boydell & Brewer, 2009.

Cotran, Eugene. "African Law." In *International Encyclopedia of Comparative Law*, 2.2:157–68. Tübingen: J. C. B. Mohr (Paul Siebeck), 1970.

Cowley, A. E., trans. *Aramaic Papyri of the Fifth Century B.C.* Ancient Texts and Translations. Eugene, OR: Wipf & Stock, 2005.

Craigie, W. A. "Gaelic Words and Names in the Icelandic Sagas." *Zeitschrift für Celtische Philologie* 1 (1897): 439–54.

———. "The Gaels in Iceland." *Proceedings of the Society of Antiquaries of Scotland* 31 (1896): 247–64.

Crawford, Barbara E. *Scandinavian Scotland*. Scotland in the Early Middle Ages 3. Leicester: Leicester University Press, 1987.

Crenshaw, James L. *Education in Ancient Israel*. New York: Doubleday, 1998.

Crüsemann, Frank. *The Torah: Theology and Social History of Old Testament Law*. 1st English-Language ed. Minneapolis: Fortress, 1996.

"Customary Law and Traditional Knowledge." Background Briefs. Geneva: World Intellectual Property Organization, 2016.

Danek, Georg. "Sänger, Dichter, Schreiber: Die Homerische Frage." In *Musiker und Tradierung*, edited by Regine Pruzsinszky and Dahlia Shehata, 33–47. Wiener Offene Orientalistik 8. Vienna: LIT Verlag, 2010.

Daube, David. *Collected Works of David Daube*. Edited by Calum M. Carmichael. Vol. 5.1. Studies in Comparative Legal History. Berkeley: Robbins, 1992.

———. *Law and Wisdom in the Bible*. West Conshohocken, PA: Templeton, 2010.

———. "The Self-Understood in Legal History." *Green Bag* 2 (1999): 413–19.

David, René. "Sources of Law." In *International Encyclopedia of Comparative Law*, 2.3:3–207. Tübingen: Mohr Siebeck, 1984.

Davies, Benedict G. *Egyptian Historical Inscriptions of the Nineteenth Dynasty*. Documenta Mundi Aegyptiaca 2. Jonsered: Åström, 1997.

Davies, Graham I. "Were There Schools in Ancient Israel?" In *Wisdom in Ancient Israel*, edited by John Day, Robert P. Gordon, and H. G. M. Williamson, 199–211. Cambridge: Cambridge University Press, 1995.

Davies, Norman de Garis. *The Tomb of Rekh-Mi-Re' at Thebes*. Publications of the Metropolitan Museum of Art Egyptian Expedition. New York: Plantin, 1943.

Dedek, Helge. "School of Life: Learned Law and the Scholastic Habitus." In *Law and Private Life in the Middle Ages*, edited by Per Andersen, Mia Münster-Swendsen, and Helle Vogt, 105–22. Copenhagen: DJØF, 2011.

Delitzsch, Franz. *A New Commentary on Genesis*. Clark's Foreign Theological Library n.s. 36–37. Edinburgh: T. & T. Clark, 1899.

Dell, Katharine J. *The Book of Proverbs in Social and Theological Context*. Cambridge: Cambridge University Press, 2006.

Delogu, Paolo. "Kingship and the Shaping of the Lombard Body Politic." In *The Langobards before the Frankish Conquest*, edited by Giorgio Ausenda, 251–88. Studies in Historical Archaeoethnology 8. Woodbridge: Boydell & Brewer, 2009.

Démare-Lafont, Sophie. "Ancient Near Eastern Laws." In *Theory and Method in Biblical and Cuneiform Law: Revision, Interpolation and Development*, edited by Bernard M. Levinson, 91–118. Journal for the Study of the Old Testament 181. Sheffield: Sheffield Academic Press, 1994.

———. "From the Banks of the Seine to the Bay of the Chesapeake: Crossglances on Ancient Near Eastern Law." *Maarav* 18 (2011): 55–62.

———. "L'ecriture du droit en Mesopotamie." In *Loi et Justice dans la Litterature du Proche-Orient ancien*, edited by Olivier Artus, 69–83. Beihefte zur Zeitschrift für altorientalische und biblische Rechtsgeschichte 20. Wiesbaden: Harrassowitz, 2013.

———. "Les lois dans le monde cuneiforme." In *Writing Laws in Antiquity*, 21–33. Beihefte zur Zeitschrift für altorientalische und biblische Rechtsgeschichte 19. Wiesbaden: Harrassowitz, 2017.

Dennis, Andrew, Peter Foote, and Richard Perkins, trans. *Laws of Early Iceland: Gragas*. Vol. 1. 2 vols. Winnipeg: University of Manitoba Press, 1980.

Dever, William G. *What Did the Biblical Writers Know and When Did They Know It?* Grand Rapids: Eerdmans, 2001.

———. *Who Were the Early Israelites and Where Did They Come From?* Grand Rapids: Eerdmans, 2003.

Dhorme, Edoard. *A Commentary on the Book of Job*. Nashville: Nelson, 1926.

Diaz, Pablo C. "Visigothic Political Institutions." In *The Visigoths: From the Migration Period to the Seventh Century*, edited by Peter Heather, 321–55. Studies in Historical Archaeoethnology 4. San Marino: Boydell, 1999.

Dobbs-Allsopp, F. W. "Inscribed in Vocality." In *Epigraphy, Philology, and the Hebrew Bible*, edited by Jeremy M. Hutton, 109–23. Atlanta: Society of Biblical Literature, 2015.

———. *On Biblical Poetry*. Oxford: Oxford University Press, 2015.

Dodds, Jeremy, trans. *The Poetic Edda*. Toronto: Coach House, 2014.

Dohmen, Christoph. *Exodus 19–40*. Herders Theologischer Kommentar zum Alten Testament. Freiburg: Herder, 2012.

Downham, Clare. *Medieval Ireland*. Cambridge Medieval Textbooks. Cambridge: Cambridge University Press, 2018.

Drew, Katherine F. "The Barbarian Kings as Lawgivers and Judges." In *Life and Thought in the Early Middle Ages*, edited by Robert S. Hoyt, 7–29. Minneapolis: University of Minnesota Press, 1967.

Drew, Katherine F., trans. *The Lombard Laws*. 5th ed. Sources of Medieval History 7. Philadelphia: University of Pennsylvania Press, 1996.

Eberhard. "Rechtgeschichte und Volkskunde." In *Die Volkskunde und ihre Grenzgebiete*, 69–125. Jahrbuch für historische Volkskunde 1. Berlin: Herbert Stubenrauch, 1925.

Eddison, E. R. *Styrbiorn the Strong (1926)*. Minneapolis: University of Minnesota Press, 2011.

Edzard, Lutz. "Oralité et écriture." In *Oralité & écriture dans la Bible & le Coran*, edited by Philippe Cassuto and Pierre Larcher, 41–52. Marseille: Presses Universitaires de Provence, 2014.

Egeler, Matthias. "A Retrospective Methodology for Using *Landnámabók* as a Source for the Religious History of Iceland?" *Retrospective Methods Network Newsletter* 10 (2015): 78–92.

———. "Icelandic Folklore, Landscape Theory, and Levity." *Retrospective Methods Network Newsletter* 12–13 (2016): 8–17.

Eissfeldt, Otto. *Geschichtsschreibung im Alten Testament*. Berlin: Evangelische Verlagsanstalt, 1948.

———. "Lade und Stierbild." *Zeitschrift für die alttestamentliche Wissenschaft* 58 (41 1940): 190–215.

Elias, Taslim Olawale. "The Problem of Reducing Customary Laws to Writing." In *Folk Law*, edited by Alison D. Renteln and Alan Dundes, 1:319–38. Garland Folklore Casebooks 3. New York: Garland, 1994.

Engnell, Ivan. *A Rigid Scrutiny*. Nashville: Vanderbilt University Press, 1969.

Ericson, J. E., and Mary P. Winston. "Civil Law and Common Law in Early Texas." *East Texas Historical Journal* 2 (1964): 26ff.

Erlanger, Howard, Bryant Garth, Jane Larson, Elizabeth Mertz, Victoria Nourse, and David Wilkins. "Is It Time for a New Legal Realism?" *Wisconsin Law Review*, Legal Studies Research Papers 1015, 2005, no. 2 (2005): 335–63.

Eska, Charlene M. "Varieties of Early Irish Legal Literature and the Cáin Lánamna Fragments." *Viator* 40 (2009): 1–16.

Evans, Paul S. "Creating a New 'Great Divide': The Exoticization of Ancient Culture in Some Recent Applications of Orality Studies to the Bible." *Journal of Biblical Literature* 136 (2017): 749–54.

Everard, Judith, and William Laurence De Gruchy, eds. *Le Grand Coutumier de Normandie: The Laws and Customs by Which the Duchy of Normandy Is Ruled*. St. Helier, Jersey, Channel Islands: Jersey and Guernsey Law Review, 2009.

Everett, Nick. "Literacy and the Law in Lombard Government." *Early Medieval Europe* 9 (2000): 93–127.

Ewald, Heinrich. *The History of Israel*. Vol. 2. London: Longman, 1883.

Falk, Zeev W. *Hebrew Law in Biblical Times*. Jerusalem: Wahrmann, 1964.

Falkenstein, A., and Wolfram Von Soden. *Sumerische und Akkadische Hymnen und Gebete*. Bibliothek der alten Welt. Stuttgart: Artemis, 1953.

Farber, Zev. "Jerubaal, Jacob and the Battle for Shechem." *Journal of Hebrew Scriptures* 13, art. 12 (2013).

Faulkes, Anthony. *What Was Viking Poetry For?* Birmingham: University of Birmingham School of English, 1993.

Fenger, O. "Danelaw and 'Danish Law.'" *Scandinavian Studies in Law* 16 (1972): 89–96.

Finkelstein, J. J. *The Ox That Gored.* Transactions of the American Philosophical Society, 71.2. Philadelphia: The American Philosophical Society, 1981.

Fisher, Ian. "Crosses in the Ocean." In *The Papar in the North Atlantic: Environment and History*, edited by Barbara E. Crawford, 39–58. St. Andrews: University of St. Andrews Press, 2002.

Fisher, Peter, trans. *Historia Norwegie.* Copenhagen: Museum Tusculanum Press, 2003.

Fix, Hans. "Poetisches im altislandischen Recht." In *Sprachen und Computer*, edited by Hans Fix, Annely Rothkegel, and Erwin Stegentritt, 187–206. Dudweiler: AQ-Verlag, 1982.

Fohrer, Georg. *Studien zur alttestamentlichen Theologie und Geschichte.* Berlin: De Gruyter, 1969.

Foote, Peter. *1117 in Iceland and England.* Dorothea Coke Memorial Lectures. London: Viking Society for Northern Research, 2002.

———. "Oral and Literary Tradition in Early Scandinavian Law." In *Oral Tradition, Literary Tradition*, 47–55. Odense: Odense University Press, 1977.

———. "Some Lines in Logrettuþattr." In *Sjötíu Ritgerðir*, edited by Einar Petursson and Jonas Kristjansson, 198–207. Stofnun Arna Magnussonar a Islandi 12. Reykjavik: Árni Magnússon Institute for Icelandic Studies, 1977.

Forte, Angelo, Richard Oram, and Frederik Pedersen. *Viking Empires.* Cambridge: Cambridge University Press, 2005.

Foster, Benjamin R. *Before the Muses: An Anthology of Akkadian Literature.* Bethesda, Md.: CDL Press, 2005.

Fox, Michael V. *Proverbs 1–9.* Anchor Bible 18A. New York: Doubleday, 2000.

———. *Proverbs 10–31.* 1st Edition edition. New Haven: Yale University Press, 2009.

Frank, Roberta. *Sex, Lies and Málsháttakvæði: A Norse Poem from Medieval Orkney.* Nottingham: Centre for the Study of the Viking Age, 2004.

Frank, Roberta, trans. "*Málsháttakvæði.*" In *Poetry from Treatises on Poetics*, 2:1213–44. Skaldic Poetry of the Scandinavian Middle Ages 3. Turnhout: Brepols, 2017.

Franklin, Simon. *Writing, Society and Culture in Early Rus, c. 950–1300.* Cambridge: Cambridge University Press, 2002.

Frendo, Anthony J. *Pre-Exilic Israel, the Hebrew Bible, and Archaeology: Integrating Text and Artefact.* Library of Hebrew Bible/Old Testament Studies 549. New York: T & T Clark, 2011.

Frese, Daniel A. *The City Gate in Ancient Israel and Her Neighbors: The Form, Function, and Symbolism of the Civic Forum in the Southern Levant.* Culture and History of the Ancient Near East 108. Leiden: Brill, 2020.

———. "The Civic Forum in Ancient Israel." Diss., University of California, San Diego, 2012.

Fried, Lisbeth S. "Historians Can Use the Scientific Method." *Transeuphratene* 31 (2006): 125ff.

Friedman, David. "Private Creation and Enforcement of Laws." *Journal of Legal Studies* 8 (1979): 399–415.

———. *The Machinery of Freedom*. 2nd ed. La Salle, IL: Open Court, 2015.

Friedrich, Rainer. *Postoral Homer*. Hermes Einzelschrift 112. Stuttgart: Franz Steiner, 2019.

Frog. "Circum-Baltic Mythology? The Strange Case of the Theft of the Thunder-Instrument (ATU 1148B)." *Archaeologia Baltica* 15 (2013): 78–96.

———. "Confluence, Continuity and Change in the Evolution of Mythology: The Case of the Finno-Karelian Sampo-Cycle." In *Mythic Discourses: Studies in Uralic Traditions*, edited by Frog, Anna-Leena Siikala, and Eila Stepanova, 205–56. Helsinki: Finnish Literature Society, 2012.

———. "German Traditions of the Theft of the Thunder-Instrument (ATU 1148B)." In *New Focus on Retrospective Methods: Resuming Methodological Discussions: Case Studies from Northern Europe*, edited by Eldar Heide and Karen Bek-Pedersen, 120–62. Folklore Fellows' Communications 307. Helsinki: Suomalainen Tiedeakatemia, Academia Scientiarum Fennica, 2014.

———. "Metamythology: The Ongoing Mythologization of Mythologies." Paper presented to the International Society for Folk Narrative Research, Miami, 2016.

———. "Multimedial Parallelism in Ritual Performance." *Oral Tradition* 31 (2017): 583–620.

———. "Mythology in Cultural Practice: A Methodological Framework for Historical Analysis." *Retrospective Methods Network Newsletter* 10 (2015): 33–57.

———. "Revisiting the Historical-Geographic Method(s)." *Retrospective Methods Network Newsletter* 7 (2013).

———. "Snorri Sturluson qua Fulcrum: Perspectives on the Cultural Activity of Myth, Mythological Poetry, and Narrative in Medieval Iceland." *Mirator* 12 (2011): 1–28.

———. "The Parallax Approach: Situating Traditions in Long-Term Perspective." *RMN Newsletter* 4 (2012): 40–59.

Frog, Kaarina Koski, and Ulla Savolainen. "At the Intersection of Text and Interpretation." In *Genre-Text-Interpretation*, 17–46. Helsinki: Finnish Literature Society, 2016.

Frog, and Karina Lukin. "Reflections on Texts and Practices in Mythology, Religion, and Research." *Retrospective Methods Network Newsletter* 10 (2015): 6–16.

Frymer-Kenski, Tikva. "Israel." In *A History of Ancient Near Eastern Law*, edited by Raymond Westbrook, 2:975–1046. Handbook of Oriental Studies. Section 1, The Near and Middle East 72. Leiden: Brill, 2003.

Fuglesang, Signe F. "A Critical Survey of Theories on Byzantine Influence in Scandinavia." 3 (1997): 35–58.

Gade, Kari Ellen, ed. *Poetry from the Kings' Sagas 2: From c. 1035 to c. 1300*. Skaldic Poetry of the Scandinavian Middle Ages 2. Turnhout: Brepols, 2009.

Gagarin, Michael. *Writing Greek Law*. Cambridge: Cambridge University Press, 2008.

Galling, Kurt. "Biblische Sinndeutung der Geschichte." *Evangelische Theologie* 8 (1948): 307–319.

Garbini, Giovanni. *Scrivere La Storia d'Israele*. Brescia: Paideia, 2008.

Gardiner, Alan H. "A New Moralizing Text." *Wiener Zeitschrift für die Kunde des Morgenlandes* 54 (1957): 43–45.

———. *Ancient Egyptian Onomastica*. Oxford: Oxford University Press, 1947.

Garner, Bryan A., ed. *Black's Law Dictionary*. 5th ed. St. Paul: Thomson Reuters, 2016.

Gaster, Moses. "An Old Hebrew Romance of Alexander." *Journal of the Royal Asiatic Society*, 1897, 486ff.

———. "The Legend of Merlin." *Folklore* 16 (1905): 965–84.

Geertz, Clifford. "Off Echoes: Some Comments on Anthropology and Law." *PoLAR* 19 (1996): 33–37.

Geisen, Christina. "The Ramesseum Dramatic Papyrus." Diss., University of Toronto, 2012.

Gemser, Berend. "The Importance of the Motive Clause in the Old Testament Law." *Supplements to Vetus Testamentum* 1 (1953): 50–66.

Gerber, W. T. *Hebraischen Verba Denominativa*. Leipzig: J. C. Hinrichs'sche, 1896.

Gerriets, Marylin. "Theft, Penitentials, and the Compilation of the Early Irish Laws." *Celtica* 22 (1991): 18–32.

Gerstenberger, Erhard S. "Life Situations and Theological Concepts of Old Testament Psalms." *Old Testament Essays* 18 (2005): 82–92.

———. *Wesen und Herkunft des "apodiktischen Rechts."* 1965; Repr. Eugene, OR: Wipf & Stock, 2009.

Gilissen, John. *La Coutume*. Typologie des Sources du Moyen Auge Occidental 41. Turnhout: Brepols, 1982.

Gisli Sigurðsson. *Gaelic Influence in Iceland*. Studia Icelandica 46. Reykjavik: Mennigarsjoðs, 1988.

———. "Medieval Icelandic Studies." *Oral Tradition* 18 (2003): 207–9.

———. *The Medieval Icelandic Saga and Oral Tradition*. Harvard University Center for Hellenic Studies eBook. Accessed January 14, 2019. https://chs.harvard .edu/CHS/article/display/6824.part-i-oral-tradition-in-iceland-in-the-twelfth-and-thirteenth-centuries-1-from-lawspeaker-to-lawbook.

Gitay, Yehoshua. *Methodology, Speech, Society: The Hebrew Bible*. Stellenbosch: SUN Media, 2011.

Goetze, Albrecht. "Mesopotamian Laws and the Historian." In *Folk Law*, edited by Alison D. Renteln and Alan Dundes, 1:485–94. Garland Folklore Casebooks 3. New York: Garland, 1994.

Goodrich, Peter. "Literacy and the Languages of the Early Common Law." *Journal of Law and Society* 14 (1987): 422–44.

Gottwald, Norman K. *The Politics of Ancient Israel*. Louisville: Westminster John Knox, 2001.

Grabbe, Lester L. "Some Recent Issues in the Study of the History of Israel." In *Understanding the History of Ancient Israel*, edited by H. G. M. Williamson,

57–70. Proceedings of the British Academy 143. Oxford: Oxford University Press, 2007.

———. "The Oral, the Written, the Forgotten, the Remembered." In *"Even God Cannot Change the Past": Reflections on Seventeen Years of the European Seminar in Historical Methodology*, edited by Lester L. Grabbe, 125–51. London: Bloomsbury, 2018.

Graham, William A. *Beyond the Written Word*. Cambridge: Cambridge University Press, 1987.

Grahn-Hoek, Heike. "The Thuringi, the Peculiarities of Their Law, and Their Legal Relationship to the *Gentes* of Their Time, Chiefly According to the Lex Thuringorum and Other *Leges Barbarorum* of the Early Middle Ages." In *The Baiuvarii and Thuringi: An Ethnographic Perspective*, edited by Janine Fries-Knoblach, Heiko Steuer, and John Hines, 289–316. Studies in Historical Archaeoethnology 9. Woodbridge: Boydell, 2014.

Gray, Ernest. "Some Proverbs of the Nyanja People." *African Studies* 3 (1944): 101–28.

Greengus, Samuel. "Legal and Social Institutions of Ancient Mesopotamia." In *Civilizations of the Ancient Near East*, edited by Jack Sasson, 1:345ff. Peabody, Mass.: Hendrickson, 1995.

———. "Some Issues Relating to the Comparability of Laws and the Coherence of the Legal Tradition." In *Theory and Method in Biblical and Cuneiform Law: Revision, Interpolation and Development*, edited by Bernard M. Levinson, 60–87. Journal for the Study of the Old Testament Supplements 181. Sheffield: Sheffield Academic Press, 1994.

Greenstein, Edward. "The Relation between Law and Narrative in the Pentateuch." Paper presented at the conference "Law and Literature, Mutual Negotiations," Tel Aviv, 2001.

Grønlie, Siân, ed. *Íslendingabók =: The Book of the Icelanders*. Text Series / Viking Society for Northern Research 18. London: Viking Society for Northern Research, 2006.

Gudrun Sveinbjarnardottir. "The Question of the Papar in Iceland." In *The Papar in the North Atlantic: Environment and History*, edited by Barbara E. Crawford, 97–106. St. Andrews: University of St. Andrews Press, 2002.

Guerber, H. A. *Myths and Legends of the Middle Ages*. 1909; Repr. New York: Dover Publications, 1993.

Guillaume, Philippe. *Waiting for Josiah: The Judges*. Journal for the Study of the Old Testament Supplements. London: T & T Clark, 2004.

Gunnar Jonsson. "Waldgang und Lebensringzaum (Landesverweisung) im alteren islandischen Recht." Diss., Hamburg University, 1987.

Gunnell, Terry. "Eddic Performance and Eddic Audiences." In *A Handbook to Eddic Poetry*, edited by Carolyne Larrington, Judy Quinn, and Brittany Schorn, 92–113. Cambridge: Cambridge University Press, 2016.

———. *Grýla, Grýlur, Grøleks and Skeklers: Folk Drama in the North Atlantic in the Early Middle Ages?* Vol. 2009. 2/19, 2000.

————. "How Elvish Were the Alfar?" In *Constructing Nations, Reconstructing Myth*, edited by Andrew Wawn, 111–30. Making the Middle Ages 9. Turnhout: Brepols, 2007.

————. "Nordic Folk Legends, Folk Traditions and Grave Mounds." In *New Focus on Retrospective Methods: Resuming Methodological Discussions: Case Studies from Northern Europe*, edited by Eldar Heide and Karen Bek-Pedersen, 17–41. Folklore Fellows' Communications 307. Helsinki: Suomalainen Tiedeakatemia, Academia Scientiarum Fennica, 2014.

————. "Walking the Dead: Folk Legends Concerning Magicians and Walking Corpses in Iceland." In *News from Other Worlds: Studies in Nordic Folklore, Mythology and Culture*, edited by Merrill Kaplan and Timothy R. Tangherlini, 235–66. Berkeley: North Pinehurst Press, 2012.

Habel, Norman C., ed. *The Book of Job: Commentary*. Cambridge Bible Commentary 16. Cambridge: Cambridge University Press, 1975.

Hadley, D. M. *The Northern Danelaw*. London: Leicester University Press, 2005.

Hallo, William W., and Hayim Tadmor. "A Lawsuit from Hazor." *Israel Exploration Journal* 27 (1977): 1–11.

Harris, Joseph. "Eddic Poetry as World Literature." *Collegium Medievale* 29 (2016): 5–28.

Harris, Richard L. "In the Beginning Was the Proverb: Communal Wisdom and Individual Deeds in the *Íslendingasögur*." Paper presented at the International Congress on Medieval Studies, Kalamazoo, 2013.

————. "Paremiological Sub-Categories and the *Íslendingasögur*: Some Applications of the Concordance to the Proverbs and Proverbial Materials in the Old Icelandic Sagas." Paper presented at the AASSC Annual Meeting, Winnipeg, 2004.

————. "The Proverbs of *Morkinskinna*." Paper presented at the International Congress on Medieval Studies, Kalamazoo, 2007.

Hart, Cyril James Roy. *The Danelaw*. London: Hambledon, 1992.

Hartman, Geoffrey. "The Voice of the Shuttle: Language from the Point of View of Literature." *The Review of Metaphysics* 23 (1969): 240–58.

Harvey, John E. *Retelling the Torah*. Journal for the Study of the Old Testament Supplements 403. Sheffield: Sheffield Academic Press, 2004.

Havelock, Eric A. *The Literate Revolution in Greece and Its Cultural Consequences*. Princeton Series of Collected Essays. Princeton: Princeton University Press, 1982.

Heather, Peter. *The Goths*. The Peoples of Europe 9. Oxford: Blackwell, 2008.

————, ed. *The Visigoths: From the Migration Period to the Seventh Century*. Studies in Historical Archaeoethnology 4. San Marino: Boydell, 1999.

Heffelfinger, Katie M. "'My Father Is King': Chiefly Politics and the Rise and Fall of Abimelech." *Journal for the Study of the Old Testament* 33 (2009): 277–92.

Heim, Knut Martin. Poetic Imagination in Proverbs: Variant Repetitions and the Nature of Poetry. *Bulletin for Biblical Research* Supplements 4. Winona Lake: Eisenbrauns, 2013.

Helgi Skuli Kjartansson. "Law Recital According to Old Icelandic Law." *Scripta Icelandica* 60 (2009): 89–103.

Hermann Pálsson, ed. *Knytlinga Saga: The History of the Kings of Denmark*. Odense: Odense University Press, 1986.

Hermann Pálsson, trans. *Njáll's Saga*. Repr. Penguin Classics. Harmondsworth: Penguin, 1983.

Hermann Palsson, and Paul Edwards, trans. *Eyrbyggja Saga*. Toronto: University of Toronto Press, 1973.

Hermann, Pernille. "Who Were the Papar?" In *The Viking Age*, edited by John Sheehan and Donnchadh O Corrain, 145–53. Dublin: Four Courts, 2010.

Hertzberg, Hans W. "Die Entwicklung der Begriffes משפט im AT." *Zeitschrift für die Alttestamentliche Wissenschaft* 30 (1923): 256–87.

Heusler, Andreas. "Sprichwörter in den eddischen Sittengedichten." *Zeitschrift des vereins für volkskunde in Berlin* 25–26 (1915): 42–57, 108–15.

Higgins, Noele. "The Lost Legal System: Pre-Common Law Ireland and the Brehon Law," in *Legal Theory Practice and Education* (Athens: Athens Institute for Education and Research, 2011), 193–205.

Hillebrand, J. H. *Deutsche rechtssprichworter gesammelt und erlautert*. Zurich: Meyer und Zelle, 1868.

Hodge, Carleton T. "Thoth and Oral Tradition." In *General and Amerindian Ethnolinguistics*, edited by Mary Ritchie Key and Stanley S. Newman, 407–14. Contributions to the Sociology of Language 55. Berlin: Mouton de Gruyter, 1989.

Hoff, Hans Henning. *Hafliði Másson und die Einflüsse des römischen Rechts in der Grágás*. Ergänzungsbände zum Reallexikon der germanischen Altertumskunde 78. Boston: De Gruyter, 2011.

Hoffmann, David Zvi. *Das Buch Deuteronomium*. Berlin: Poppelauer, 1913.

Hoffner, Harry A. "Legal and Social Institutions of Hittite Anatolia." In *Civilizations of the Ancient Near East*, edited by Jack Sasson, 1:555ff. Peabody, Mass.: Hendrickson, 1995.

Hoftijzer, J., K. Jongeling, Richard C. Steiner, Bezalel Porten, A. Mosak Moshavi, and Charles-F. Jean. *Dictionary of the North-West Semitic Inscriptions*. Handbuch Der Orientalistik. Erste Abteilung, Der Nahe Und Mittlere Osten, 21. Bd., pts. 1–2. Leiden: E.J. Brill, 1995.

Holmes, Oliver Wendell. "Introduction to the General Survey (1913)." In *Collected Legal Papers*. New York: Peter Smith, 1952.

———. "Law in Science and Science in Law (1899)." In *Collected Legal Papers*. New York: Peter Smith, 1952.

———. *The Fundamental Holmes*. Edited by Ronald K. L. Collins. Cambridge: Cambridge University Press, 2010.

———. "The Theory of Legal Interpretation (1899)." In *Collected Legal Papers*. New York: Peter Smith, 1952.

Honko, Lauri. "Comparing the Textualization of Oral Epics." *Folklore Fellows Newsletter* 13 (1996): 2–3, 7–8.

Hountondji, Paulin J. "Tradition: Hindrance or Inspiration?" *Quest* 14 (2000): 5–11.

Hrisztova-Gotthardt, Hrisztalina, and Melita A. Varga. *Introduction to Paremiology*. Berlin: De Gruyter, 2015.

Hudson, John G. H. "Customs, Laws, and the Interpretation of Medieval Law." In *Custom: The Development and Use of a Legal Concept in the Middle Ages: Proceedings of the Fifth Carlsberg Academy Conference on Medieval Legal History 2008*, edited by Per Andersen and Mia Münster-Swendsen, 1st ed., 1–16. Copenhagen: DJØF Pub, 2009.

Hulstaert, G. *Traditions Orales Mongo*. Bandundu: Ceeba, 1979.

Hunter, James. *Last of the Free: A Millennial History of the Highlands and Islands of Scotland*. Edinburgh: Mainstream, 1999.

Jackson, Bernard S. "Evolution and Foreign Influence in Ancient Law." *American Journal of Comparative Law* 16 (1968): 372–85.

———. "Exodus 21:18–19 and the Origins of the Casuistic Form." *Israel Law Review* 33 (1999): 798–820.

———. "Law in the Ninth Century: Jehoshaphat's 'Judicial Reform.'" In *Understanding the History of Ancient Israel*, edited by H. G. M. Williamson, 369–97. Proceedings of the British Academy 143. Oxford: Oxford University Press, 2007.

———. "Literal Meaning: Semantics and Narrative in Biblical Law and Modern Jurisprudence." *International Journal for the Semiotics of Law* 13 (2000): 433–57.

———. "Modelling Biblical Law." *Chicago-Kent Law Review* 70 (1995): 1745–1827.

———. "Models in Legal History: The Case of Biblical Law." *Journal of Law and Religion* 18 (2002): 1–30.

———. *Studies in the Semiotics of Biblical Law*. Journal for the Study of the Old Testament Supplements 314. Sheffield: Sheffield Academic Press, 2000.

———. "The Original Oral Law." In *Jewish Ways of Reading the Bible*, edited by George J. Brooke, 3–19. Journal of Semitic Studies Supplement 11. Oxford: Oxford University Press, 2000.

———. *Wisdom-Laws: A Study of the* Mishpatim *of Exodus 21:1–22:16*. Oxford: Oxford University Press, 2006.

Jackson, Elizabeth. *Old Icelandic Truce Formulas*. Viking Society for Northern Research. London: University College London Press, 2016.

Jackson, Samuel A. *A Comparison of Ancient Near Eastern Law Collections Prior to the First Millennium BC*. Gorgias Dissertations 35. Piscataway, NJ: Gorgias, 2008.

Jacobs, Sandra. *The Body as Property: Physical Disfigurement in Biblical Law*. Library of Hebrew Bible/Old Testament Studies 582. London: Continuum, 2015.

Jacobsen, Thorkild. "Oral to Written." In *Societies and Languages of the Ancient Near East*, edited by J. Nicholas Postgate, 129–37. Warminster: Aris and Phillips, 1982.

Janssen, C. "Samsu-Iluna and the Hungry *Naditums*." *Northern Akkad Project Reports* 5 (1991): 3–40.

Jastrow, Morris. *The Book of Job*. Philadelphia: Lippincott, 1920.

Jeremias, Alfred. *The Old Testament in the Light of the Ancient East*. London: Williams, 1911.

Jeremias, Jörg. "Prophetenwort und Prophetenbuch." *Forschungen zum Alten Testament* 99 (1990): 19–35.

Jesch, Judith. "Murder and Treachery in the Viking Age." In *Crime and Punishment in the Middle Ages*, edited by Timothy Shaw Haskett, 63–85. Victoria, BC: Humanities Centre, University of Victoria, 1998.

Jhutti, Sundeep S. *The Getes*. Sino-Platonic Papers 127. Philadelphia: Department of East Asian Languages and Civilizations, University of Pennsylvania, 2003.

Jón Hnefill Aðalsteinsson. *Under the Cloak: A Pagan Ritual Turning Point in the Conversion of Iceland*. 2nd ed. Reykjavík: Háskólaútg, 1999.

Jon Viðar Sigurðsson. "The Court and Assembly Organisation in Iceland." In *Legislation and State Formation*, edited by Steinar Imsen, 211–28. Norgesveldet Occasional Papers 4. Trondheim: Akademika, 2013.

———. "The Education of Sturla Þórðarson." In *Sturla Þórðarson: Skald, Chieftain, and Lawman*, edited by Jon Viðar Sigurðsson and Sverrir Jakobsson, 20–30. The Northern World 78. Leiden: Brill, 2017.

Jon Viðar Sigurðsson, Frederik Pedersen, and Anders Berge. "Making and Using the Law in the North, c. 900–1350." In *Making, Using and Resisting the Law in European History*, edited by Gunther Lottes, Eero Medijainen, and Jon Viðar Sigurðsson, 37–64. Pisa: Plus, 2008.

Jurasinski, Stefan. *Ancient Privileges: Beowulf, Law, and the Making of Germanic Antiquity*. Medieval European Studies 6. Morgantown: West Virginia University Press, 2006.

Justel, Daniel. "Ancient Near Eastern Law." *Journal of Ancient Civilizations*, 2019, 69–81.

Katz, Marilyn A. "Ox-Slaughter and Goring Oxen." *Yale Journal of Law & the Humanities* 4 (1992): 249–78.

Kaufmann, Ekkehard. "Rechtssprichwort." In *Handworterbuch zur deutschen Rechtsgeschichte*, 4:364–67. Berlin: Erich Schmidt, 2017.

Kelly, Fergus. *A Guide to Irish Law*. Early Irish Law 3. Dublin: Institute for Advanced Studies, 1988.

Kent, Charles F., and Millar Burrows. *Proverbs and Didactic Poems*. The Student's Old Testament 6. New York: Charles Scribner's Sons, 1927.

King, Paul D. *Law and Society in the Visigothic Kingdom*. Cambridge Studies in Medieval Life and Thought, 3.5. Cambridge: Cambridge University Press, 1972.

———. "The Character of Visigothic Legislation." Diss., University of Cambridge, 1967.

Kleefeld, John C. "From Brouhahas to Brehon Laws." *Law and Humanities* 4 (2010): 21–61.

Knierim, Rolf P. "Customs, Judges, and Legislators in Ancient Israel." In *Early Jewish and Christian Exegesis: Studies in Memory of William Hugh Brownlee*, edited by Craig A. Evans and William F. Stinespring, 3–16. Scholars Press Homage Series 10. Atlanta: Scholars, 1987.

Knight, Douglas A. *Law, Power, and Justice in Ancient Israel*. Library of Ancient Israel 9. Louisville: Westminster John Knox, 2011.

———. "Tradition-History-Criticism: The Development of the Covenant Code." In *Method Matters: Essays on the Interpretation of the Hebrew Bible in Honor of David L. Petersen*, edited by David L. Petersen, Joel M. LeMon, and Kent Harold

Richards, 97–116. Society of Biblical Literature Resources for Biblical Study 56. Atlanta: Society of Biblical Literature, 2009.

Konidaris, Ioannis M. "The Ubiquity of Canon Law." In *Law and Society in Byzantium: Ninth–Twelfth Centuries*, edited by Angelikē E. Laïu-Thōmadakē and Dieter Simon, 131–50. Washington, DC: Dumbarton Oaks Research Library and Collection, 1994.

Kropotkin, Peter. *Law and Authority*. London: International, 1886.

Kuenen, Abraham. *The Religion of Israel to the Fall of the Jewish State*. London: Williams and Norgate, 1882.

Kutsch, Ernst. *Verheissung und Gesetz*. Berlin: De Gruyter, 1973.

Lagarde, Paul de. *Deutsche Schriften*. Gottingen: Dieterich, 1891.

Lambert, W. G. *Babylonian Wisdom Literature*. Winona Lake: Eisenbrauns, 1996.

Landau, Peter. "The Importance of Classical Canon Law in Scandinavia in the 12th and 13th Centuries." In *How Nordic Are the Nordic Medieval Laws*, edited by Per Andersen, Ditlev Tamm, and Helle Vogt, 2nd ed., 23–39. Copenhagen: DJØF Pub, 2011.

Larrington, Carolyne. *A Store of Common Sense: Gnomic Theme and Style in Old Icelandic and Old English Wisdom Poetry*. Oxford: Clarendon, 1993.

Larrington, Carolyne, trans. *The Poetic Edda*. Oxford World's Classics. Oxford: Oxford University Press, 2008.

Larson, Laurence M., trans. *The Earliest Norwegian Laws, Being the Gulathing Law and the Frostathing Law*. New York: Columbia University Press, 1935.

Larsson, Inger. "The Role of the Swedish Lawman in the Spread of Lay Literacy." In *Along the Oral-Written Continuum*, edited by Slavica Rankovic, 411–27. Utrecht Studies in Medieval Literacy. Turnhout: Brepols, 2010.

Larusson, Olafur, ed. *Staðarhólsbók: The Ancient Lawbooks Gragas and Járnsíða*. Corpus Codicum Islandicorum Medii Aevi 1. Copenhagen: Levin & Munksgaard, 1936.

Lassen, Annette, trans. *Hrafnagaldur Óðins*. Viking Society for Northern Research Text Series 20. London: University College London Press, 2011.

Lauhakangas, Outi. *The Matti Kuusi International Type System of Proverbs*. Folklore Fellows' Communications 275. Helsinki: Suomalainen Tiedeakatemia, 2001.

———. "Use of Proverbs and Narrative Thought." *Folklore: Electronic Journal of Folklore* 35 (2007): 77–84. https://doi.org/10.7592/FEJF2007.35.lauhakangas.

Lemche, Niels Peter. "Justice in Western Asia in Antiquity: or Why No Laws Were Needed." *Chicago-Kent Law Review* 70 (1995): 1695–1716.

———. *The Old Testament between Theology and History: A Critical Survey*. Louisville: Westminster John Knox, 2008.

———. "The Same Old Story." In *Finding Myth and History in the Bible: Scholarship, Scholars and Errors: Essays in Honor of Giovanni Grabini*, edited by Łukasz Niesiołowski-Spanò, Chiara Peri, and Jim West, 85–95. Sheffield: Equinox, 2016.

Leo VI the Wise. *Les Novelles de Leon VI Le Sage*. Translated by P. Noailles and A. Dain. Paris: Societe d'Edition "Les Belles Lettres," 1944.

Leuchter, Mark. "The Cult at Kiriath Yearim." *Vetus Testamentum* 58 (2008): 526–43.

Levin, Saul. "The 'Qeri' as the Primary Text of the Hebrew Bible." *General Linguistics* 35 (1995): 181–223.

————. "The Traditional Chironomy of the Hebrew Scriptures." *Journal of Biblical Literature* 87 (1968): 59–79.

Levine, Baruch A., ed. *Numbers 1–20: A New Translation with Introduction and Commentary.* The Anchor Bible 4. New York: Doubleday, 1993.

Levinson, Bernard M. "The Case for Revision and Interpolation within the Biblical Legal Corpora." In *Theory and Method in Biblical and Cuneiform Law: Revision, Interpolation and Development,* edited by Bernard M. Levinson, 37–59. Journal for the Study of the Old Testament 181. Sheffield: Sheffield Academic Press, 1994.

————. *"The Right Chorale": Studies in Biblical Law and Interpretation.* Forschung zum alten Testament 54. Tubingen: Mohr Siebeck, 2008.

Lichtheim, Miriam. *Ancient Egyptian Literature.* Vol. 1. 3 vols. Berkeley: University of California Press, 1975.

Lindal, Sigurður. *Law and Legislation in the Icelandic Commonwealth.* Stockholm: Stockholm Institute for Scandinavian Law, 2009.

————. "The Law Books." In *Icelandic Sagas, Eddas, and Art,* ed. Jónas Kristjánsson (New York: Pierpont Morgan Library, 1982), 39–48.

Linklater, Eileen. "Udal Law—Past, Present and Future?" LLB Diss., University of Strathclyde, 2002.

Lippert, Sandra L. "Ancient Egypt." *Journal of Ancient Civilizations,* 2019, 83–111.

Llewellyn, Karl N. *Jurisprudence.* Chicago: University of Chicago Press, 1962.

Locher, Clemens. *Die Ehre einer Frau in Israel: exegetische und rechtsvergleichende Studien zu Deuteronomium 22, 13–21.* Gottingen: Vandenhoeck & Ruprecht, 1986.

Logan, Robert K. *McLuhan Misunderstood: Setting the Record Straight.* Toronto: Key, 2013.

Lokin, J. H. A. "The Significance of Law and Legislation in the Law Books of the Ninth to Eleventh Centuries." In *Law and Society in Byzantium: Ninth–Twelfth Centuries,* edited by Angelikē E. Laïu-Thōmadakē and Dieter Simon, 71–92. Washington, DC: Dumbarton Oaks Research Library and Collection, 1994.

Long, Ann-Marie. *Iceland's Relationship with Norway c.870–c.1100.* The Northern World 81. Leiden: Brill, 2017.

Lorton, David. "Legal and Social Institutions of Pharaonic Egypt." In *Civilizations of the Ancient Near East,* edited by Jack Sasson, 1:345ff. Peabody, Mass.: Hendrickson, 1995.

Loubser, J. A. *Oral & Manuscript Culture in the Bible.* Stellenbosch: SUN Media, 2007.

Lugmayr, Helmut, Björg Árnadóttir, and Andrew Cauthery. *The Althing at Thingvellir.* Reykjavík: Iceland Review, 2002.

Lundstedt, A. Vilhelm. *Legal Thinking Revisited.* Stockholm: Almqvist & Wiksell international, 1956.

Lupoi, Maurizio. "A European Common Law before Bologna?" In *Law before Gratian,* edited by Per Andersen, Mia Münster-Swendsen, and Helle Vogt. Proceedings of the Carlsberg Academy Conferences on Medieval Legal History 3. Carlsberg: DJOF, 2007.

Mac Airt, Seán, trans. *Annals of Inisfallen*. Dublin: Dublin Institute for Advanced Studies, 1951.

Mac Airt, Seán, and Gearóid Mac Niocaill, eds. *The Annals of Ulster (to A.D. 1131)*. Dublin: Dublin Institute for Advanced Studies, 1983.

Mac Neill, Eoin, and D. A. Binchy. "Prolegomena to a Study of the 'Ancient Laws of Ireland.'" *Irish Jurist* n.s. 2 (1967): 106–15.

MacDonald, Aidan. "On 'Papar' Names in N. and W. Scotland." *Northern Studies* 9 (1977): 25–30.

Macdonald, M. C. A. "Literacy in an Oral Environment." In *Writing and Ancient Near Eastern Society*, edited by Piotr Bienkowski, Christopher Mee, and Elizabeth A. Slater, 49–118. New York: T & T Clark, 2005.

Machinist, Peter B. "The Voice of the Historian in the Ancient Near Eastern and Mediterranean World." *Interpretation*, 2003, 117–37.

MacLean, Magnus. *The Literature of the Celts*. Kennikat Press Scholarly Reprints in Irish History and Culture. Port Washington, N.Y.: Kennikat, 1970.

Madden, M. Stuart. "Paths of Western Law after Justinian," *London Law Review* 2 (2006): 1–40.

Magdalene, F. Rachel. "Legal Science Then and Now: Theory and Method in the Work of Raymond Westbrook." *Maarav* 18 (2011): 17–54.

Magnusson, Eirikr, and William Morris, trans. *The Tale of Roi the Fool*. In Parenthesis Publications Old Norse Series. Cambridge, Ontario: In parenthesis, 2000.

Malul, Meir. "Review of *Inventing God's Law* by David P. Wright (Oxford: Oxford University Press, 2009)," *Strata* 29 (2011): 155–59.

———. "Review of *Studies in Biblical and Cuneiform Law* by Raymond Westbrook (Paris: Gabalda, 1988)," *Orientalia* n.s. 59 (1990): 85–90.

———. *The Comparative Method in Ancient Near Eastern and Biblical Legal Studies*. Alter Orient und Altes Testament 227. Kevelaer: Butzon & Bercker, 1990.

Mar Jonsson. "Uses and Usability of Icelandic Medieval Books of Law." In *Libert Amicorum Ditlev Tam*, edited by Per Andersen, Pio Letto-Vanamo, Kjell A. Modeer, and Helle Vogt, 153–62. Copenhagen: DJØF, 2011.

Marwick, Hugh. "Antiquarian Notes on Papa Westray." *Proceedings of the Orkney Antiquarian Society* 3 (1924): 31–47.

Matthews, Victor H. "Entrance Ways and Threshing Floors." *Fides et Historia* 19 (1987): 25–40.

Mattioli, Vittorio. "Grímnismál: A Critical Edition." Diss., University of St. Andrews, 2017.

Maunier, Rene. *Introduction au folklore juridique*. Paris: Les Editions d'Art et d'Histoire, 1938.

Mayes, Andrew D. H. "Deuteronomistic Royal Ideology in Judges 17–21." *Biblical Interpretation* 9 (2001): 241–58.

McAuley, Gay. "Place in the Performative Experience." *Modern Drama* 46 (2003): 598–613.

McGlynn, Michael P. "Orality in the Old Icelandic Grágás: Legal Formulae in the Assembly Procedures Section." *Neophilologus* 93 (2009): 521–36.

McLeod, Neil. "The Concept of Law in Ancient Irish Jurisprudence." *Irish Jurist* 17 (1982): 356–67.

McLuhan, Marshall. "Achieving Relevance (1970)." In *The Medium and the Light: Reflections on Religion*, edited by Eric McLuhan and Jacek Szlarek, 136–40. Toronto: Stoddart, 1999.

———. "Alphabet, Mother of Invention." *Etc., A Review of General Semantics*, January 1977.

———. "Communication Media (1959)." In *The Medium and the Light: Reflections on Religion*, edited by Eric McLuhan and Jacek Szlarek. Toronto: Stoddart, 1999.

Megill, Allan. *Historical Knowledge, Historical Error: A Contemporary Guide to Practice*. Chicago: University of Chicago Press, 2007.

Meyer, Berend. *Das Apodiktische Recht*. Beiträge zur Wissenschaft vom Alten und Neuen Testament 213. Stuttgart: Kohlhammer, 2017.

Michaelis, Christian B. *Hagiographos*. 3 vols. Halle, Germany: Orphanotrophei, 1720.

Michaelis, Johann D. *Commentaries on the Laws of Moses*. Translated by A. Smith. Vol. 1. London: F. C. and J. Rivington, 1814.

———. *Deutsche Übersetzung des Alten Testaments: Mit Anmerkungen für Ungelehrte*. Vol. 8. Gottingen: Johann Christian Dieterich, 1779.

Mieder, Wolfgang. "Origin of Proverbs." In *Introduction to Paremiology*, edited by Hrisztalina Hrisztova-Gotthardt and Melita A. Varga, 28ff. Berlin: De Gruyter, 2015.

Millar, Suzanna. "A Proverb in a Collection Is Dead?" Paper presented at the conference "Reframing Wisdom," London, 2019.

Miller II, Robert D. "Deuteronomistic Theology in the Book of Judges?" *Old Testament Essays* 15 (2002): 411–16.

———. "Early Israel and Its Appearance in Canaan." In *Ancient Israel's History: An Introduction to Issues and Sources*, edited by Bill T. Arnold and Richard S. Hess. Grand Rapids: Baker, 2014.

———. "History, Folkore, and Myth in the Book of Judges." *Melita Theologica* 69 (2019): 173–88.

———. "How Post-Modernism (and W. F. Albright) Can Save Us from Malarkey." *Bible and Interpretation*, November 2003. www.bibleinterp.com.

———. "Performance of Oral Tradition in Ancient Israel." In *Contextualizing Israel's Sacred Writing: Ancient Literacy, Orality, and Literary Production*, edited by Brian B. Schmidt, 175–96. Atlanta: Society of Biblical Literature, 2015.

Miller, William I. *Bloodtaking and Peacemaking: Feud, Law, and Society in Saga Iceland*. Chicago: University of Chicago Press, 1996.

———. "Of Outlaws, Horsemeat, and Writing: Uniform Laws and Saga Iceland." *Michigan Law Review* 89 (1991): 2081–95.

———. "Where's Iceland?," 76–95. Leiden: Brill, 2016.

Milstein, Sara J. "Making a Case: The Repurposing of 'Israelite Legal Fictions' as Post-Deuteronomic Law." In *Supplementation and the Study of the Hebrew Bible*, edited by Saul M. Olyan and Jacob L. Wright, 161–81. Brown Judaic Studies 361. Providence: Brown Judaic Studies, 2018.

————. *Tracking the Master Scribe: Revision through Introduction in Biblical and Mesopotamian Literature.* New York: Oxford University Press, 2016.

Minchin, Elizabeth. *Homer and the Resources of Memory.* Oxford: Oxford University Press, 2001.

————. "Ring-Patterns and Ring-Composition." *Helios* 22 (1995): 23–33.

Mirelman, Sam. "Performative Indications in Late Babylonian Texts." In *Musiker und Tradierung*, edited by Regine Pruzsinszky and Dahlia Shehata, 241–64. Wiener Offene Orientalistik 8. Vienna: LIT Verlag, 2010.

Mitchell, Stephen A. "The Mythologized Past: Memory in Medieval and Early Modern Gotland." In *Minni and Muninn: Memory in Medieval Nordic Culture*, edited by Pernille Hermann, Stephen A. Mitchell, and Agnes S. Arnórsdóttir, 155–74. Acta Scandinavica 4. Turnhout: Brepols, 2014.

Monod, Jean-Claude. "Vanishing Point: *Les Mots et Les Choses*, History, and Diagnosis." *History and Theory* 55 (2016): 23–34.

Moore, Megan Bishop. "Beyond Minimalism." *Bible and Interpretation*, March 2010. www.bibleinterp.org.

Morgenstern, Julian. "The Book of the Covenant, Part II." *Hebrew Union College Annual* 7 (1930): 19–258.

Morris, L. L. "Judgment and Custom." *Australian Biblical Review* 7 (1959): 72–74.

Morrow, William. "Legal Interactions: The *MISPATIM* and the Laws of Hammurabi." *Bibliotheca Orientalis* 70 (2013): 309–31.

Mqhayi, S. E. K. *Iziganeko Zesizwe: Occasional Poems (1900–1943).* Translated by Jeff Opland and Peter T. Mtuze. Publications of the Opland Collection of Xhosa Literature 4. Pietermaritzburg, South Africa: University of KwaZulu-Natal Press, 2017.

Müller, David H. "Himjarische Studien," *ZDMG* 30 (1876): 671–708.

Mullins, Robert A. "A City and a Mother in Israel." *Bible Study Magazine*, April 2019.

Murhard, J. G. "Discovery of Ancient Greek Tablets Relative to Music." *The Harmonicon: A Journal of Music* 4 (1825): 55–57, 74–77.

Musset, Lucien, Michel Fleury, and François-Xavier Dillmann. *Nordica et normannica: recueil d'études sur la Scandinavie ancienne et médiévale, les expéditions des Vikings et la fondation de la Normandie.* Studia Nordica 1. Paris: Société des études nordiques, 1997.

Nagy, Gregory. "An Evolutionary Model for the Making of Homeric Poetry." In *Homeric Questions*, edited by Gregory Nagy, 163–79. Austin: University of Texas Press, 2009.

————. "'Life of Homer' Myths as Evidence for the Reception of Homer." Paper presented at the IV International Conference on Comparative Mythology, Cambridge, MA, 2010.

Nedkvitne, Arnved. *The Social Consequences of Literacy in Medieval Scandinavia.* Utrecht Studies in Medieval Literacy 11. Turnhout: Brepols, 2004.

Newsom, Carol A. "Scenes of Reading." In *Reading for Faith and Learning: Essays on Scripture, Community, & Libraries in Honor of M. Patrick Graham*, edited by John B. Weaver, 19–30. Abilene: Abilene Christian University Press, 2017.

Niditch, Susan. *Judges: A Commentary*. The Old Testament Library. Louisville: Westminster John Knox, 2008.

Niles, John D. "The Myth of the Anglo-Saxon Oral Poet." *Western Folklore* 62 (2003): 7–61.

Nissinen, Martti. "Reflections on the 'Historical-Critical' Method." In *Method Matters: Essays on the Interpretation of the Hebrew Bible in Honor of David L. Petersen*, edited by Joel M. LeMon and Kent Harold Richards, 479–504. Society of Biblical Literature Resources for Biblical Study 56. Atlanta: Society of Biblical Literature, 2009.

———. "Spoken, Written, Quoted, and Invented: Orality and Writtenness in Ancient Near Eastern Prophecy." In *Writings and Speech in Israelite and Ancient Near Eastern Prophecy*, edited by Ehud Ben Zvi and Michael H. Floyd, 235–71. Society of Biblical Literature Symposium Series 10. Atlanta: Society of Biblical Literature, 2000.

Nordal, Sigurður. *Icelandic Culture*. Ithaca, NY: Cornell University Press, 1990.

Nordgren, Ingemar. *The Well Spring of the Goths*. New York: iUniverse, 2004.

Norrick, Neal R. "Subject Area, Terminology, Proverb Definitions, Proverb Features." In *Introduction to Paremiology*, edited by Hrisztalina Hrisztova-Gotthardt and Melita A. Varga, 7ff. Berlin: De Gruyter, 2015.

Noth, Martin. "The Background of Judges 17–18." In *Israel's Prophetic Heritage*, edited by Bernhard Anderson and Walter Harrelson. New York: Harper, 1962.

———. *The Laws in the Pentateuch*. Philadelphia: Fortress, 1968.

Nyika, Hillary. "The Traditional Israelite Legal Setting." In *Wisdom, Science, and the Scriptures: Essays in Honor of Ernest Lucas*, edited by Stephen Finamore and John Weaver, 34ff. Eugene, OR: Pickwick, 2014.

Ó Cathasaigh, Tomás. *Coire Sois, The Cauldron of Knowledge: A Companion to Early Irish Saga*. South Bend: University of Notre Dame Press, 2014.

Ó Corrain, Donnchadh. "Nationality and Kingship in Pre-Norman Ireland." In *Nationality and the Pursuit of National Independence*, edited by T. W. Moody, 1–35. Historical Studies 9. Belfast: Appletree, 1978.

Ó Sidodhachain, Patricia H. "Oral Tradition to Written Word." *Studies: An Irish Quarterly Review* 101 (2012): 323–34.

Ojoade, J. Olowo. "Proverbial Evidences of African Legal Customs." *International Folklore Review* 6 (1988): 26–38.

Olason, Pall E., ed. *Codex Regius of Gragas*. Corpus Codicum Islandicorum Medii Aevi 3. Copenhagen: Levin & Munksgaard, 1932.

Olrik, Axel. *Viking Civilization*. New York: American Scandinavian Foundation, 1930.

Orfield, Lester B. *The Growth of Scandinavian Law*. Union, N.J: Lawbook Exchange, 2002.

Östborn, Gunnar. *Cult and Canon*. Uppsala Universitets Arsskrift 10. Leipzig: Harrassowitz, 1950.

———. *Tora in the Old Testament*. Lund: Hakan Ohlssons, 1945.

Pálsson, Hermann. "A Florilegium in Norse from Medieval Orkney." In *The Northern and Western Isles in the Viking World*, edited by Alexander Fenton and Hermann Pálsson. Edinburgh: John Donald, 1981.

Panitz-Cohen, Nava, and Naama Yahalom-Mack. "The Wise Woman of Abel Beth Maacah." *Biblical Archaeology Review*, October 2019.

Pardee, Dennis. *Ritual and Cult at Ugarit*. Atlanta: Society of Biblical Literature, 2002.

Pardee, Dennis, and Robert Hawley. "Les textes juridiques en langue ougaritique." In *Trois Millenaires de formulaires juridiques*, edited by Sophie Démare-Lafont and André Lemaire, 125–40. Haute Etudes Orientales—Moyen et Proche-Orient, 4.48. Geneva: Droz, 2010.

Pasqualino, Catarina. "La littérature orale comme performance." *Cahiers de la littérature orale* 63–64 (2008): 1–6.

Patrick, Dale. *Old Testament Law*. Eugene, OR: Wipf & Stock, 2011.

Patron, Sylvie. "Les catégories narratologiques et la (non-)distinction oral-écrits dans la théorie narrative." In *Narrativité, oralité et performance*, edited by Alain Gignac, 19–42. Collection Terra Nova 4. Leuven: Peeters, 2018.

Paul the Deacon. *History of the Lombards*. Translated by William D. Foulke. Philadelphia: University of Pennsylvania Press, 2003.

Peden, Joseph R. "Property Rights in Celtic Irish Law." In *Anarchy and the Law*, edited by Edward P. Stringham, 565–85. New Brunswick, N.J.: Transaction, 2017.

Peel, Christine, trans. *Guta Lag: The Law of the Gotlanders*. Viking Society for Northern Research Text Series. London: University College London Press, 2009.

Pencak, William. *The Conflict of Law and Justice in the Icelandic Sagas*. Value Inquiry Book Series 21. Amsterdam: Rodopi, 1995.

Pennington, Kenneth. "Learned Law, Droit Savant, Gelehrtes Recht." *Syracuse Journal of International Law and Commerce* 20 (1994): 205–15.

Pfoh, Emanuel. "On Finding Myth and History in the Bible." In *Finding Myth and History in the Bible: Scholarship, Scholars and Errors: Essays in Honor of Giovanni Grabini*, edited by Łukasz Niesiołowski-Spanò, Chiara Peri, and Jim West, 196–208. Sheffield: Equinox, 2016.

Phillpotts, Bertha S. *Kindred and Clan*. New York: Octagon, 1974.

Pientka-Hinz, Rosel. "Schlangenauge." In *Von Gottern und Menschen: Beitrage zu Literatur und Geschichte des Alten Orients*, edited by Brigitte Groneberg, Dahlia Shehata, Frauke Weiershauser, and Kamran V. Zand, 170–86. Leiden: Brill, 2010.

Piltz, Elisabeth. "Byzantium and Islam in Scandinavia." In *Byzantium and Islam in Scandinavia*, edited by Elisabeth Piltz, 27–37. Studies in Mediterranean Archaeology 126. Jonsered, Sweden: Paul Astroms, 1998.

Pioske, Daniel. "Retracing a Remembered Past: Methodological Remarks on Memory, History, and the Hebrew Bible." *Biblical Interpretation* 23 (2015): 291–315.

Pound, Roscoe. *An Introduction to the Philosophy of Law*. Rev. ed. New Haven: Yale University Press, 1982.

Powels, Sylvia. "Samaritan Proverbs." *Abr-Nahrain* 28 (1990): 76–95.

Poyatos, Fernando. *Nonverbal Communication across Disciplines*. Vol. 2. Philadelphia: John Benjamins, 2002.

Pressler, Carolyn. "Sexual Legislation." In *The Oxford Encyclopedia of the Bible and Law*, edited by Brent A. Strawn, 1:290–302. Oxford: Oxford University Press, 2019.

Propp, Vladimir Jakovlevic. *The Russian Folktale*. Translated by Sibelan Forrester. Detroit: Wayne State University Press, 2012.

Puech, Emile. "Les écoles dans l'israël préexilique." In *Congress Volume Jerusalem*, 189–203. Vetus Testament Supplement 40. Leiden: Brill, 1996.

Quinn, Judy. "From Orality to Literacy in Medieval Iceland." In *Old Icelandic Literature and Society*, edited by Margaret Clunies Ross, 30–60. Cambridge Studies in Medieval Literature 42. Cambridge: Cambridge University Press, 2000.

Redford, Donald B. *Pharaonic King-Lists, Annals and Day-Books*. Benben Publications, 1986.

Reviv, Hanoch. *The Elders in Ancient Israel*. Jerusalem: Magnes, 1989.

Riisøy, Anne I. "Outlawry." In *New Approaches to Early Law in Scandinavia*, edited by Stefan Brink and Lisa Collinson, 101–30. Acta Scandinavica 3. Turnhout: Brepols, 2014.

Rofè, Alexander. "Clan Sagas As a Source in Settlement Traditions." In *"A Wise and Discerning Mind": Essays in Honor of Burke O. Long*, edited by Saul M. Olyan and Robert C. Culley, 191–203. Brown Judaic Studies 325. Providence: Brown Judaic Studies, 2000.

———. "Ephraimite versus Deuteronomistic History." In *Storia e Tradizioni Di Israele*, edited by D. Garrone and F. Israel. Brescia: Paideia, 1991.

Rohrbach, Lena. "Matrix of the Law?" In *The Power of Book: Medial Approaches to Medieval Nordic Legal Manuscripts*, edited by Lena Rohrbach, 99–128. Berliner Beiträge zur Skandinavistik 19. Berlin: Nordeuropa Institut, Humboldt-Universität, 2014.

———, ed. *The Power of Book: Medial Approaches to Medieval Nordic Legal Manuscripts*. 1. Auflage. Berliner Beiträge zur Skandinavistik 19. Berlin: Nordeuropa Institut, Humboldt-Universität, 2014.

Rollston, Christopher A. "Scribal Curriculum during the First Temple Period." In *Contextualizing Israel's Sacred Writings*, edited by Brian B. Schmidt, 71–101. Society of Biblical Literature: Ancient Israel and Its Literature 22. Atlanta: SBL, 2015.

———. "The Phoenician Script of the Tel Zayit Abecedary and Putative Evidence for Israelite Literacy." In *Literate Culture and Tenth-Century Canaan: The Tel Zayit Abecedary in Context*, edited by Ron E. Tappy and P. Kyle McCarter, 61–96. Winona Lake, Ind: Eisenbrauns, 2008.

———. *Writing and Literacy in the World of Ancient Israel: Epigraphic Evidence from the Iron Age*. Archaeology and Biblical Studies 11. Atlanta: Society of Biblical Literature, 2010.

Ronayne, Liam. "Seandlithe Na NGael: An Annotated Bibliography of the Ancient Laws of Ireland." *Irish Jurist* 17 (1982): 131–44.

Roper, Jonathan. "Ronald or Donald: Vernacular Theorizing on Language." Paper presented to the International Society for Folk Narrative Research, Miami, 2016.

Ross, Alf. *On Law and Justice*. London: Stevens & Sons, 1958.

Ross, Margaret C., ed. *Poetry on Christian Subjects*. Skaldic Poetry of the Scandinavian Middle Ages 7. Turnhout: Brepols, 2007.

Rossouw, Johann. "The Politics of Liturgy between Tradition and Modernity in South Africa." *Acta Theologica* 25 (2017): 111–25.

Rost, Leonhard. *Die Vorstufen von Kirche und Synagoge im alten Testament*. Darmstadt: Wissenschaftliche Buchgesellschaft, 1967.

Roth, Martha T. *Law Collections from Mesopotamia and Asia Minor*. Writings from the Ancient World 6. Atlanta: Scholars, 1997.

Rowe, Ignacio Marquez. "Alalakh." In *A History of Ancient Near Eastern Law*, edited by Raymond Westbrook, 2:693–718. Handbook of Oriental Studies. Section 1, The Near and Middle East 72. Leiden: Brill, 2003.

Rupert, Christopher T. "Hebrew Poetry: Patterned for Performance." In *From Babel to Babylon*, edited by Joyce R. Wood, John E. Harvey, and Mark Leuchter, 455:80–97. New York: T and T Clark, 2006.

Russell, D. A. *Greek Declamation*. Cambridge: Cambridge University Press, 1983.

Russell, Paul. "Law, Glossaries, and Legal Glossaries in Early Ireland." *Zeitschrift Für Celtische Philologie* 51 (1999): 85–115.

Rüterswörden, Udo. "Das kasuistische Recht die Weisheit." In *Ex oriente Lux: Studien zur Theologie des Alten Testaments*, edited by Angelika Berlejung and Raik Heckl, 323–32. Arbeiten zur Bibel und ihrer Geschichte 39. Leipzig: Evangelische Verlagsanstalt, 2012.

Ryder, Jane. "Udal Law: An Introduction." *Northern Studies* 25 (1988): 1–20.

Sachs, Albie. *The Strange Alchemy of Life and Law*. Oxford: Oxford University Press, 2011.

Saintyves, P. "Le Folklore juridique." *Etudes de Sociologie et d'Ethnologie juridiques* 12 (1932): 65–108.

Sánchez del Rio, Carlos. "Teoria del Derecho en Israel." *Relaciones Internacionales* 28 (2019): 107.

Sanders, Seth L. "Writing and Early Iron Age Israel." In *Literate Culture and Tenth-Century Canaan: The Tel Zayit Abecedary in Context*, edited by Ron E. Tappy and P. Kyle McCarter, 97–112. Winona Lake, Ind: Eisenbrauns, 2008.

Sanmark, Alexandra. *Viking Law and Order: Places and Rituals of Assembly in the Medieval North*. Edinburgh: Edinburgh University Press, 2017.

Saxo. *The History of the Danes, Books–IX*. Suffolk: D.S. Brewer, 1998.

Scelles-Millie, J. *Contes arabes du Maghreb*. Collection documentaire de Folklore 11. Paris: G.-P. Maisonneuve et Larose, 1970.

Schaper, Joachim. "Exilic and Post-Exilic Prophecy and the Orality / Literacy Problem." *Vetus Testamentum* 55 (2005): 324–42.

Scheel, Roland. "Byzantium—Rome—Denmark—Iceland." In *Transcultural Approaches to the Concept of Imperial Rule in the Middle Ages*, edited by Christian Scholl, Torben R. Gebhardt, and Jan Clauß, 278–94. Frankfurt: Peter Lang, 2017.

Schei, Liv Kjørsvik, Gunnie Moberg, and Tróndur Patursson. *The Faroe Islands*. Edinburgh: Birlinn, 2003.

Schipper, Bernd U. "'Teach Them Diligently to Your Son!' The Book of Proverbs and Deuteronomy." In *Reading Proverbs Intertextually*, edited by Katherine Dell and Will Kynes, 21–34. New York: T & T Clark, 2019.

Schniedewind, William M. "Scripturalization in Ancient Judah." In *Contextualizing Israel's Sacred Writings*, edited by Brian B. Schmidt, 305–21. Society of Biblical Literature: Ancient Israel and Its Literature 22. Atlanta: SBL, 2015.

Schorn, Brittany. *Speaker and Authority in Old Norse Wisdom Poetry.* Trends in Medieval Philology 34. Berlin: De Gruyter, 2017.

Schott, Rudiger. "Main Trends in German Ethnological Jurisprudence and Legal Ethnology." In *Folk Law*, edited by Alison D. Renteln and Alan Dundes, 1:201–30. Garland Folklore Casebooks 3. New York: Garland, 1994.

Schuol, Monika. *Hethitische Kultmusik: eine Untersuchung der Instrumental- und Vokalmusik anhand hethitischer Ritualtexte und von archäologischen Zeugnissen.* Orient-Archäologie 14. Rahden: Marie Leidorf, 2004.

Schweid, Eliezer. *The Philosophy of the Bible as Foundation of Jewish Culture. Philosophy of Biblical Law.* Reference Library of Jewish Intellectual History. Boston: Academic Studies Press, 2008.

Scodel, Ruth. "Prophetic Hesiod." Paper presented at the conference "Orality and Literacy VI," Ann Arbor, 2012.

Scott, S. P., ed. *The Visigothic Code: (Forum Judicum).* Library of Iberian Sources Online, 1908.

Selma Jonsdottir. *An 11th Century Byzantine Last Judgement in Iceland.* Reykjavik: Almenna, 1959.

Shehata, Dahlia. *Musiker und ihr vokales Repertoire.* Göttinger Beiträge zum Alten Orient 3. Göttingen: Universitätsverlag, 2009.

Shepherd, Simon. *The Cambridge Introduction to Performance Theory.* Cambridge: Cambridge University Press, 2016.

Sherzer, Joel. *Verbal Art in San Blas.* Cambridge Studies in Oral and Literate Culture 21. Cambridge: Cambridge University Press, 1990.

Simpson, William Kelly, ed. *The Literature of Ancient Egypt: An Anthology of Stories, Instructions, Stelae, Autobiographies, and Poetry.* 3rd ed. New Haven: Yale University Press, 2003.

Ska, Jean-Louis. "The Tablet of the Heart and the Tablets of Stone: Orality and Jurisprudence in Ancient Israel." In *Stones, Tablets, and Scrolls*, edited by Peter Dubovsky and F. Giuntoli, 39–61. Tubingen: Mohr Siebeck, 2020.

Skladny, Udo. *Die altesten Spruchsammlungen in Israel.* Göttingen: Vandenhoeck & Ruprecht, 1962.

Slater, Niall. "Speaking Verse to Power: Circulation of Oral and Written Critique in the *Lives of the Caesars*." Paper presented at the conference "Orality and Literacy VI," Ann Arbor, 2012.

Smend, Rudolf. *Yahweh War and Tribal Confederation.* Nashville: Abingdon, 1970.

Smith, Brian. "Dull as Ditch Water or Crazily Romantic: Scottish Historians on Norwegian Law in Shetland and Orkney." In *Legislation and State Formation*, edited by Steinar Imsen, 117–32. Norgesveldet Occasional Papers 4. Trondheim: Akademika, 2013.

Smith, Mark S. "The Passing of Warrior Poetry in the Era of Prosaic Heroes." In *Worship, Women and War*, edited by John J. Collins, T. M. Lemos, and Saul M. Olyan, 5–15. Brown Judaic Studies. Atlanta: Society of Biblical Literature, 2015.

———. "Warrior Culture in Early Israel and the Voice of David in 2 Samuel 1." Paper presented at the Catholic Biblical Association Annual Meeting, Omaha, 2009.

———. "Warrior Culture in Ugaritic Literature." Paper presented at the Society of Biblical Literature Annual Meeting, New Orleans, 2009.

Smyth, Alfred P. *Scandinavian Kings in the British Isles*. Oxford: Oxford University Press, 1977.

———. *Scandinavian York and Dublin*. Vol. 2. Dublin: Templekieran, 1979.

Smyth, Alfred P. *Warlords and Holy Men: Scotland AD 80–1000*. Edinburgh: Edinburgh University Press, 1998.

Snorri Sturluson. *Óláfr Haraldsson (The Saint)*. Translated by Alison Finlay and Anthony Faulkes. Heimskringla 2. London: Viking Society for Northern Research, 2014.

Søby Christensen, Arne. *Cassiodorus, Jordanes and the History of the Goths: Studies in a Migration Myth*. Copenhagen: Museum Tusculanum Press, 2002.

Sonkowsky, Robert P. "Latin Verse-*Ictus* and Multimodal Entrainment." *Electronic Antiquity* 8 (2005): 7–23.

Sørensen, Preben M. "Social Institutions and Belief Systems of Medieval Iceland (c. 870–1400) and Their Relations to Literary Production." In *Old Icelandic Literature and Society*, edited by Margaret Clunies Ross, 8–29. Cambridge Studies in Medieval Literature 42. Cambridge: Cambridge University Press, 2000.

Speiser, E. A. "The Stem *PLL* in Hebrew." *Journal of Biblical Literature* 82 (1963): 301–6.

Stacey, Robin C. "Learning Law in Medieval Iceland." In *Tome: Studies in Medieval Celtic History and Law*, edited by Fiona Edmonds and Paul Russell, 135–44. Boydell, 2011.

Stacey, Robin Chapman. *Dark Speech: The Performance of Law in Early Ireland*. The Middle Ages Series. Philadelphia: University of Pennsylvania Press, 2007.

Starcke, Viggo. *Denmark in World History*. Philadelphia: University of Pennsylvania Press, 1969.

Staubli, Thomas. *Musik in biblischer Zeit*. BIBEL+ORIENT Museum. Stuttgart: Katholisches Bibelwerk, 2007.

Steere, Allen C. "An Introduction to the Law of Community Property." *Indiana Law Journal* 23 (1947): 34ff.

Stein, Peter. *Regulae Iuris: From Juristic Rules to Legal Maxims*. Edinburgh: Edinburgh University Press, 1966.

Stewart, Columba. *Cassian the Monk*. New York: Oxford University Press, 1998.

Stoddard, Willam H. "Law and Institutions in the Shire." *Mythlore*, no. 70 (Autumn 1992): 4–8.

Stokl, Jonathan. "Schoolboy Ezekiel: Remarks on the Transmission of Learning." *Die Welt des Orients* 45 (2019): 50–61.

Stone, Lawson G. "From Tribal Confederation to Monarchic State." Diss., Yale University, 1988.

Sulzberger, Mayer. *The Status of Labor in Ancient Israel*. Philadelphia: Dropsie College for Hebrew and Cognate Learning Press, 1923.

Sunde, Jorn O. "Daughters of God and Counsellors of the Judges of Men." In *New Approaches to Early Law in Scandinavia*, edited by Stefan Brink and Lisa Collinson, 131–84. Acta Scandinavica 3. Turnhout: Brepols, 2014.

Sundqvist, Olof. *Freyr's Offspring: Rulers and Religion in Ancient Svea Society*. Acta Universitatis Upsaliensis 21. Uppsala: Uppsala universitet, 2002.

Sven Aggesen. *The Works of Sven Aggesen, Twelfth-Century Danish Historian*. Translated by Eric Christiansen. Viking Society for Northern Research Text Series 9. London: Viking Society for Northern Research, 1992.

Tamm, Ditlev. "How Nordic Are the Old Nordic Laws?" In *How Nordic Are the Nordic Medieval Laws: Proceedings from the First Carlsberg Conference on Medieval Legal History*, edited by Per Andersen, Ditlev Tamm, and Helle Vogt, 2nd ed. Copenhagen: DJØF Pub, 2011.

———. "How Nordic Are the Old Nordic Laws—Ten Years Later?" In *How Nordic Are the Nordic Medival Laws? Ten Years after: Proceedings of the Tenth Carlsberg Academy Conference on Medieval Legal History 2013*, edited by Per Andersen, Kirsi Salonen, Helle I. M. Sigh, and Helle Vogt. Copenhagen: DJØF Publishing, 2014.

———. *The History of Danish Law: Selected Articles and Bibliography*. Bibliotek for Ret Og Kultur = Law and Culture Series 5. Copenhagen: DJØF Publishing, 2011.

Tarkany-Szucs, Erno. "Results and Tasks of Legal Ethnology in Europe." In *Folk Law*, edited by Alison D. Renteln and Alan Dundes, 1:161–86. Garland Folklore Casebooks 3. New York: Garland, 1994.

Tarkka, Lotte. "Intertextuality, Rhetorics and the Interpretation of Oral Poetry." In *Nordic Frontiers*, edited by Pertti J. Anttonen and Reimund Kvideland, 165–95. NIF Publications 27. Turku: Nordic Institute of Folklore, 1993.

———. "The Poetics of Quotation." In *Genre—Text—Interpretation*, edited by Kaarina Koski and Frog, 175–99. Studia Fennica Folkloristica / Suomalaisen Kirjallisuuden Seura 22. Helsinki: Finnish Literature Society, 2016.

Taylor, Archer. *The Proverb*. Cambridge: Harvard University Press, 1931.

Taylor, Paul B. "Volundarkvida, Þrymskvida, and the Function of Myth." *Neophilologus* 78 (1994): 263–81.

Tegner, Esias, ed. *Frithiof's Saga*. Translated by W. L. Blakely. New York: Leypoldt & Holt, 1867.

Theocharous, Myrto. "Response to John Walton, Understanding Torah: Ancient Legal Text, Covenant Stipulation, and Christian Scripture." Paper presented at the Institute for Biblical Research Annual Meeting, Boston, 2017.

Thomas, Rosalind. "Performance Literature and the Written Word." *Oral Tradition* 20 (2005): 1–6.

———. "Written in Stone? Liberty, Equality, Orality and the Codification of Law." *Bulletin of the Institute of Classical Studies* 40 (1995): 59–74.

Thompson, E. A. *The Goths in Spain*. Oxford: Clarendon, 1969.

Thompson, John M. *The Form and Function of Proverbs in Ancient Israel*. The Hague: Mouton, 1974.

Thomson, William P. L. *The New History of Orkney*. 3rd ed. Edinburgh: Birlinn, 2008.

Thorsteinn Gundjonsson. *Thingvellir*. Reykjavik: Formprent, 1985.

Tigay, Jeffrey H. *The Evolution of the Gilgamesh Epic*. Wauconda, Ill.: Bolchazy-Carducci, 2002.

Tobin, Brendan, and Rodrigo de la Cruz. "Customary Law, Traditional Knowledge and Intellectual Property." Geneva: World Intellectual Property Organization Secretariat, 2013. www.wipo.int/export/sites/www/tk/en/resources/pdf/overview_customary_law.pdf.

Tobolowsky, Andrew. "Israelite and Judahite History in Contemporary Theoretical Approaches." *Currents in Biblical Research* 17 (2018): 33–58.

Togeby, Knut. "Les relations litteraires entre le monde Roman et le monde Scandinave." In *Les relations litteraires Franco-Scandinaves au Moyen Age*, edited by Pierre Halleux, 299–329. Bibliotheque de La Faculte de Philosophie et Lettres de l'Universite de Liege 208. Paris: Societe d'Edition "Les Belles Lettres," 1975.

Tolkien, Christopher, trans. *The Saga of King Heidrek the Wise*. Icelandic Texts. London: Thomas Nelson and Sons, 1960.

Tolkien, J. R. R. *The Lost Road and Other Writings: Language and Legend before "The Lord of the Rings."* Edited by Christopher Tolkien. The History of Middle-Earth 5. Boston: Houghton Mifflin, 1987.

Tooman, William A. "Authenticating Oral and Memory Variants in Ancient Hebrew Literature." *Journal of Semitic Studies* 64 (April 1, 2019): 91–114.

Tuori, Kaius. *Lawyers and Savages: Ancient History and Legal Realism in the Making of Legal Anthropology*. Milton Park, UK: Routledge, 2015.

Van Arkel, Andrea. "Die Mantel Þorgeir Ljósvetningagoði." In *Maukastella*, edited by Jonas Kristjansson, 5–7. Reykjavik: Arni Magnusson Institute, 1974.

Van der Ploeg, J. "Šāpaṭ et Mišpāṭ." In *Lijst van de voornaamste geschriften van Prof. Dr. B. D. Eerdmans*, edited by Joh De Groot and F. Dykema, 144–55. Oudtestamentische Studien 2. Leiden: Brill, 1943.

———. "Studies in Hebrew Law." *Catholic Biblical Quarterly* 12 (1950): 248–59.

Van der Toorn, Karel. "Judges XVI 21 in the Light of the Akkadian Sources." *Vetus Testamentum* 36 (1986): 248–52.

———. *Scribal Culture and the Making of the Hebrew Bible*. Cambridge, MA: Harvard University Press, 2009.

Van Seters, John. *A Law Book for the Diaspora: Revision in the Study of the Covenant Code*. Oxford: Oxford University Press, 2003.

———. "A Response to G. Aichelle, P. Miscall and R. Walsh, 'An Elephant in the Room: Historical-Critical and the Postmodern Interpretations of the Bible.'" *Journal of Hebrew Scriptures* 9, Article 26 (2010).

———. "Cultic Laws in the Covenant Code and Their Relationship to Deuteronomy and the Holiness Code." In *Studies in the Book of Exodus*, 319–45. Bibliotheca Ephemeridum Theologicarum Lovaniensium 126. Leuven: Peeters, 1996.

———. "Revision in the Study of the Covenant Code and a Response to My Critics." *Scandinavian Journal of the Old Testament* 21 (2007): 5–28.

Vayntrub, Jacqueline. *Beyond Orality: Biblical Poetry on Its Own Terms.* The Ancient Word 2. London: Routledge, 2019.

———. "The Book of Proverbs and the Idea of Ancient Israelite Education." *Zeitschrift für die alttestamentliche Wissenschaft* 128 (2016): 96–114.

Veenhof, Klaas R. "Hebrew *Pelilim* and Old Assyrian *Palalum.*" In *Biblical Hebrew in Context: Essays in Semitics and Old Testament Texts in Honour of Professor Jan P. Lettinga,* 12–27. Leiden: Brill, 2018.

Veldhuis, Niek. "The Cuneiform Tablet as an Educational Tool." *Dutch Studies on Near Eastern Languages and Literatures* 2 (1996): 11–26.

Verena, Höfig. "A Pre-Modern Nation? Icelanders' Ethnogenesis and Its Mythical Foundations." *Scandinavian Studies* 90 (2018): 110–32.

VerSteeg, Russ. *Law in the Ancient World.* Durham, N.C: Carolina Academic Press, 2002.

Vestein Olason. *The Traditional Ballads of Iceland.* Stofnun Arna Magnussonar a Islandi 22. Reykjavik: Arni Magnusson Institute, 1982.

Viberg, Ake. *Symbols of Law.* Coniectanea Biblica Old Testament Series 34. Stockholm: Almqvist & Wiksell International, 1992.

Viðar Hreinsson, ed. *The Complete Sagas of Icelanders, Including 49 Tales.* Viking Age Classics. Reykjavík: Leifur Eiríksson, 1997.

Vinyals, Ramon d'Abadal i de. "A propos du Leges Visigothique en Espagne." *Settimane di Studio del centro italiano di studi sul'alto medioevo* 5 (1958): 541–85.

Vogt, Helle. "Secundum Consuetudinem et Leges Patrie." In *Custom: The Development and Use of a Legal Concept in the Middle Ages: Proceedings of the Fifth Carlsberg Academy Conference on Medieval Legal History 2008,* edited by Per Andersen and Mia Münster-Swendsen, 1st ed., 67–80. Copenhagen: DJØF Pub, 2009.

Vogt, Helle, and Ditlev Tamm, eds. *The Danish Medieval Laws: The Laws of Scania, Zealand and Jutland.* Medieval Nordic Laws. London: Routledge, 2016.

Volkwein, Bruno. "Masoretisches `edut, `edwot, `edot." *Biblische Zeitschrift* 13 (1968): 18–40.

Von Rad, Gerhard. *The Problem of the Hexateuch and Other Essays.* New York: McGraw-Hill, 1984.

Wagner, V. "Die Gerichtsverfassung Israel nach der Weisheitliteratur des alten Testaments." *Biblische Zeitschrift* 56 (2012): 96–106.

Wainwright, Frederick T. *The Northern Isles.* New York: Thomas Nelson and Sons, 1964.

Walton, John H. "No Books, No Authors." In *Write That They May Read,* 263–77. Eugene, OR: Pickwick, 2020.

———. "Understanding Torah: Ancient Legal Text, Covenant Stipulation, and Christian Scripture." Plenary address to the Institute for Biblical Research Annual Meeting, Boston, 2017.

Walzer, Michael. "The Legal Codes of Ancient Israel." *Yale Journal of Law & the Humanities* 4 (1992): 335–49.

Watts, James W. *Reading Law*. The Biblical Seminar 59. Sheffield: Sheffield Academic Press, 1999.

Weeks, Sindiso Mnisi. "Women Seeking Justice at the Intersection between Vernacular and State Laws and Courts in Rural KwaZulu-Natal, South Africa." In *The New Legal Realism*, edited by Heinz Klug and Sally E. Merry, 2:113–42. Cambridge: Cambridge University Press, 2016.

Weeks, Stuart. *Early Israelite Wisdom*. New York: Oxford University Press, 1994.

Wells, Bruce. "Biblical Law (Old Testament)." In *The Oxford Encyclopedia of the Bible and Law*, edited by Brent A. Strawn, 1:39–50. Oxford: Oxford University Press, 2019.

———. "Review of *Inventing God's Law* by David P. Wright (Oxford: Oxford University Press, 2009)." *The Journal of Religion* (2010): 558–60.

———. "The Covenant Code and Near Eastern Legal Traditions: A Response to David Wright." *Maarav* 13 (2006): 85–118.

Wénin, André. "À vouloir être trop dissuasif: Rhétorique et oralité en 1 S 8, 11–18." In *Narrativité, oralité et performance*, edited by Alain Gignac, 155–62. Collection Terra Nova 4. Leuven: Peeters, 2018.

Westbrook, Raymond. "Biblical and Cuneiform Law Codes." In *Folk Law*, edited by Alison D. Renteln and Alan Dundes, 1:495–512. Garland Folklore Casebooks 3. New York: Garland, 1994.

———. "Biblical and Cuneiform Law Codes (1985)." In *Law from the Tigris to the Tiber: The Writings of Raymond Westbrook*, edited by Bruce Wells and F. Rachel Magdalene, Vol. 1. Winona Lake: Eisenbrauns, 2009.

———. "The Character of Ancient Near Eastern Law." In *A History of Ancient Near Eastern Law*, edited by Raymond Westbrook, 1:1–92. Handbook of Oriental Studies. Section 1, The Near and Middle East 72. Leiden: Brill, 2003.

———. "Codification and Canonization (2000)." In *Law from the Tigris to the Tiber: The Writings of Raymond Westbrook*, edited by Bruce Wells and F. Rachel Magdalene, Vol. 1. Winona Lake: Eisenbrauns, 2009.

———. "Cuneiform Law Codes and the Origins of Legislation (1989)." In *Law from the Tigris to the Tiber: The Writings of Raymond Westbrook*, edited by Bruce Wells and F. Rachel Magdalene, Vol. 1. Winona Lake: Eisenbrauns, 2009.

———. "Emar and Vicinity." In *A History of Ancient Near Eastern Law*, edited by Raymond Westbrook, 2:657–92. Handbook of Oriental Studies. Section 1, The Near and Middle East 72. Leiden: Brill, 2003.

———. "Judges in Cuneiform Sources." In *Law from the Tigris to the Tiber: The Writings of Raymond Westbrook*, edited by Bruce Wells and F. Rachel Magdalene, Vol. 2. Winona Lake: Eisenbrauns, 2009.

———. *Studies in Biblical and Cuneiform Law*. Cahiers de La Revue Biblique 26. Paris: Gabalda, 1988.

———. "The Laws of Biblical Israel." In *The Hebrew Bible: New Insights and Scholarship*, edited by Frederick E. Greenspahn, 99–119. Jewish Studies in the 21st Century. New York: New York University Press, 2008.

———. "What Is the Covenant Code?" In *Theory and Method in Biblical and Cuneiform Law: Revision, Interpolation and Development*, edited by Bernard M.

Levinson, 15–36. Journal for the Study of the Old Testament Supplements 181. Sheffield: Sheffield Academic Press, 1994.

Westbrook, Raymond, and Bruce Wells. *Everyday Law in Biblical Israel: An Introduction.* Louisville: Westminster John Knox, 2009.

Westermann, Claus. *Basic Forms of Prophetic Speech.* London: Lutterworth, 1967.

———. *Roots of Wisdom.* Louisville: Westminster John Knox, 1995.

Widengren, Geo. *Literary and Psychological Aspects of the Hebrew Prophets.* Uppsala Universitets Arsskrift 10. Leipzig: Harrassowitz, 1948.

———. "Tradition and Literature in Early Judaism and in the Early Church." *Numen* 10 (1963): 42–83.

Wilson, Robert R. "Orality and Writing in the Creation of Exilic Prophetic Literature." In *Worship, Women and War*, edited by John J. Collins, T. M. Lemost, and Saul M. Olyan, 83–96. Brown Judaic Studies. Atlanta: Society of Biblical Literature, 2015.

Wolf, C. Umhau. "Traces of Primitive Democracy in Ancient Israel." *Journal of Near Eastern Studies* 6 (1947): 98–108.

Wolfram, Herwig. *History of the Goths.* Translated by Thomas J. Dunlap. 2nd ed. Berkeley: University of California Press, 1990.

Wood, I. "Social Relations in the Visigothic Kingdom from the Fifth to the Seventh Century." In *The Visigoths: From the Migration Period to the Seventh Century*, edited by Peter Heather, 191–207. Studies in Historical Archaeoethnology 4. San Marino: Boydell, 1999.

Woolf, Lex. *From Pictland to Alba.* New Edinburgh History of Scotland 2. Edinburgh: Edinburgh University Press, 2014.

Wormald, Patrick. *Legal Culture in the Early Medieval West.* London: Hambledon, 2004.

———. *The Making of English Law.* Vol. 1. Oxford: Blackwell, 1999.

Wright, David P. "How Exodus Revises the Laws of Hammurabi." *The Torah.Com* (blog), 2019. thetorah.com/how-exodus-revises-the-laws-of-hammurabi.

———. "Intertextuality in the Laws of Hammurabi, the Covenant Code, and Deuteronomy, and the Date of the Covenant Code." Paper presented to the International Society for Old Testament Research, Helsinki, 2010.

———. *Inventing God's Law: How the Covenant Code of the Bible Used and Revised the Laws of Hammurabi.* Oxford: Oxford University Press, 2009.

———. "Laws of Hammurabi." *Maarav* 10 (2003): 87.

———. "Origin, Development, and Content of the Covenant Code." In *The Book of Exodus: Composition, Reception, and Interpretation*, edited by Thomas B. Dozeman, Craig A. Evans, and Joel N. Lohr, 220–44. Supplements to Vetus Testamentum 164. Leiden: Brill, 2014.

Wundt, Wilhelm M. *The Language of Gestures.* 1921; Repr. The Hague: Mouton, 1973.

Yankah, Kwesi. "Proverb Rhetoric and African Judicial Process." *Journal of American Folklore*, 1986, 280–303.

Yelena Helgasdóttir. "Retrospective Methods in Dating Post-Medieval Rigmarole-Verses from the North Atlantic." In *New Focus on Retrospective Methods:*

Resuming Methodological Discussions: Case Studies from Northern Europe, edited by Eldar Heide and Karen Bek-Pedersen, 98–119. Folklore Fellows' Communications 307. Helsinki: Suomalainen Tiedeakatemia, Academia Scientiarum Fennica, 2014.

———. "When Law Becomes Poetry?" Paper presented to the 17th International Saga Conference, Reykholt, Iceland, 2018. http://fornsagnathing2018.hi.is/ efnisagrip-fyrirlestra/#Yelena%20SesseljaHelgad%C3%B3ttir.

Yona, Shamir. "The Influence of Legal Style on the Style of the Aphorisms." In *Birkat Shalom*, edited by Chaim Cohen, 413–23. Winona Lake: Eisenbrauns, 2008.

Zakovitch, Yair. "Some Remnants of Ancient Laws in the Deuteronomic Code." *Israel Law Review* 9 (1974): 346–51.

Ziegler, Nele. "Teachers and Students: Conveying Musical Knowledge in the Kingdom of Mari." In *Musiker und Tradierung*, edited by Regine Pruzsinszky and Dahlia Shehata, 119–33. Wiener Offene Orientalistik 8. Vienna: LIT Verlag, 2010.

Zimmer, H. *The Irish Element in Mediaeval Culture*. Translated by Jane L. Edmands. New York: G. P. Putnam's Sons, 1891.

Zorn, Jeffrey R. "An Inner and Outer Gate Complex at Tell En-Nasbeh." *Bulletin of the American Schools of Oriental Research* 307 (1997): 53–66.

———. "Tell En-Nasbeh: A Re-Evaluation of the Architecture and Stratigraphy of the Early Bronze Age, Iron Age and Later Periods." Diss., University of California, Berkeley, 1993.

Zumthor, Paul. *Oral Poetry*. Theory and History of Literature 70. Minneapolis: University of Minnesota Press, 1990.

Index

About the Author

Dr. Robert D. Miller II, O.F.S., is Ordinary Professor of Old Testament at the Catholic University of America and a Research Affiliate with the Faculty of Theology and Religion at the University of Pretoria. He is a Secular Franciscan and a Life Member of St. John's College, Cambridge. Dr. Miller has published eight monographs and three edited volumes, most recently *Yahweh: Origins of the Desert God* (Vandenhoeck & Ruprecht, 2021).

Milton Keynes UK
Ingram Content Group UK Ltd.
UKHW010802150524
442746UK00006B/290

9 781978 715233